DATE

Media, Memory, and Human Rights in Chile

Media, Memory, and Human Rights in Chile

Kristin Sorensen

MEDIA, MEMORY, AND HUMAN RIGHTS IN CHILE
Copyright © Kristin Sorensen, 2009.

All rights reserved.

First published in 2009 by PALGRAVE MACMILLAN® in the
United States—a division of St. Martin's Press LLC,
175 Fifth Avenue, New York, NY 10010

Where this book is distributed in the UK, Europe and the rest of
the world, this is by Palgrave Macmillan, a division of Macmillan
Publishers Limited, registered in England, company number 785998,
of Houndmills, Basingstoke, Hampshire RG21 6XS. Palgrave
Macmillan is the global academic imprint of the above companies and
has companies and representatives throughout the world.

Palgrave® and Macmillan® are registered trademarks in the United
States, the United Kingdom, Europe and other countries.

ISBN-13: 978-0-230-61283-9

Library of Congress Cataloging-in-Publication Data is available from
the Library of Congress.

A catalogue record of the book is available from the British Library.
Design by Scribe Inc.

First edition: June 2009

10 9 8 7 6 5 4 3 2 1

Printed in the United States of America.

This book is dedicated to the memory of
Ana Luisa Rojas Castañeda and Inelia Hermosilla Silva.
They dedicated their lives to seeking truth and justice
for the disappearance of their sons
and never received truth or justice.
They are my inspiration.

Este libro está dedicado a la memoria de
Ana Luisa Rojas Castañeda e Inelia Hermosilla Silva.
Ellas dedicaron sus vidas a buscar la verdad y la justicia
por la desaparición de sus hijos
y nunca recibieron ni la verdad ni la justicia.
Ellas son mi inspiración.

Contents

Acknowledgments		ix
1	Introduction	1
2	Television: Self-censorship, Sensationalism, and Structured Absences	29
3	Documentaries and Contested Historical Memories	57
4	The *Machuca* Phenomenon	75
5	Print Media: Significant Discourses If You Know Where to Look	105
6	Public Protests: Responding to Silences and Omissions	133
7	Conclusion	143
Notes		153
Bibliography		159
Index		179

Acknowledgments

This book was produced with the support of many people. First, I wish to thank María Rebeca Cartes, who, through sharing her life experiences, introduced me to Chile and its recent history. Without her, I would never have embarked on this research. I also thank Liliana Mason for believing in the importance of this project and motivating me to finish the book.

An earlier version of this book first appeared as my doctoral dissertation at Indiana University. My adviser and dissertation director, Professor Barbara Klinger, was an invaluable source of encouragement. She also serves, with her commitment, professionalism, and integrity, as a role model for me as I continue in my career. The other three members of my advisory committee receive my deep gratitude as well. Professor Michael Curtin encouraged my international media research, especially in the context of postrepressive regimes. Professor Darlene Sadlier ensured that I was well read in Latin American cinema and encouraged me to position my work in relation to this area that deserves more academic and popular attention. In Professor Emeritus Russell Salmon, I found a kindred spirit whose love for Chile and concern for what Chileans had suffered under the Pinochet dictatorship, as well as the role that our own U.S. government had played in Chile's affairs, was as deep as mine. The staff, faculty, and graduate students of Indiana University's Department of Communication and Culture supported me in multiple ways throughout my project. I received support from Indiana University's Graduate and Professional Student Organization and Indiana University's Center for Latin American and Caribbean Studies.

Since finishing my degree and arriving at Bentley University as an assistant professor in the Department of Global Studies, I have received generous support, especially through the Valente Center for the Arts and Sciences Research Fellowship, Bentley's summer research grants, and the Dean's Fund for International Travel. Thanks go to my dozens of friends and colleagues and hundreds of students who make Bentley such a wonderful place to work.

Thanks also to Anna Siomopoulos (Bentley) and Gonzalo Bacigalupe (University of Massachusetts, Boston) who served as my commentators at Bentley's Valente Center for the Arts and Sciences Working Seminar Series. Gonzalo also first introduced me to Nicole Senerman's film, *The Day Pinochet Died*. I also wish to thank the many colleagues I met at numerous academic conferences, especially those hosted by the Latin American Studies Association, the New England Council of Latin American Studies, the National Communication Association, and Syracuse University's Department of Communication and Rhetorical Studies, who gave me feedback and inspired me with their own research projects.

I am grateful to Anthony Grahame, editorial director of Sussex Academic Press, for allowing me to borrow ideas published in my contributing chapter to the 2005 book *Democracy in Chile: The Legacy of September 11, 1973*, edited by Silvia Nagy-Zekmi and Fernando Leiva. Ideas in this book also first appeared in *SECOLAS Annals* 35 (2003): 82–109; thanks to Gregory Crider, coeditor of *SECOLAS Annals*, for his support. Parts of Chapter 3 appeared as "Truth and Justice, Transience and Doubt in Chilean Documentary" in the *Journal of Human Rights* (*JHR*) 7, no. 4, available at http://www.informaworld.com. Thanks to Richard Hiskes and Aaron Paterson at *JHR* and John Banionis at Taylor and Francis.

I am eternally grateful to Lucía Cartes, who so enthusiastically offered her talent to create the beautiful artwork on the cover of this book. Thanks to all of my supporters at Palgrave Macmillan, including, among others, Julia Cohen, Colleen Lawrie, Luba Ostashevsky, and Rachel Tekula. Thanks especially to Jennifer Kepler at Scribe for her attention to detail in the copyediting of this manuscript.

I thank my parents, Erl and Cilla, for teaching me the values of education and compassion. I thank Ramón Bannister for frequently serving as my research assistant, providing continuous emotional support, and most importantly, sharing his life with me.

Finally, I wish to thank the countless people in Chile who were and are so willing to talk with me about what can be a painful subject. In their homes and offices, they have shared their stories over cups of tea. I also appreciate how eager they are to talk with my students when I bring new groups to Chile each year. This *gringa* values their friendship and trust.

CHAPTER 1

INTRODUCTION

In October 1998, the status quo in Chile was turned on its head. Former dictator, retiring commander of the armed forces, and senator-for-life General Augusto Pinochet Ugarte, was recovering from minor back surgery at a London hospital, The Clinic, while on his annual vacation trip to the United Kingdom, during which he enjoyed visiting his favorite department stores and seeing his longtime friend and ally, Margaret Thatcher, the former prime minister. To his surprise as well as that of the rest of the world, his hospital recovery room was stormed by British police officers who pronounced him under arrest. Spanish Judge Baltasar Garzón was requesting his extradition to Spain, where he would be tried for the torture, murder, and the disappearance of Spanish citizens in Chile.

Suddenly, a story that had received scant attention—Pinochet's visit to England—was making front-page news in TV outlets and newspapers across the globe. With great interest and much caution, Chilean media began to cover this story as well. In fact, one group of Chilean Generation Xers created their own periodical called *The Clinic*.

While Pinochet's immunity from prosecution was being challenged in Europe, the climate was entirely different back in Chile. Simply discussing Pinochet's detention was touchy, especially if the discussant suggested that the United Kingdom and Spain were justified in their actions against Pinochet. Even Socialist presidential candidate Ricardo Lagos argued that Pinochet should be returned to Chile, that this was a domestic issue, and that Chile should take care of its own affairs. During Pinochet's detention in London, the office of the Chilean Commission of Human Rights, a barebones facility running on a meager budget and hidden in a building next to Santa Lucía Hill in downtown Santiago, was robbed. The commission's sole computer, containing important records about what happened to the victims of Pinochet's dictatorship, was stolen. The timing of the event is suspicious and illustrates the power that Pinochet still had eight years after the return to democratic rule in Chile as well as the degree to which information about the dictatorship was still restricted.

Fast-forward eight years to January 15, 2006. Under the late afternoon sun of this warm summer day, rhythmic honking can be detected on Alameda, the main east–west thoroughfare of Santiago. As time passes, it gets louder and more frequent and is accompanied by drivers and passengers cheering and waving Chilean flags out their windows. Socialist Party candidate Michelle Bachelet, daughter of a murdered military general who did not agree with the coup that led to Pinochet's dictatorship, and survivor herself of the most notorious dictatorship-era detention center in Chile, Villa Grimaldi, has just won the elections to become the first female president of Chile. TV cameras capture the swelling crowds congregating in the plaza where Bachelet will speak.

Jump ahead another eleven months to early December 2006. General Pinochet's supporters are holding candlelight vigils outside the hospital where he lies, gravely ill. Chilean and international journalists covering the situation get attacked by Pinochet's faithful—the journalists are targets of tossed water bottles, verbal abuse, spit, and technological interference with their cameras and microphones. On the afternoon of December 10, International Human Rights Day and the birthday of Pinochet's wife, Lucía Hiriart, the news breaks: Pinochet has died. Blogger and filmmaker Nicole Senerman runs outside with a borrowed video camera and records the public response, creating her short documentary, *The Day Pinochet Died* (*El día en que murió Pinochet*). The streets are filled with celebrators who opposed Pinochet, while others later wait in line for hours to kiss his coffin and bid a final farewell. The mourners are outraged that Pinochet does not receive an official state funeral, only a military one. What led to this?

During the dictatorship that began with a U.S.-supported military coup on September 11, 1973, in which the democratically elected, Socialist President Dr. Salvador Allende Gossens was killed, a military junta led by four generals, including Augusto

Pinochet, shut down congress, banned all unions and political organizations, and supervised the actions of the military, police, and civilian personnel who detained, tortured, exiled, and killed thousands of people. Virtually all media centers, schools, universities, and hospitals were shut down or taken over by members of the military. There was absolute censorship, and civil liberties were abolished. The nightmare continued, with slight variations, for seventeen years.

In 1990, Chile returned to a democratic form of government, although Pinochet remained the commander in chief of the army until 1998. Because he had declared himself president in 1980 in his revision of the Chilean constitution, he also became a senator for life, since according to this constitution, former presidents became senators for life. In order to prevent a return to military rule, center-left civilian political parties—no longer banned—formed an alliance called *Concertación*. All four presidents that Chile has had since the end of Pinochet's regime (two Christian Democrats and two Socialists) have come from this coalition. Throughout the 1990s, politicians and other government and professional leaders cautiously proceeded with Chilean democracy. Life under military rule was rarely mentioned, and then only in hushed tones. The military still held enough power to pose a threat—in fact, on a couple occasions, they actually did threaten, quite explicitly, to intervene—and many Chileans just wanted to put the dreadful past behind them by ignoring it and moving on.[1]

The year 1998 was a turning point with Pinochet's international detention. Ultimately, Pinochet was released from the United Kingdom and returned to Chile in 2000. Subsequently, the Chilean courts tried to prosecute him in his own country. Judge Juan Guzmán Tapia, charged with pursuing the investigations and prosecutions, successfully made the argument that the cases of the disappeared did not fall under the protection of immunity that Pinochet had instituted for all crimes that took place between 1973 and 1978 because—since the disappeared had not been found—the crimes were ongoing. In August 2002, the Supreme Court deemed Pinochet unfit to stand trial for reasons of health and mental ability. Just when it appeared that he would never be prosecuted, the Santiago Appeals Court stripped Pinochet of his immunity.[2]

Pinochet died in 2006 without ever being convicted of his crimes. Cases against him have been dropped. The courts are still attempting to prosecute high-ranking military officials who worked under Pinochet, but progress is slow. In June 2007, General Raúl Iturriaga Neumann, who was supposed to report to prison to begin a five-year sentence for ordering the 1974 kidnapping of a "disappeared" member of the Revolutionary Left Movement (MIR), Luis San Martín Vergara, went into hiding. He left behind a video statement in which he proclaimed, "I openly rebel against this arbitrary, biased, unconstitutional and illegal sentence . . . I was subjected to undue prosecution, just like approximately 500 other members of the armed forces, several of whom have been convicted for the same reason, under the complacent gaze of the government and institutions that do not defend our rights, which we are justly claiming" (Estrada, "General in Hiding a 'Coward,' Say Activists," *Inter Press Service News Agency* June 14, 2007). Former naval captain Hernan Bayas, serving as a spokesman for retired officers, announced, "We have knocked on all the doors seeking a re-encounter among Chileans. Sooner or later, there will be a storm," threatening military consequences if human rights cases were not dropped (Lagos and McDonnell, June 16, 2007). Current commander of the army, General Óscar Izurieta, has offered gestures of cooperation, especially with some of the most notorious cases of human rights violations, including the assassination of General Carlos Prats and his spouse, Sofía Cuthbert, in Argentina in 1974 and the alleged poisoning of former President Eduardo Frei Montalva in a Santiago hospital in 1982. However, he also speaks about how members of the military implicated in these crimes are "innocent until proven guilty" and that they should not be condemned until they have had a complete and fair trial in the courts. This all sounds perfectly reasonable despite the fact that the military and secret police *never* granted the same protections to those whom they rounded up during the dictatorship.

Until November 2004, most Chilean media coverage of dictatorship-era human rights violations was limited to the cases of the detained-disappeared and executed. Part of the reason for this focus on the disappeared and the executed was the Rettig Report, known internationally as the report of the National Commission for Truth and Reconciliation, released in 1991 and based on testimony of individuals from the military, human rights groups, and other members of Chilean society. While torture was systematically used on an estimated hundreds of thousands of political detainees during the dictatorship, this would not be addressed in the report; neither would issues of exile, job blacklisting, and other secondary effects of state repression. The report focused only on the politically executed and disappeared, and along with Pinochet's amnesty for all crimes committed between 1973 and 1978, set the parameters for what types of judicial procedures could take place in postdictatorship democracy. In November 2004, however, the Chilean government released the report by the National Commission on Political Prison and Torture—better known as the Valech Report—an extensive document that reveals where torture centers were located in Santiago and the rest of Chile, what methods of torture were used, and the names and identification numbers of former political prisoners who have testified to being tortured in these detention centers. The report is available on the Internet.[3]

Torture, a formerly taboo subject that affected a much larger number of Chileans than disappearances and executions, is a subject that is now also circulating through the Chilean media, but still scarcely. When the topic does get covered, it may, in some cases, do more harm than good since media producers may use the stories for sensational appeal, potentially violating the survivors and further tormenting the loved ones of the dead and disappeared without helping in any way to bring the perpetrators to justice. However, at least the Valech Report itself, if not the mainstream media coverage that has been available so far, may open the door for judicial procedures against those who committed torture against survivors, even though that has not happened much yet.

Human Rights and the Media

Contemporary media discourses in Chile play a significant role in determining how Chileans deal with human rights violations that occurred during the dictatorship as well as those that still exist today. Audiences are not passive consumers of media—they interpret their media with a repertoire of meaning-making tools. Nevertheless, media and culture play an agenda-setting function. They suggest appropriate points of departure for discussion and debate, as they define which issues are important and which are not, as well as which issues are allowed to be discussed and which are not. However, the media does not only affect Chileans' reactions to their recent traumatic past and their conflicted present—the media responds to activities taking place in the larger culture and society. There is a crucial interplay of human rights discourses that occurs in Chile among the media institutions, the courts, the congress, the Presidential Palace, the armed forces, schools, human rights activists, survivors, audiences, artists, and grassroots media producers.

In addition, there is a dynamic relationship among these same discourses as they flow between local, national, and international arenas. As Andreas Huyssen argues, "Even in places where memory practices have a very clear political focus, such as South Africa, Argentina, Chile, and most recently Guatemala, they are affected and to a degree even created by international media coverage and its memory obsessions" ("Present Pasts," 75). Indeed, it was the framing of Pinochet and his legacy as an international issue that allowed for an opening up of media and public discourses in Chile in 1998.

Scholars have generated a number of theories as to why Chile was not able to make more progress during the 1990s to remove the shackles of the dictatorship.[4] Now, new discussions need to take place about the speed at which Chilean society has been making these changes, starting in 1998 with Pinochet's detention in the United Kingdom and progressing more quickly in recent years with constitutional reforms, the election of former political prisoner Michelle Bachelet for president, the death of General Pinochet, and the intransigence of some dictatorship legacies. What is missing from most of these discussions is consideration of the role that the media play in making certain discourses available to the public that may or may not encourage social change and suggesting how Chileans should react to these changes and continuities.

By investigating the circulation of media discourses of human rights, issues of censorship, and opportunities for *aperturas*, or openings, in the communicational tapestry of contemporary Chile, I intend to offer a new dimension to the understanding of how Chilean society is dealing with dictatorship-era human rights violations. Looking more closely at the content, production, and reception of media, global and local media flows, and the role and characteristics of historical memory in Chile will address key questions that pertain to other national contexts as well. One such question is, how do different types of media available in a postrepressive regime address sensitive social and political issues? What sorts of opportunities and limitations exist under such conditions for the articulation of different types of ideas that can contribute to a cultural dialogue? How have the opportunities and limitations changed with the introduction of new forms of media and different conditions for the production, distribution, and exhibition of media? How can individuals participate in dialogues that circulate through the media? How much ability do they have to contribute to these dialogues, especially through the use of new technologies?

To answer these questions, I borrow from cultural studies, globalization studies, political-economic media studies, media reception studies, historical memory studies, and psychological studies of posttraumatic stress. I also consider the work of other authors who have investigated Chilean media, cinema, and journalism.[5] By investigating conditions in Chile through these approaches, I intend to offer an analysis that is sensitive to the significant role of media and cultural communication in such a national context. Furthermore, I will demonstrate that media and cultural discourses in Chile circulate in a restricted and oftentimes unusual fashion due in part to the severe degree of trauma inflicted on Chileans during and after the dictatorship.

My project focuses on different types of media that engage with the issue of human rights in Chile. Specifically, I consider how the media has treated Pinochet's violent legacy—the human rights violations that were systematically committed throughout his regime. As others have remarked,[6] until the Chilean nation and the Chilean state confront this past, acknowledge what happened to the victims, and punish those responsible for the violence, the country will remain an "open wound," interminably festering. Under such conditions, it is argued, Chile will be unable to move toward a more positive and democratic future. The role that the media play in these confrontations needs to be considered more thoroughly, and I hope that this investigation encourages others, especially those concerned about Chile, to pay closer attention to this neglected area. Media discourses of human rights situations that still exist today, such as hate crimes committed against members of the lesbian, gay, bisexual, transgender, queer/questioning (LGBTQ) community, domestic violence, illnesses and deaths caused by air and water pollution, the dangers of illegal abortions, and allegations of the continued use of torture and excessive violence by various members of Chilean security personnel are also worthy of further study; however, they are not the primary focus of this book.

When discussing the media in Chile, I consider both mass commercial media and alternative media, although the boundaries between these two categories are somewhat permeable. For example, the biweekly satirical newspaper *The Clinic* had very alternative beginnings in 1999 but could arguably be labeled now as mainstream and commercial. I also consider the Internet, which plays a significant role in the circulation of both mainstream and alternative media discourses. In general, the alternative media discuss dictatorship-era human rights violations frequently and extensively, but not always. Mainstream media rarely discuss these themes and when they do discuss them, the format for discussion is normally quite restrictive; but there are notable exceptions to this generalization as well. Since the inauguration of President Bachelet and the death of General Pinochet as well as recent reforms in press laws and the elimination of cinema censorship, media producers appear to have more freedom to address sensitive themes, if they choose to pursue these themes at all.

Both types of media—mainstream and alternative—are available to most citizens, although access to the alternative media is more challenging. Newsstand prices are higher for alternative newspapers and magazines, and hence these materials are more difficult for Chileans to afford. Documentaries may or may not be available at the local video rental store but are frequently available for viewing or ordering via the Internet. Not all Chileans can afford a computer with Internet access, but Internet cafés do exist, which makes Internet access more attainable, granted one can pay the fee. Despite the relative availability of the alternative media that I investigate,[7] consumers of this media tend to be a selective sector of the population—frequently those who identify with the political Left, intellectuals, artists, and youth. While much alternative media does address human rights violations extensively, the impact of this coverage must be questioned due to the limited readership and consumption of these products.

Mainstream commercial media, what is most consumed, is primarily owned by those who were aligned with, and supported, the right-wing dictatorship. Although many contemporary media studies scholars caution against simplistic political economic explanations of the media, in the case of Chile, these factors must be considered. If, for no other reason, attention must be given to patterns of ownership of the major media companies because Chileans believe this is important. Almost everyone I interviewed in Chile, regardless of whether or not they actually worked in the media industry and regardless of their political perspective, mentioned this factor as a cause for censorship and self-censorship in Chilean media.

In their book *The Global Media*, Edward Herman and Robert McChesney paint a grim picture of the state of the world—one where the U.S.-Western commercial media have essentially obliterated all alternatives both within and outside the United States. There is no denying that many of these concerns are justified, especially in Chile, where a democratically elected socialist government was overthrown, with U.S. support, by a military coup that ensured Chile's future status as a capitalist state open to foreign investment. Herman and McChesney describe the influence of the United States in Latin America during the 1960s and 1970s, when the United States helped install many anticommunist military dictators as heads of state: "The United States was an active or behind-the-scenes participant in many of these transfers of power. The new regimes invariably attacked and decimated trade unions and other social democratic forces, opened up the economies, and encouraged neoliberal transformations, and if they did not immediately commercialize the media at least created a political environment that helped expedite commercialization after the military regimes retreated to the barracks. The dominant media of the West treated these lengthy interludes of state terror and class cleansing in a low-key manner and as regrettable features of Cold War policy" (Herman and McChesney, 155).

As Herman and McChesney indicate, not only did U.S.–cold war policies influence media environments in the countries under dictatorship, they also influenced the amount and type of information the rest of the world received about these military coups and dictatorships and the democratic governments that they had replaced.

There is certainly evidence of this in Chile. In contrast to coverage of the coup, coverage of Salvador Allende's presidential election victory in 1970 was depicted as threatening to the existing sociopolitical order of the western hemisphere. *Time magazine* ran a cover story about the election in its October 19, 1970, issue. The cover contains two different imposing images of President Allende in various shades of red, a literal indication of the "red menace." Seven months before the coup, on February 21, 1973, the *New York Times* ran a brief article buried near the entertainment section, titled, "Wealthy in Chile Still Find Beef and Scotch." The article, by Jonathan Kandell,[8] appears sympathetic to the wealthy who hint that they expect a coup to take place in the coming months. Five days after the coup, on September 16, 1973, the *New York Times* ran an article titled, "A Devastating End for a Unique, Troubled Venture." No mention was made of U.S. involvement in the events of Chile, but to be fair, the extent to which the United States was involved would not be publicized until years later.[9] Constantin Costa-Gavras's feature film *Missing* (1982), based on the novel by Thomas Hauser and starring Jack Lemmon and Sissy Spacek, relates the true story of the disappearance of Charles Horman, an American journalist in Chile. The film does make explicit the U.S. collusion with Chilean military in Horman's disappearance. As a consequence, the film was lambasted by the *New York Times* upon its release[10] but then proceeded to win multiple film awards, including an Oscar. Now that declassified CIA documents reveal that Costa-Gavras's version of events was more accurate than that of the sources that 1982 *New York Times* film critics used to blast the film, he ponders, "One wonders how much could have been revealed about Chile if, years earlier, *New York Times* reporters had been pressing Washington for the truth, instead of parroting the official story in the guise of movie criticism" (22).

Inside of Chile, after the coup, almost all media outlets were taken over or shut down by the military regime. Those that remained, although state-controlled, were open to U.S.-friendly programming and investments. In fact, Chile's most prestigious conservative commercial newspaper, *El Mercurio*, was partially funded by the CIA before and after Pinochet's coup because it was considered a crucial propaganda tool for the Right.[11] Incidentally, a member of the Edwards family, which owned *El Mercurio*, had fled to the United States during the socialist government of President Allende and worked as an executive at Pepsi, a company that is demonized, through the brand's juxtaposition with violence and the military, by Costa-Gavras in *Missing*.[12]

Globalization of Media and Culture

The scholarship that does not celebrate the emancipating potential of an interconnected world tends to depict the spread of capitalist, transnational media as the demise of local, "authentic" cultures, especially in third-world countries that are too poor and dependent on international loans and investment to put up a fight to protect their own interests. Furthermore, scholars, such as Herbert Schiller, Herman, and McChesney, argue that issues of great concern to particular regions of the world or groups of people within them get virtually no, or very mediated, coverage at the international level.

Ideas such as these inspired many developing nations to challenge Western control of global media in the United Nations in the 1970s. This Non-Aligned Movement (NAM) called for more control of global media flows for the developing nations. These nations wanted more access to production and distribution of their film and TV programming as well as more restrictions placed on Western media pouring into their countries. The New World Information and Communication Order (NWICO) debates ended, however, in the 1980s, when the United States and United Kingdom withdrew from the talks.

The 1980s were a time of political conservatism and market liberalization in the Western/Northern nations, which had global repercussions. U.S. President Ronald Reagan supported media deregulation. TV, radio, film, and print media corporations had many restrictions regarding ownership and control of their companies lifted. Antitrust concerns were dropped from the national agenda. Companies were allowed to acquire more stations, more theaters, and a greater number of different types of media and technologies, with no one seeming especially concerned about conflicts of interest. Globally, more Hollywood films and TV programming started to flow into countries around the world as many nations that were struggling to survive the global recession realized it was much less expensive to import films and TV programming than to produce media content themselves.

However, as countries like Chile experienced an influx of Western/Northern media and culture, the Western/Northern countries received media and culture from the developing nations as well. Despite the repressive and suppressive climate in Chile after September 11, 1973, and the grim picture conceptualized by globalization critics, some disparate voices did manage to get out of the country after the coup and throughout the time of the dictatorship. Many voices were those of exiles who were able to share their stories with the rest of the world after they fled their home country. Other voices came from those still living within Chile, especially through *arpilleras*,[13] the craftwork made by women of the Association of Relatives of the Detained-Disappeared (AFDD). As Rosalind Bresnahan (2002) and Juan Poblete (2006) have demonstrated, radio played a crucial role in the dispersal of anti-Pinochet discourses during the dictatorship, and continues to be an outlet for alternative perspectives today. With improved access to video production equipment in the 1980s, many Chileans smuggled out video footage that ended up in documentaries. Today, video footage and documentaries are distributed and exhibited more easily than ever before through the Internet.

Contemporary media globalization scholars tend to offer a more nuanced perspective on the cultural impact of an increasingly globalized world. Annabelle Sreberny-Mohammadi argues that "modernity has created a paradoxical global unity which remains deeply problematic in its patterns of inequality and domination. Yet it may also hold some opportunity. A recognition of the many inextricable linkages that bind us is part of an emergent global consciousness that might just do some good" ("The Many Faces of Cultural Imperialism," 68). She suggests that cultural imperialism is a dynamic process that has taken place since the original European conquests. Examples of this imperialism include missionaries and European formal education systems; Western/Northern notions of professionalism, languages, travel, and tourism, including sex exploitation; and technology. She also points out that sometimes these forms of "cultural imperialism" have given an advantage to the people usually considered the victims of such imperialism. Many people in "developing" countries now understand more languages than people in "developed" countries, as they were often forced to learn the languages of the colonizers while also maintaining their own, and the colonizers rarely learned much of the languages used by the colonized. This phenomenon often remains the same today. Tourists and business travelers from the "developed" countries are limited in their knowledge of the languages spoken in the "developing" countries they visit. Citizens of "developing" countries have often learned additional languages as a survival skill in order to conduct business with those visiting from the "developed" world or as a consequence of spending time in the "developed" world in order to earn a living, attend university, or escape political persecution. In addition, many in the developing world are exposed to other languages from the large quantity of imported Northern/Western media that they consume. A result of this today is that many people in developing nations can engage with a larger diversity of media texts offered in the various languages that they understand.

John Tomlinson (1991, 1999) argues that in today's global environment, where companies are trying to maintain and create new audiences for new media in addition to more traditional forms of film and TV, there is no unified or organized intent or effect on audiences and consumers. The global environment is saturated with an overabundance of media products, consumer goods, and competing ideas. Tomlinson does not deny that there is an uneven distribution of power for nations, institutions, and individuals to communicate through media. Nonetheless, he believes that our complex global media environment often allows unexpected voices and messages to be heard in creative and unconventional ways. He reminds us that globalization allows for a "complex connectivity." As local cultures are exposed to more global media, products, and ideas, the global environment is also changing as it incorporates more elements of different local cultures. He also claims that the idea of preserving a "national culture" is problematic. For this argument, Tomlinson refers to Benedict Anderson.

Anderson describes how the concept of nationalism relies on an "imagined community." A nation is imagined since most individuals within a nation will never know each other, yet they feel a horizontal alliance and sense of brother- and sisterhood even though many of these brothers and sisters are much better or worse off than their siblings and they actually have very different living conditions and life experiences. Anderson argues that nationalism as a concept did not exist until the development of the printing press, which both allowed people to read in their vernacular languages and condensed the reader's sense of time and space in a way that created a feeling of unity. Today's electronic media has enhanced these conceptions of nation. However, this sense of unity was, and is, imaginary, as there has never been a unified national culture.

Tomlinson refers to "the ambiguous gift of capitalist modernism" (1991, 108). He believes that many critics of globalization perceive transnational global media as a monolithic, unilateral entity with no positive effects. These critics fail "to probe the contradictions of capitalist culture" (108). One of the contradictions important to this project is that increased capitalist globalization has opened up spaces for alternative cultural texts, often oppositional to the status quo, that may reach large audiences through increased channels of international distribution.

Joseph Straubhaar points to another phenomenon that further deconstructs concerns about media imperialism. He agrees with Tomlinson that current global media discourse that concentrates on nations should be more sensitive to regions and other transnational dimensions: "While globalization increasingly dominates current discussion of television flows and impacts, Tomlinson (1991, pp. 23–24) observes that most of the media imperialism and cultural imperialism discussion assumes that the primary actors are nations . . . However, the view of the nation as a cultural unit is changing" (Straubhaar, 286).

Straubhaar's concept of the geocultural market—"multi-country markets linked by geography, language, and culture"—can help us appreciate the complex channels through which media can flow (291). In Spanish-speaking Latin America, there is a Spanish language geocultural market, where Mexico, Spain, and Miami, Florida, are significant centers, along with Brazil, with Spanish dubbed over the Portuguese, which distributes a lot of programming to smaller countries with fewer resources for the production of their own media. On network television, Chile imports a far greater number of programs from these Hispanic and Latin American sources, although on cable, there are more networks and programming from the United States and elsewhere.

Conceptualizing Chilean media audiences, consumers, users, and producers is complex because of the huge Chilean diaspora communities scattered across the globe. Arjun Appadurai's characterization of the five dimensions of global cultural flow—*ethnoscapes*,[14] *mediascapes*,[15] *technoscapes*,[16] *finanscapes*,[17] and *ideoscapes*[18]—is useful to consider as we attempt to conceive a Chilean-global community that interacts with media. The Internet has played a significant role in the advancement of these cultural flows. Although the Internet is not easily accessible to all Chileans, it does offer new opportunities for some groups, especially the exiles and children of exiles, to come together across geographic barriers.

Sonia Serra explains the importance of this dynamic relationship that exists across national boundaries as well as across concepts of "centers" and "peripheries": "In routine modes, the initiative in agenda-setting and policy-making lies with the center of the political system, but as Habermas (1997, 381) argues the great issues of the last decades were not initiated by central powers. Instead, they were brought up by intellectuals, concerned citizens, radical professionals and self-proclaimed advocates" (154).

To understand how those on the fringe can be heard in the mainstream, we need to imagine multiple public spheres, including an international public sphere. Serra explains how human rights activists in Brazil, with the help of groups, such as Amnesty

International and the Children's Defense Fund, were able to get their story about the execution of abandoned street children covered by the international media (151–72). This started a discussion at the international level about the cruelty of Brazilian police and the inhumanity of murdering homeless children. A large international public became outraged. The Brazilian media did not cover the issue until the issue was discussed at the international level. In this case, a domestic problem within Brazil was not resolved until Brazilian officials and media executives felt outside pressure to address the issue.

Media and the Public Sphere

Some scholars believe that Habermas's concept of the public sphere is too romanticized and unrealistic because he does not acknowledge the degree to which all semblances of a public sphere are mediated. Nancy Fraser has criticized Habermas's idea of a unified, all-inclusive public sphere as inaccurate and undesirable. She argues that such a sphere has never existed. The idealized sphere that Habermas first imagined really only included white, upper-class men. Furthermore, even if an all-inclusive public sphere could exist, it would not be enough. There are so many differences among individuals and their communication styles that for us to presume that each person's voice could be heard in one place is naive. She suggests that there are multiple public spheres: "The bourgeois public was never *the* public. On the contrary, virtually contemporaneous with the bourgeois public there arose a host of competing counter-publics, elite women's publics, and working-class publics" (Fraser, 523).

This does not mean, however, that these smaller, multiple spheres take the place of a larger, more inclusive sphere. Rather, these smaller spheres allow group members to organize and give strength to individual members who can then carry their message to a larger, mainstream public sphere: "I propose to call these *subaltern counterpublics* in order to signal that they are parallel discursive arenas where members of subordinated social groups invent and circulate counter-discourses to formulate oppositional interpretations of their identities, interests, and needs. . . . On the one hand, they function as spaces of withdrawal and regroupment; on the other hand, they also function as bases and training grounds for agitational activities directed toward wider publics" (Fraser, 527–28).

Although those who care about Chile are scattered across the globe, we can still think of them as unified in a virtual space: their concern for the same issues brings them together. During Chile's dictatorship, chapters of the Victor Jara Foundation, named after the Chilean folksinger and songwriter who was tortured and killed after the coup, and Amnesty International organized at the local level around the world. These groups took their message to a larger public, educating people about the issues they cared about. As they raised the level of awareness in their own communities, the story of what was happening in Chile got picked up by the local press and eventually by the mainstream press of larger regions. Here we see an international issue channeling into local communities and then these local communities affecting responses at the international level.

A dynamic interaction among subaltern spheres and a larger, more inclusive and hegemonic sphere is occurring inside of Chile as well. Alternative Chilean media, which tends to circulate more extensive and diverse discourses of human rights, serves the role that Fraser describes for "counterpublics." The alternative media, combined with public demonstrations and protests, art, literature, music, and the theater, interact with a wider public sphere arena found in Chile's mainstream, commercial media. In contemporary Chile, as well as in most other countries, commercial media is the largest gatherer of the public: it brings more Chileans together than any other venue, and its power to influence the shaping of the nation's consciousness must be considered.

CENSORSHIP AND SELF-CENSORSHIP

In addition to my investigation of media and communicational flows, I pay particular attention to censorship, emphasizing the multiple and nuanced roles censorship plays in Chilean media. First, there are remnants of official state censorship as it was mandated in the Chilean Constitution of 1980,[19] written primarily with the advice of former Senator Jaime Guzmán, who was assassinated at the beginning of Chile's return to democracy. Second, there is the censorship commonly found in any capitalist, global media environment—a type that aims to enhance the mood and messages of paid advertising and diminish risk for offending any important sector (from a commercial point of view) of the audience. Third, and perhaps most significant in the context of Chile, is the practice of self-censorship as exercised by media writers, editors, news anchors, and producers working in media institutions with high concentrations of conservative ownership. In Chile, there are unwritten rules understood by professionals in the postdictatorship era regarding what is acceptable for discussion and what is not. Those breaking the rules can lose their jobs and get blacklisted.

Historical Memory and Media Interpretation in a Posttraumatic Nation

In coordination with an investigation of censorship and self-censorship, we must consider the role of historical memory, and more specifically, historical memory in a posttraumatic context. Historical memory studies offer a significant dimension to this research.[20] I aspire to contribute to these dialogues by incorporating media studies more concretely into their conceptual frameworks. These scholars emphasize how key cultural moments and their representations offer framing devices and perspectives for interpreting history through memory, while also indicating that individual responses to these moments and representations will vary according to the individual's background and experience. This argument—that individual responses to media texts will depend on background and experience—has been made, as well by media reception scholars.[21]

I pay heed particularly to scholars, such as Staiger, Klinger, and Gripsrud, who suggest that a closer look at the historical context in which media are released and circulate over time indicates what discourses are available to viewers and how those discourses interact with a specific culture or ideology. Similarly, I approach audience reception primarily through consideration of the sociohistoric context in which contemporary media discourses circulate. I agree with Gripsrud's suggestion that media texts should be analyzed with respect to the historical contexts through which individual audience members engage with these texts.

Annette Kuhn, who looks at the role of memory, including post-traumatic memory, in our interpretation of media texts, describes memory as having personal and collective aspects, and she suggests how memories can change over time. In one of her studies, older female film viewers watching a film that they first watched when they were young describe their inner, "true" selves as the younger versions of themselves. Those initial experiences of their younger selves remained vivid in their memories, and it is those experiences that they hold onto most strongly.

Anyone who has seen Patricio Guzmán's documentary *Chile: Obstinate Memory* (1997) has witnessed the same process at play as Chileans in postdictatorship Chile watched and reacted to Guzmán's documentary trilogy, *The Battle of Chile* (1975–79). Many Chileans who experienced the years of Popular Unity and then the military coup that led to Pinochet's dictatorship also hold on to vivid memories of these historical moments that sometimes feel even more real than their present. Those defining moments were formative in the construction of their identities, and the realities that they experience today are filtered through their experiences in those crucial earlier years.

Marita Sturken takes the idea of subjectivity as social construct and pays particular attention to the role of visual media and cultural texts in the cultivation of historical memory: "Camera images—photographic, cinematic, televisual, documentary, and docudrama—play a vital role in the development of national meaning by creating a sense of shared participation and experience in the nation . . . It does not follow, however, that the collective experience of watching 'national' events on television leaves all viewers with similar and singular interpretations. Rather, in watching national television events, viewers engage with, whether in agreement or resistance, a concept of nationhood and national meaning" (Sturken, 24).

All types of media and communication that I investigate in this project have an important visual element. Consideration of human rights media and public culture discourses in Chile requires spending just as much time on the images that may pervade our consciousness and linger in our memories as on the spoken and silenced words. For example, as a woman and a feminist, what stands out to me most when I watch an episode of *Chilevisión*'s Sunday talk show, *Tolerancia Cero (Zero Tolerance)*, is that the regular panelists sitting around the table include four men and zero women. That image of four prestigious men talking about the state of affairs in Chile and the world interferes with my paying attention to what they are saying because I cannot stop thinking about who is being excluded from these discussions. However, another viewer can have a completely different response to this media text. Likewise, images of General Pinochet victoriously standing up out of his wheelchair upon his return from the United Kingdom in 2000—after convincing the courts that he was too weak and frail to stand trial for crimes against humanity—can affect very different reactions in Chileans. Some see that image as justice personified—the savior of the *patria* back on his native soil, as strong and courageous as ever, away from the inappropriate and inexcusable interventions of the European courts. Others see the image as one more example of the general's deceptions and lies and, in hindsight, his escape from the moment that came closest to his proper prosecution and judgment in the form of a trial outside of Chile.

In response to arguments that Chile did not deal more directly with the legacy of the dictatorship in the 1990s because Chileans suffered from a national amnesia, historian Steve J. Stern suggests that the Chilean people do *not* suffer from collective amnesia of the violence and repression of the military government. Rather, they do remember the violence, but they understand and interpret it in different ways depending on their proximity to the violence and their social and class positions in society. He posits four major methods that Chileans use to interpret the violence that took place during the military government and discusses them under the rubric of *emblematic memories*.

According to Stern, there are four emblematic memories that have competed for dominance in Chile: the memory of salvation,[22] the memory of an open wound,[23] the memory of a test of democracy and ethical values,[24] and the memory of a closed box.[25] He describes memory as a process, using the metaphor of *memory knots* to describe how certain events, groups, and ideas can stir up memories. Stern identifies three types of memory knots: human groups, actions and dates, and locations or physical remains. For example, exposure to a workers' union, a political party, or a human rights organization—any group of people in which individuals have shared a collective history—may trigger memories. So can anniversaries of historical events, such as the military coup or the date of a loved one's disappearance or departure from the country into exile. In addition, memory knots also emerge when observing military parades or police officers monitoring a contemporary street protest, and also in the National Stadium, once used as a concentration camp, and at a memorial site for the disappeared. All three types of memory knots elicit multiple memories and "demand the construction of bridges between collective memory and forgetting" (13). Clearly, the media can play a special role in bringing these memories to the forefront of a nation's consciousness when what triggers memories is represented and addressed in the media. Decisions *not* to represent these groups, events, and related issues also have a tremendous impact.

As an example, on August 13, 2008, I found a story in the Chilean mainstream media on the Internet that retired military officials—three generals, one brigadier, and one colonel in the army—are being processed for the 1992 (postdictatorship) assassination of their colleague, Colonel Gerardo Huber ("Cinco altos oficiales del Ejército procesados por caso Huber"). For thirteen years, Colonel Huber's twenty-day disappearance after giving testimony on the illegal trafficking of arms to Croatia, and then the discovery of his body in the Maipo River with a bullet wound in his head, had been classified as a suicide. The five who are charged are believed to be responsible for the assassination of Colonel Huber's driver as well. At least on their Web sites, the most mainstream media outlets, including the newspapers *El Mercurio* and *La Tercera*, as well as the TV networks *Televisión Nacional de Chile* and *Chilevisión*, deemed the story not worth mentioning. Most likely, the absence of coverage is due to one of two reasons (or a combination of both): (1) covering the story may be considered too dangerous and (2) the story may not be considered newsworthy because the case has been active since 2006 and because there have been so many examples of outrageous acts committed by members of the Chilean military and security forces. An event that an outsider may perceive as extremely unusual may seem very "normal" to Chileans. Either scenario is deeply disturbing.

While the most common reaction of Chilean mainstream media is to silence memory knots, there have been significant moments of their coverage as well. Pinochet's detention in London was one of these instances of a cautious *apertura*, or opening, in discourses. Another was in May 2002, when Judge Juan Guzmán Tapia was investigating the case of Charles Horman, one of two American journalists who disappeared and were found dead shortly after the coup. Coverage was extensive. Clips were shown on the news from the previously mentioned movie, *Missing* (Costa-Gavras, 1983). The former U.S. Consul General in Santiago, Frederick Purdy,[26] was asked by reporters about the role the United States played in supporting the coup (and his belligerent response, which includes a denial of the existence of declassified CIA documents that prove U.S. involvement in the planning and implementation of the coup—available to anyone with Internet access, interspersed with English profanity, which I captured on videotape, would embarrass any thinking, compassionate U.S. citizen). The National Stadium, where thousands of citizens were detained and tortured and hundreds were executed, was visited, with former prisoners explaining to the judge what had happened there in 1973. Under the façade of an "international story," the locker room torture chambers of the National Stadium were shown on TV. The plight of Charles Horman became the plight of the thousands of Chilean citizens who were once victimized there.

Stern ultimately argues that Chileans have been slow to resolve and seek justice for the events of the recent past as a result of a cultural impasse due to competing emblematic memories. What makes the situation more complicated is that many Chileans have different emblematic memories but share a conviction that the way to resolve those competing memories is by ignoring the past and refusing to confront its legacy.

Macarena Gómez-Barris suggests that "the process of national identification gains traction through a kind of selectivity that condenses particular meaning formations, while banishing others from public visibility" (5). She offers the term *memory symbolic* to explain how the Chilean public sphere negotiates state-led, top-down initiatives with alternative, bottom-up processes of memory discourse. The intentions of the former often clash with the intentions of the latter, causing a constant, dynamic struggle in competing explanations and reactions to recent national history.

Elizabeth Jelin looks more broadly at the role of historical memory in relation to the legacy of human rights violations in the Southern Cone region of South America. She describes the early 1990s as a grim period at the political and judicial level in the postrepressive regimes of these countries, while historical memory was still engaged through cultural and artistic venues, a phenomenon that she suggests helps to explain the resurgence of these issues at all levels of the public sphere in the late 1990s and beginning of the twenty-first century:

> In fact, at the level of state institutions, the first half of the 1990s was a low point in actions and initiatives related to human rights violations during dictatorship in South America. . . . At the societal and cultural level, however, there were fewer silences. Human rights movements in these countries have maintained a significant presence, linking the demands to settle accounts with the past (demands for justice) with the founding principles of democratic institutions. Those directly affected by repression bear their suffering and pain, which they translate into various types of public action. Artistic expressions in film, narrative, fine arts, theater, dance, and music often incorporate that past and its legacies. (Jelin, xiv–xv)

Jelin approaches the study of historical memory according to three principles:

> First, memories are to be understood as subjective processes anchored in experiences and in symbolic and material markers. Second, memories are the object of disputes, conflicts, and struggles. This premise involves the need to focus attention on the active and productive role of participants in these struggles. It is they who generate meanings of the past, framed by the power relations in which their actions are embedded in the present. Third, memories must be looked at historically; that is, there is a need to 'historicize' memories, which is to say that the meanings attached to the past change over time and are part of larger, complex social and political scenarios. There are also variations in the place assigned to memories in different societies and cultural settings and across the distinct spaces in which political and ideological struggles take place. (xv)

Jelin's articulation of historical memory complements that of Stern when she describes historical memory as a power struggle that is performed by competing groups of people with different experiences and backgrounds that fight to impose their perceptions of a given historical moment on the larger public sphere: "In every case, *once sufficient time has elapsed to make possible the establishment of a minimum degree of distance between past and present*, alternative (even rival) interpretations of that recent past and its memory occupy a central place in cultural and political debates. These interpretations constitute an inescapable subject for public debate in the difficult road toward forging democratic societies. These memories and interpretations are also key elements in the processes of (re)construction of individual and collective identities in societies emerging from periods of violence and trauma" (xvii–xviii).

Also, just as Stern describes historical amnesia, or the closed box, as actually full of memory, so does Jelin: "Slogans such as 'memory against oblivion' or 'against silence' hide an opposition between distinct and rival memories (each one with its own forgetfulness). In truth, what is at stake is an opposition of 'memory against memory'" (xviii). This struggle to articulate competing historical memories plays out through the arenas of media and public culture—visible and audible in the content of media but also in the responses to media and its surrounding culture as voiced by media producers, journalists, human rights activists, members of the military, politicians, and "regular" citizens.

When we consider individual responses to media texts in a posttraumatic historical context, it is useful to remember cultural studies scholar Stuart Hall's classic article, "Encoding, Decoding." According to his model, individuals can respond in three different ways to the dominant ideology of the text. They can agree with it, negotiate its meaning, or oppose it. If they oppose the dominant meaning altogether, they can look for gaps and fissures in the text that allow for alternative readings. Citizens of repressive and postrepressive regimes develop talents for reading messages between the official lines of media texts.

There are many examples of significant discourses slipping through or past repressive and postrepressive media institutions.

Annabelle Sreberny-Mohammadi and Ali Mohammadi looked at the role of small media during the Iranian revolution of the late 1970s and early 1980s. In the case of Iran, television was controlled by the state (by the shah who supported Western modernization without political freedom). TV was supposed to unify the Iranian people and encourage them to support the shah. Ironically, the shah's push for modernization and the introduction of Western TV programming had the opposite effect. For many Muslims and Muslim leaders, it demonstrated the evils of the West and the need to return to a more "traditional" society. For others, it allowed exposure to representations of other ways of life and encouraged them to fight for more political freedom and to imagine different systems of government. All of the people who were critical of the shah's regime and desired a revolution could not, however, use TV to call for change since it was controlled by the state. Instead, they used other forms of communication, including audiocassette tapes and mimeographed letters and poetry that were circulated throughout Iran and back and forth over its national borders. Many Iranian exiles, including Ayatollah Khomeini, were able to communicate with the Iranian people in the nation through these channels. Here again, we see these alternative, subaltern discourses circulating past the more hegemonic venue of television, offering diverse interpretations to the observing public.

In China, James Lull has looked at the role of television in the lives of urban Chinese before, during, and after the Tiananmen Square uprising. In the 1980s, television sets suddenly became available and affordable to most urban Chinese families. Since Chinese TV is run by the state, officials hoped that they could use the medium to unify the people and continue to promote authoritarian Communism. However, Lull found that TV actually helped the Chinese people reflect on their way of life and think critically about party officials. For example, when the Chinese watch the state news, they know that they are getting the Chinese Communist Party's point of view, and they have learned to watch critically and read between the lines. Further, international flows of communication played a key role during the Tiananmen Square uprising. Many Chinese student activists, when trying to communicate with students at other universities, would phone or send faxes and letters to points outside of the country. Also, many people relied on the news they received from radio networks, such as the BBC, that they picked up on shortwave radio. Thus, while the Chinese leadership offered a specific interpretation of events, many Chinese depended on information available from outside of the country to get a different perspective.

In India, Purnima Mankekar has looked at how working-class and lower middle-class urban Indian women engaged with state-run television representations of women, the family, and the nation in the 1980s, and she suggested how conditions were changing in the 1990s with the introduction of more commercial, regional, and international programming. Mankekar found that in the 1980s, programming from *Doordarshan*, the national station, represented the appropriate roles for women as submissive and dutiful wives and mothers. At the same time, women were hailed by advertisers in often contradictory manners. When Mankekar looked at the media environment in India in the 1990s, she was hopeful that more alternative programming of different types from different sources would allow women to reimagine themselves in new and more empowering ways. Also, the introduction of satellite regional programming offered audiences in many parts of India programs in their own languages for the first time, paying more attention to specific regional concerns.

Many media texts in Chile also offer alternative readings through the systemic use of certain types of structured absences. A key theme or idea will be noted by audience members because its very lack of discussion and representation is obvious to Chileans familiar with their specific culture and history. This is a legacy of the dictatorship, but it remained as a tactic in the 1990s[27] and continues to this day. In 2002, *Televisión Nacional de Chile* produced a documentary on Latin American dictatorships but neglected discussion of Chile. Also in 2002, a photograph of members of the AFDD holding a burial service for the identified remains of a victim formerly classified as missing[28] was included in Chile's daily commercial newspaper, *El Mercurio*, but there was no article attached. Orlando Lübbert's popular feature film released in 2001, *Taxi para tres* (*Taxi for Three*), does not refer to the dictatorship directly, but a police officer character acts similarly to how members of Pinochet's secret police forces behaved, and one of the main characters mentions that he was raised by his grandparents because his parents were "taken away." On August 16, 2008, an article on *La Tercera*'s Web site announced how photographer Ricardo Portugueis received the 2008 Rodrigo Rojas DeNegri prize ("Fotógrafo Ricardo Portugueis recibió premio Rodrigo Rojas Denegri 2008"). Rodrigo Rojas DeNegri was a nineteen-year-old photojournalist who was severely beaten, covered in gasoline, and burned alive by members of the Chilean military in 1986. The article said that he "died in a protest during the Military Government," a much milder and vaguer description than "violently killed by the military during the dictatorship," but anyone familiar with the case, or even anyone familiar with recent history, will be able to interpret additional meanings.[29]

CASE STUDIES OF CHILEAN MEDIA AND CULTURE

In this book, I discuss the discursive media flows of human rights issues in a variety of media. However, my discussion focuses primarily on specific examples from each of the following types of media: alternative newspapers including *The Clinic*, programming on the TV network *Chilevisión*, the documentaries *Fernando ha vuelto (Fernando Is Back;* Silvio Caiozzi, 1998) and *El día en que murió Pinochet (The Day Pinochet Died;* Nicole Senerman, 2006), and the feature narrative film *Machuca* (Andrés Wood, 2004). *Chilevisión* is one of the big five TV networks of Chile and was owned by foreigners in the early part of the new millennium; it is now owned by presidential candidate for the conservative National Renovation Party and owner of *LAN Chile* airlines, Sebastián Piñera. Caiozzi and Senerman have produced short documentaries that offer significant discourses on Chile's violent legacy and various approaches to the articulation of national memory. Wood has produced feature films that have been popular with both cultural critics and general audiences. *Machuca* approaches Chile's recent history through the eyes of adolescent children and managed to appeal to diverse sectors of Chile's divided society. Arguably, this film text and the reception it received in Chile upon its release have played a significant role in bringing all Chileans to a common table needed to begin a process of national healing. *The Clinic* is an alternative to the two corporate newspaper giants of Chile—*El*

Mercurio and *La Tercera*. Finally, this book considers the role of protests in public culture and investigates the cases of the Funa organization, whose members and their allies demonstrate outside of the homes and workplaces of men who committed human rights violations during the dictatorship but continue to live in impunity, and weekly demonstrations that take place every Thursday night at Londres 38, a former torture center in downtown Santiago.

Interdisciplinary Approach to This Research

My research is informed by a combination of methods: analysis of media texts, consideration of the industrial and cultural institutions through which these texts circulate, analysis of the larger cultural context that colors these national memory discourses, and the ways in which media producers and consumers perceive and discuss media within a specific historical context (postdictatorship Chile). I have conducted interviews with media professionals, members of human rights organizations, and regular citizens. In this project, I look closely at the concerns raised and the language used by media producers and media consumers because I believe them to be crucial components in an investigation of Chilean media and discourses of human rights.

Consideration of the effect of these multiple media discourses on current cultural, political, and judicial processes taking place within and outside of post-Pinochet Chile not only demonstrates the crucial role that media can play in raising awareness and expediting procedures for bringing perpetrators of crimes against humanity to justice, but it also demonstrates the degree to which media, serving as an agenda-setter, can aid a nation in continuing along a path of avoidance, apathy, and impunity. This study also demonstrates how media communication can influence the ways in which members of a divided society choose to deal with a traumatic past and negotiate their competing historical memories. Media and its surrounding culture play a key role in the shaping of local, national, and global identities and consciousness. This book investigates that role in the context of contemporary Chile.

Chapter 2

Television

Self-censorship, Sensationalism, and Structured Absences

The media plays a major role introducing [human rights] issues—albeit with short and only intermittent incursions—into the public sphere.

—Roniger and Synajder, *The Legacy of Human-Rights Violations in the Southern Cone*

The concept of hegemony shows us how powerful institutions like media are involved in a perpetual struggle (never fully won, always ongoing) to incorporate social conflict and reach popular consensus.

—Spigel and Curtin, *The Revolution Wasn't Televised*

Chilean broadcast television illustrates the complicated ways in which mainstream commercial media can address sensitive issues, often through shared understandings of the unspoken—pushing human rights discourses into programming despite tremendous pressures for censorship and self-censorship. This chapter looks at television, arguably the most powerful form of media due to its accessibility to a large, diverse public as well as the impact of the blend of visual language with dialogue. Then this chapter investigates the case of one of the five major broadcast networks in Chile—*Chilevisión*.

Television plays a central role in the ways that Chileans choose to deal with the legacy of General Augusto Pinochet's regime as well as move forward in the struggle toward a real democracy.

According to Stephen Crofts Wiley, "The dictatorship maintained a tight grip on programming through censorship and the production of vast amounts of pro-Pinochet propaganda, all the while imposing a thorough commercialization of broadcasting and permitting the unregulated private development of cable television . . . Television, during this period, reinforced the authoritarian project of controlling national public space and reorganizing 'Chile' as a territory of uncontested, transnationally dependent capitalist development" ("Assembled Agency," 2006). After the dictatorship, the military generals stepped down as network heads, but many of the staff who had sympathized with Pinochet remained. Others who had worked during the regime may not have sympathized with Pinochet but they had learned that, in order to preserve their jobs and their safety, they needed to be careful. The result during the transition to democracy was extreme network conservatism.

In the early 1990s, television exposed Chilean citizens who had been removed from the violence of the dictatorship to many of the atrocities for the first time. Those who had denied that the human rights violations had been committed were faced with irrefutable evidence. But by the mid-1990s, "public interest" in the violent legacy of Pinochet had declined. As former *Chilevisión* news director and anchor Alejandro Guillier described, "People were very informed of human rights violations. After the first few years of the return to democracy, when there had been much dealing with human rights, especially after 1994, we said okay, we know what happened; now we need to move on; change themes" (personal interview, April 8, 2002).

In their book on postrepressive regimes in the southern countries of South America, Luis Roniger and Mario Synajder write, "While certain minorities progressively adopted human rights as their banner for opposing military rule, wide sectors of the demobilized societies of the Southern Cone accepted the official versions and others reacted with apathy" (1999, 39). This phenomenon existed during and after the dictatorship in Chile. Justice was not meted out to most leaders of the military, and while many citizens sympathized with the victims, many also believed that the victims had been "enemies of the state." In addition, the media industry and the *Concertación* government were under the watchful eyes of the armed forces. They were threatened on multiple occasions throughout the 1990s when the generals did not agree with the decisions of media professionals and government representatives. According to Guillier, "The military regime was successful in many aspects. The economic and political power supported Pinochet. They negotiated the transition to democracy. There were tacit agreements, not written, about what would be discussed and done, and what would not. We knew that Pinochet would not spend time in prison" (personal interview, April 8, 2002).

When Pinochet was arrested in England in October 1998 with the possibility of being extradited to Spain to be tried for "crimes against humanity," and as the British courts debated Pinochet's case, the Chilean media opened up. With a newfound sense of freedom due to their former dictator being held thousands of miles away and the knowledge that the international community was watching, they reopened their human rights dialogues and discussed how they could achieve real justice and social change. As Roniger and Synajder state, "The massive publicity of these issues in the global mass media [added] another dimension of difficulty in any attempt to cover up, favoring public accountability" (1999, 146). When Pinochet was returned to Chile in 2000, some of these dialogues were stifled again, but others remained. As with the rest of the media, television could no longer be so tightly controlled. More journalists and producers were willing to test the limits with a bold, reinvigorated sense of righteousness and intolerance for restrictive media policies and practices.

While Chile has a productive domestic television industry in relation to smaller Latin American countries with fewer resources, production pales in comparison to larger Latin American television industries such as Mexico and Brazil. Most of Chile's domestic TV production is nonfiction, in part because this programming tends to be cheaper to produce, but Chile does produce some soap operas or *telenovelas* as well. Chile exports some programs to other Latin American countries and imports many more. Until recently, Chileans who could afford cable and satellite TV got virtually no domestic programming through these outlets. At least 80 percent of paid television has been imported programming (Getino 1998, 201). In late 2008, CNN began offering Chile-centered news programming on its new network, CNN Chile. In early 2009, Chile's public broadcast network, Televisión Nacional de Chile (TVN), began offering a competing cable news network—Canal 24 Horas.

Coverage of themes and issues related to the dictatorship and human rights is partial and cryptic. While Pinochet was in London, the Chilean government appointed special Judge Juan Guzmán Tapia to investigate cases of the disappeared. Judge Guzmán convinced the courts that the perpetrators of these crimes could not be granted amnesty under the law written by Pinochet because the crimes were ongoing. Chilean news does cover these cases of the disappeared regularly. Yet, especially until 2004, there was virtually no coverage or discussion of the systematic use of torture that was practiced on what many estimate to be hundreds of thousands of Chileans and non-Chileans detained during the dictatorship, many of whom are still living. As Guillier explained, "We're more sensitive to cases of finding the detained-disappeared. It's not an editorial decision, but a sensation that with the tortures, twenty years later, we're not going to have a way to resolve them. It's a defensive, psychological instinct, a tendency to concentrate on what happened with those killed, less on those still living" (personal interview, April 8, 2002). Guillier was detained himself during the dictatorship and experienced the repression firsthand. But omitting these themes *is* an editorial decision as well. Likewise, only infrequently is there a story about the individuals and families who have been affected by internal or external exile.

The reasons for the selectiveness of television coverage regarding these themes and issues are multiple, and not all of the reasons are media-specific. One factor is the Rettig Report. Composed by a government-appointed committee in the early 1990s and known internationally as the *Truth and Reconciliation Commission Report*, this mandate asked that everything possible be done for the families of individuals who were killed or who disappeared during Pinochet's regime. The report did not suggest that any action be taken on behalf of survivors who experienced the violence. Thus, the report established an agenda detailing what was and was not to be addressed. The tacit agreement that was made between the leaders of the fledgling democracy and the military was that only the most egregious crimes against humanity—namely, those that resulted in death—would be investigated. The reasoning was that in order to heal rifts among different sectors of the political and social structure and protect the democracy, other cases would not be mentioned or approached. As Lawrence Kirmayer contends, "The social world fails to bear witness for many reasons. Even reparative accounts of the terrible things that happen to people (violations, traumas, losses) are warded off because of their capacity to create vicarious fear and pain and because they constitute a threat to current social and political arrangements" (1996, 192). These conditions could not have been clearer in Chile when even President Ricardo Lagos of the Socialist Party—the same political party of former President Salvador Allende—beseeched the British courts to release General Pinochet and allow him to return to Chile.

Another possible reason for the avoidance of certain themes on television is that many torture survivors and citizens who were once exiled do not want to talk about their experiences. Personal remembrances of these traumatic events in Chile are very complex. In their own memories, survivors must continuously relive the horrors that they experienced. At the same time, those who committed the violence against the detained prisoners, facing threats to their own lives if they disobeyed, must confront their own guilt. Furthermore, many who survived torture were spared their lives because they revealed names and information to their captors that led to the tortures and deaths of their friends, family members, and colleagues. As a result, some survivors feel shame and remorse for what may have happened to people they named. Kirmayer argues, "A private space of trauma places the victim in a predicament, since the validation of suffering depends on recovering enough memory to make it real for others, but this memory can be retrieved only be reliving or representing the place of victimization. Of course, this experience of reliving is vigorously resisted by rememberer and audience alike" (190).

However, there are factors specific to Chile's media system and its relationship to the nation's social, political, and economic structures that also strongly contribute to either the complete avoidance of human rights issues or a circuitous manner in dealing with them. Before taking a closer look at mainstream Chilean media and its discourses, consider the notion of structuring absences, or what Althusser once called "the internal shadows of exclusion"—the strategic withholding of certain themes, discourses, or ideologies within textual systems.

Just because the media may concentrate on certain themes does not mean that viewers will avoid considering others. The overdetermination of those themes can lead some to question. The Chilean public can fill in the gaps as well when delicate topics from the era of the dictatorship are avoided or indirectly addressed. Viewers are well aware of the limitations of media discourse—they experienced state censorship during Pinochet's regime. Yet, even then, messages were encoded and decoded through structured absences. For example, when newspaper and magazine censors forbade the publication of certain photographs, bold editors would leave blank spaces where photographs would have appeared so that viewers would know something else was supposed to be there. When reporters wanted to share sensitive information in their articles, they often buried the information in a brief phrase or sentence somewhere near the end. Radio journalists were able to emphasize the degree to which they were constrained by only reporting international news that had absolutely no relevance to the lives of Chileans.

The structuring absences of human rights discourse are not just a result of Chile's military repression and the threats that the armed forces still pose today. The economic structure of Chile's media industry is also an important factor. Ever since the economic reforms of Pinochet's regime, Chile has been a hypercapitalistic society with extreme concentration of ownership. The same is true for the media industry. "Anticipating the transfer of power, the Pinochet government initiated a radical transformation of the political and economic framework that had structured Chilean television under authoritarian rule. University-run television stations were privatized, broadcast licensing was deregulated, and cable television was allowed to develop in a regulatory vacuum . . . In short, before stepping down, the Pinochet government had set the parameters for the development of a postauthoritarian cultural environment that was morally conservative but, at the same time, thoroughly transnationalized and radically neoliberal in economic terms" (Wiley, "Transnation," 2006). In addition, virtually all media was owned by only a few different individuals and families who were staunch supporters of the Pinochet regime.

The responsibility of network executives is to earn as much money for their networks as possible through commercial advertising. One strategy, then, has been to attract mass audiences with entertainment—what not only appeals to a diverse public but also does not detract from or trivialize the commercials. Another strategy has been to attract smaller, more affluent, niche audiences—namely, those who can afford cable and frequently choose internationally imported networks, such as CNN, BBC, or Discovery instead. In both cases, product placements and product endorsements by program stars and hosts are common. Transitioning from a discourse on torture to one on cell phones, shoes, aspirin, or soda cannot be done smoothly. However, that does not mean that hard-hitting themes are entirely avoided. Disruptive, awkward transitions from news programs to commercials occur all the time. How those news stories are shaped, though, especially regarding the degree to which audiences may be perceived to tolerate unpleasant descriptions and images, must be considered carefully to avoid alienating the commercial sponsors.

The restrictions imposed on a capitalist television system do not prevent all significant discourse. Individual programs as well as individual producers and journalists have found ways to work through the system, introducing controversial subjects and material. In fact, sometimes a program's "subversiveness" can have market appeal. If enough of a sponsor's target audience is interested in the programming, discussing normally taboo topics may appear as an excellent business decision. To compete against the other networks, producers seek to offer something different and unique through counterprogramming. A show's "specificity" can sell.

In *The Revolution Wasn't Televised*, Spigel and Curtin contend that by 1974, oppositional TV programming that challenged the status quo had found room on broadcast television in the United States: "In 1974, the opposition suddenly seemed popular and powerful. It was a moment inextricably connected to years of organizing and struggle in the streets, but it was also a moment at which those working within the culture industries who sympathized with oppositional movements saw the opportunity to promote the politics of change and to justify their work to superiors by touting its popular appeal" (1997, 8). Much in their description resonates with current conditions in Chile. Controversial programming and news stories can have popular appeal to a commercial audience.

Chilean journalists and media professionals appear to be attempting different strategies and techniques to get their socially and politically charged topics on the air. One effective strategy is that of converting a local or national story into an international one, a technique with a legacy that dates back to the dictatorship. Once a story reaches international status, it seems to be more protected for the Chilean press and perhaps more newsworthy for certain sectors of the audience. Although journalists have become adept at making these conversions themselves, sometimes, international angles and events are handed to them. Such was the case in 1998 when Pinochet was arrested in London. Pinochet's international detention allowed the national media to revisit themes and issues that had been shut down since the early 1990s when they were briefly aired after the dictatorship had ended but then effectively silenced again.

What is more common is the blatant absence of discourse regarding Pinochet's regime. This was especially clear in 2002 when Channel 7, *Televisión Nacional de Chile*, aired a special documentary that they produced on Latin American dictatorships. Chile was never mentioned! But what would be the point of Chilean television producers spending resources on such a documentary if the viewers were not supposed to deduce that the story was also about Chile? Here, the international stood in for the national. No Chilean could have watched this documentary without thinking of Pinochet's dictatorship. The absence is noticed.

There is also a special evasive language common in spoken parlance as well as that which is found on television. For example, on TV, the term "dictatorship," *dictadura*, is rarely used to describe the Pinochet years. Rather, these years are described as *régimen militar* (military regime), *régimen de Pinochet* (Pinochet's regime), *gobierno militar* (military government), *gobierno de Pinochet* (Pinochet's government), or *aquella época* ("that era" or "that time"). Every word spoken on Chilean nonfiction television is chosen with care and codification, and richly layered.

The Spectrum of Broadcast Television in Chile

As mentioned previously, in addition to the constraints imposed on television due to Chile's recent history, the market forces of global capitalism, combined with a high concentration of media ownership, impose their own restrictions on the discourses that circulate on Chile's networks. Chilean TV producers usually try to appeal to a large, diverse audience, and exploitative entertainment is the rule of thumb. Even the morning "news" shows are not immune. Normally, women's bodies are objectified or not represented at all, and discussions circulate around star gossip as the "journalists" drink their Chilean juice or tea. In fact, throughout most of the day, when it is presumed that most audiences are women and children, Chilean television could be classified as a "media circus." Indeed, that is how many self-deprecating television professionals have labeled it themselves. The exception occurs during the evenings, when networks try to appeal to a more professional, educated, masculine, and affluent audience.

In Santiago, watching TV without cable leaves you a handful of choices. The five big broadcast networks are Channel 4, *La Red*; Channel 7, *Televisión Nacional de Chile* (*TVN*); Channel 9, *Megavisión*; Channel 11, *Chilevisión*; and Channel 13, *Canal 13* or *UC13*, of Catholic University (*Universidad Católica*). Historically, most of the networks have been aligned with the political right. During the dictatorship, the two main networks, *TVN* and *UC13*, along with other university networks, were under virtually complete control of Pinochet's regime.

Televisión Nacional de Chile was the official network of Pinochet's regime. Since the country's return to democracy, it has been run by a directorate of representatives from every political party represented in the congress. All decisions made at the network need to be accepted by all political party representatives on the directorate. Many producers and journalists who have at one time worked at this network complain that this causes inefficient bureaucracy. In recent years, though, this network has offered the most extensive lineup of programming and subject matter on the legacy of the Pinochet regime and other hard-hitting themes, offering programs such as *Informe Especial (Special Report)*; *Vía Pública: La Política sin Restricción (Public Way: Politics without Restriction)*; *360°: Ventana al Mundo (360°: Window to the World)*; *Estado Nacional (National Condition*—also very similar in appearance and pronunciation to *Estadio Nacional [National Stadium]*, which was used as a concentration camp after the coup); and *Esto No Tiene Nombre: Porque todos tenemos derechos (This Has No Name: Because We All Have Rights).*

Canal 13 is run by the Catholic University of Chile and serves as the official network of the Catholic Church. Although it has always been a conservative network, during the dictatorship it was able to sneak some criticism toward Pinochet through its channel due to the unique position of power and respect that the Catholic Church has always maintained in Chile. Human rights was a cause that some elements of the Catholic Church took up during the dictatorship; indeed, during Pinochet's regime, the church was the only relatively safe place for human rights victims. Since the return to democracy, its concentration on these issues has diminished, but the network still demonstrates a concern for the theme of poverty and the responsibility of viewers to help those less fortunate. It also offers fairly consistent coverage of judicial cases pertaining to those killed and disappeared during the coup. *Canal 13* offers some of its news broadcasts with a sign language interpreter in the corner of the screen.

Megavisión is not a key player in the circulation of human rights discourses, although many of its shows receive high ratings. Its mission has been almost exclusively entertainment-based. The owner of the network was, until his death in 2008, conservative Chilean billionaire Ricardo Claro, who also owned and controlled the cable television company Metrópolis-Intercom (León-Dermota, 153). During the dictatorship, Claro criticized the media that did attempt to cover human rights violations, describing the coverage as irresponsible and unpatriotic. *Megavisión* began in 1990 by the Ricardo Claro financial group. In 1992, 49.5 percent of its stock was sold to the Mexican television company *Televisa*

(Wiley, "Transnation"). According to Ken León-Dermota, Claro's purchasing of several Mexican *telenovelas* led to a large financial loss, which influenced *Televisa*'s decision to reduce its share to 37 percent and then 0 percent (152).

La Red is also not a significant contributor to human rights discourses. This network was created in 1991 by the COPESA media group (owners of the powerful *La Tercera* and affiliated newspaper and magazine print media conglomerate). In 1993, 49 percent of its stock was sold to the Canadian company CanWest Global Communications (Wiley, "Transnation"). In 2006, the network was owned by Mexican business magnate Ángel González.

This chapter concentrates on *Chilevisión*. Despite the constraints that we would expect to find on any commercial network, as well as the nuanced restrictions imposed on Chilean television that are unique to Chile's recent history, this network managed to get some truly revolutionary "reality" TV programming on the air during the first decade of the new millennium. Indeed, in the earlier part of the decade, it unquestionably was the boldest of the big five networks, offering the largest amount of controversial, sensitive subject matter. As will be discussed, though, this no longer appears to be the case. By conducting a "symptomatic reading" of some of the network's most innovative programming, we can see that significant human rights discourses have materialized within the gaps and fissures characteristic of the structuring absences of Chilean television discourse, but we can also see how those discourses have been contained, and in some cases, completely eliminated.

Chilevisión: Tu Mirada (Your Viewpoint)

Channel 11, *Chilevisión*, was formerly the network of the University of Chile. The University of Chile was one of the military junta's first targets after Chile's coup since it was considered a bastion of left-wing ideology. The network was completely controlled by the military generals during the dictatorship and, with the return to democracy, completely privatized. In 1993, the network sold 49 percent of its stock to *Venevisión*. *Venevisión* had acquired 99 percent of the company by 1997 (Wiley, "Transnation"). Until 2005, the owners were not Chilean, but rather Venezuelan Gustavo

Cisneros of *Venevisión* and Claxson Interactive Group Inc., headquartered in Buenos Aires, Argentina, and Miami, Florida, in the United States. In 2002 and 2003, journalists at *Chilevisión* cited the network's international, nonnative owners as a reason for the greater independence and freedom of expression experienced at this network in relation to the two other most significant networks, *TVN* and *UC13*.

In 2005, *Chilevisión* was purchased by Chilean billionaire Sebastián Piñera, owner and shareholder of, among other companies, LAN Chile Airlines and the *Colo Colo* soccer team. He is a political conservative and member of the National Renovation (*Renovación Nacional*) political party who ran for president in 2005. In 2008, he ran for president again as leader of the National Renovation Party, and in December 2008, he has become the only candidate for the politically conservative Alliance (*Alianza*) coalition of the National Renovation and extreme-right *Unión Democrata Independiente*/Independent Democrat Union (UDI) party. In 2009, he will be campaigning against centrist Christian Democrat and former President Eduardo Frei Ruiz-Tagle (1994–2000), whose father, Eduardo Frei Montalva, was also a president of Chile (1964–1970) and allegedly killed by Pinochet's men while he was recovering from surgery in 1982. If Piñera's ambition was to influence the content of the network's relatively progressive programming in order to favor his 2005–2006 election, the attempt failed. Time will tell if he has greater success this time. Piñera's ownership of *Chilevisión* does correlate with a noticeable difference in programming and editorial decisions, and when he does appear on his own network, he seems to receive especially gentle treatment in comparison to the appearances of other political leaders and candidates, especially those from the Left.

Before the Piñera takeover, *Chilevisión* displayed unique network identification and self-promotional spots. Each spot showed "regular" Chileans standing on different street corners in Santiago, holding up hand-painted placards with slogans such as, "I want more freedom of expression" and "We need less fear," in sepia-toned camera images playing to the upbeat music of an individual whistling. A voice-over accompanied a digital graphic reading, "*Chilevisión: Tu canal*" (*Chilevisión*: Your Channel) or "*Chilevisión: Tu Mirada*" (*Chilevisión*: Your Viewpoint).

Unlike the "reality" TV programming that was available on other networks in Chile (especially *Canal 13*'s versions of *American Idol* and *The Amazing Race*—*Protagonistas de la música en Bruto* [*Musical Protagonists in the Rough*] and *Conquistadores del fin del mundo* [*Conquistadors from the End of the World*]), *Chilevisión*'s programming confronted its nation's real societal problems and engaged diverse segments of the Chilean public, allowing them to have a voice in a mediated, semipluralistic public sphere. While audiences for other reality shows could register their votes by phone or e-mail for who they believed should become the next pop music icon, viewers of *Chilevisión's* debate show, *El Termómetro* (*The Thermometer*), voted on how effectively their government had controlled smog in Santiago, whether their police forces had succeeded in hunting down pedophiles, and whether these same police forces used excessive violence during street protests and demonstrations. Furthermore, on another *Chilevisión* program called *Ciento*, which aired in 2002, the producers handed out cameras to their viewers and encouraged them to go where they wanted to go and interview who they wanted to interview. The program then broadcasted the interviews during primetime TV.

EL TERMÓMETRO: THE PULSE OF THE CHILEAN PUBLIC

The program on *Chilevisión* that most consistently offered a unique opportunity for the discussion of significant and sensitive topics was *El Termómetro*. *El Termómetro* aired Monday through Friday, usually from 8:00 p.m. to 9:00 p.m., leading into Chilean television primetime (9:00 p.m. to midnight). Most of the networks—*Chilevisión*, *TVN*, *UC13*, and *Megavisión*—show the national news from 9:00 p.m. to 10:00 p.m., followed by feature films, documentaries, specials, or other programming. The network heads of *Chilevisión* wanted to attract more lucrative primetime audiences by offering counterprogramming—a live show in the 8:00 p.m. to 9:00 p.m. lead-in slot. As Pablo Alvarado, editorial director of the program in 2002, described the decision to create this program,

"*Chilevisión* is not political or religious like other channels. It was not an ideological decision, but a commercial decision" (personal interview, April 4, 2002). Alvarado suggested that *Chilevisión* was unique. The fact that *Chilevisión* did not, previous to its purchase by Piñera, have to deal with local or national constraints to the extent that most other networks did seemed to make a difference.

John Caldwell explains in *Televisuality*, "At the same time that networks publicly applaud viewer activity and choice, they counterprogram to ensure audience share against the new and volatile viewing practices" (1995, 259). This was the case for *Chilevisión*. Not many *telenovela* viewers who religiously tuned in to the other channels were going to switch over to *El Termómetro*; rather, the network was clinching a favored target audience for the following evening news. Even though the number of viewers for *El Termómetro* may have been quite small in relation to the number of viewers for the *telenovelas* and other shows on the competing networks, the upscale, educated audiences so sought after by advertisers were already tuned in for the 9:00 news, when the selections on most of the major networks are almost identical. "Counterprogramming, a marketing strategy that helps fuel stylistic individuation, has also taken on increased importance in the face of heightened competition" (Caldwell 1995, 294).

The share of viewers (percentage of households with their television sets turned on to a specific network) for *Chilevisión* during this time slot was actually quite small compared to the other major networks (on July 15, 2003, 6.7 percent, compared with 41.2 percent for *TVN*, 24.5 percent for *Megavisión*, 19.9 percent for *UC13*, and 6.7 percent for *La Red*). But the audience that the channel did get was one highly esteemed by advertisers—that is, one composed of professional, educated, and affluent viewers who could afford cable and would probably watch CNN instead of a *telenovela*. According to Alvarado, "Upper classes like the show, watch, participate. We are receiving some information on who is watching. Mainly about socio-economic groups; to allow a better choice of themes; we need to cater to the audience" (personal interview, April 4, 2002). In this case, the network was less concerned with broadcasting to a wide audience than it was with narrowcasting to a more lucrative select audience.

El Termómetro was usually the only live program broadcast on any of the five major networks in the pre-evening news timeslot. That "liveness" can be attractive to viewers, especially those who want to feel connected to their community and their nation. They might want something not only serious and engaging but also Chilean (not cable outlets such as CNN or BBC).

El Termómetro was hosted until 2005 by Iván Núñez, a charismatic young journalist. After the change in ownership of the network, he moved to *Televisión Nacional de Chile*. *El Termómetro* continued with two more charismatic young journalists, first with Macarena Pizarro, and eventually with regular host Matías del Río, until 2007. Each evening, four guests were invited to participate. In his 2002 interview, Alvarado explained, "People are usually invited before topics are chosen. We make a panel with both poles. From conservative to liberal. Right to left. Some people ask to be on the show, but we have absolute freedom to choose." Many panelists were repeat performers who came back every couple of weeks. Most were prestigious professionals—mayors, representatives from congress, journalists, lawyers, business owners, filmmakers, and pop stars. By 2006, the diversity of guests was wider. In an interview with host Matías del Río that year, he explained, "Every day we try to invite one or two new people who have never been on the show. Audiences prefer guests who are validated for what they know, not who they are" (personal interview, July 11, 2006).

In addition to the four panelists, others had the opportunity to participate through phone calls and e-mail messages. The host dedicated some time in every show to sharing these responses. In addition, every show had a poll in which you could vote on a "yes"–"no" question through the phone or Internet. Results of the poll were revealed at the end of the program. Occasionally, there was a live studio audience that sometimes posed questions and opinions at the end of the program. However, the audience that was visible behind the panelists did not always appear so "alive," and Núñez admitted that the producers needed to do a better job of integrating the audience into the discussion (personal interview, July 16, 2003).

Nancy Fraser advises, "One task for critical theory is to render visible the ways in which societal inequality infects formally inclusive existing public spheres and taints discursive interaction within them" (1999, 526). Her admonition emphasizes our need to consider who was allowed to participate in these *El Termómetro* discourses, and to what extent they could in fact participate. Social class, gender, political affiliation, and education level all played significant roles here, not only in terms of who was invited, but also in relation to who had access to the technology—the television for viewing and a phone or Internet access for responding. Added to these issues is the fact that advertisers were seeking the exclusive, upwardly mobile, and economically comfortable sector of the viewing public to which the program was catering. According to Wiley, "the capitalist construction of the public as potential consumers leads to a dual society and, some argue, to the social disarticulation of one sector (the globally connected elites and upper middle class) from the other (the mass audience constituted by broadcast television and radio) . . . in other words, in a deregulated context where capitalist logics drive infrastructural development, the wealthy are incorporated into a broader range of global media flows and those who lack value as consumers are left out" ("Transnation"). Nonetheless, despite its limitations and constraints, this show did allow a public forum for the airing of sensitive issues. For six years, *El Termómetro* seemed to have struck an appropriate balance between "edginess" and network decorum.

Alvarado highlighted an interesting tension between the show's content and its audience. He mentioned that research showed that *El Termómetro* was watched especially by members of the socioeconomic elite, yet this sector of the Chilean public tended to be conservative. Confronting sensitive themes on the program, especially those regarding the legacy of the Pinochet dictatorship, must have been a delicate operation, since it was very likely that large sectors of the audience confronted these themes with much resistance. Alvarado stated, "You can mention certain things, but only things on the periphery." That is what *El Termómetro* did so well in its early years. Via this circuitous route, what was normally taboo material for network television slipped through.

Several episodes contained elements of a controversial nature with issues that addressed human rights. In 2002, one episode aired in response to international news about the priests who were under investigation in Boston for allegations of child sexual abuse. Chile has many priests who have been accused of child sexual abuse as well. In fact, several priests who had been accused of sex abuse in the United States had been sent overseas to countries like Chile. The most emotional moment in this episode of *El Termómetro* came when an adult in his fifties called to say that he had been sexually abused by a priest when he was a young child and that he was still damaged and traumatized by that experience.

Another episode addressed the police search for Paul Schäfer—the leader of *Colonia Dignidad*, a German commune in Chile—who was accused of sexually abusing dozens of children from the commune and from neighboring communities who had attended the school or been treated at the hospital on its grounds. During the dictatorship, the leaders of *Colonia Dignidad* sympathized with the leaders of Pinochet's regime. A torture center was located on their land in underground caves. While most of the debate addressed the child sexual abuse and the Chilean police force's inability or disinterest in finding and capturing the leader, the role that the commune played in the tortures and disappearances of many victims of Pinochet's regime was also mentioned. Schäfer was later found and arrested in 2005 with the cooperation of the Argentine police.

Other episodes indirectly approached the legacy of Pinochet and his regime. For example, one program dealt with the purchase by the mayor of Providencia—a *comuna*, or borough, of Santiago—of the dining room table that Pinochet used when he was under house arrest in London. The question was whether the mayor had the right to use public funds to purchase this table, but mention was also made that the interest in purchasing this table at all was disturbing. In another episode, a young man who had been assaulted by the grandson of Pinochet when he was coming out of a nightclub was interviewed. The question for the panelists and the viewers at home was, is justice the same for everyone in Chile? While this case purported to be about justice being served to the grandson on behalf of the victim of the assault, the question could also be interpreted as being directed toward Pinochet himself.

Another program addressed the alleged excessive use of force and violence of the *carabineros*, the Chilean police forces, during public protests and demonstrations. On May 21, 2002, President Lagos gave his annual state of the union address to congress in the city of Valparaíso. Political groups, unions, and university students marched and protested in the streets outside of the congress building. Some protestors became violent, looting stores, spray-painting graffiti, and throwing Molotov cocktails at the police water cannon trucks. Several people were injured as the police tried to barricade streets, and protestors tried to break down the barricades. Hundreds of people were arrested. During the program's debate, emphasis was placed on police actions in contemporary times. However, the issue was also portrayed as a legacy of the dictatorship when those who dared to demonstrate were routinely beaten, humiliated, imprisoned, and sometimes killed. Again, this topic became a strategy of reference without head-on treatment of the repression of the dictatorship.

In April 2002, when members of the opposition to the administration of President Hugo Chávez in Venezuela attempted a coup to topple his regime, *El Termómetro* covered it. Several times, Núñez and panelists referenced Chile's own coup in 1973, suggesting that the events in Venezuela had much in common with those that had taken place in Chile. By making the analogy, they warned that the future did not bode well for Venezuela. They even insinuated that the United States was probably involved in this attempted coup. They froze an image from news footage that showed a man shooting into a crowd with a handgun and suggested that he was a member of the CIA trying to instigate trouble and cause violence that would be blamed on Chávez's security forces. All of these examples demonstrate how peripherals—themes that are tangential to the human rights violations of the dictatorship—became displacements for a more direct confrontation of Chile's recent past.

El Termómetro allowed a space on network TV for the airing of sensitive topics and an opportunity for members of a diverse audience to express their concerns in a public forum. Nonetheless, *El Termómetro* was not a utopia for public discourse and freedom of expression. For every individual who joined the panel, aired her opinion on the air over the phone, or got his e-mail read aloud by Núñez, Pizarro, or del Río, there were countless others who did not. Especially in the early years, most voices were screened before they were broadcasted and silenced if they were too direct in their criticism of social and political conditions, or if they belonged to human rights groups or extreme left political parties. Furthermore, the host often had to become the good-natured harmonizer, with twinkling eyes and a broad smile, soothingly coaxing the contending panelists to calm down and not be so "extreme." In these regards, the discourses available through *El Termómetro* certainly were compromised. According to Alvarado, "We have certain public enemies, but we don't bow to pressures." Nonetheless, there must have been a high degree of self-censorship.

As the show achieved higher ratings, more advertisers were interested in placing commercials during the program. Moreover, the host was often their spokesperson, appearing in the commercials or plugging the sponsors' products during the actual program. In one ad, Núñez looked straight into the camera and said, "There are some opinions that I *don't* like to hear. Before you speak, use *Listerine*." And during the show, the host encouraged the audience to use their *Telefónica* cell phone plan to call in and give their comments. As commercials increased, the length of the actual program decreased. Indeed, time given to commercials sometimes seemed about equal to actual program time.

After the Piñera takeover of *Chilevisión* in the later part of the decade, *El Termómetro* changed. This evolution, in some ways, allowed more diversity of guests and opinions but there was also a noticeable shift in political tone. For example, guests included leaders of human rights organizations, leaders of lesbian, gay, bisexual, transgender, queer/questioning (LGBTQ) organizations, members of nonmoderate political parties, members of Nazi youth organizations, and student leaders. In June and July of 2006, significant time and attention was given to the national student strikes, the largest grassroots movement in post-Pinochet Chile in which high school and college students from different socioeconomic classes and political perspectives united to oppose the state of the Chilean education system. Other topics that received attention during this time period included violence committed between neo-Nazi gangs and anti-Nazi skinheads, discrimination and violence committed against members of the LGBTQ community, the annual flooding of poor people's homes and communities during the winter rainy season, and house break-ins and assaults, especially in the wealthier regions of Santiago.

An emphasis was placed on violence, but especially violence that concerned the advertisers' target audience—individuals with higher incomes and, frequently, more conservative politics. Embedded in this discourse of violence, as well as the attention paid to the student movements, was a critique of Socialist President Michelle Bachelet and her administration. Oftentimes, guest speakers suggested that Chile's first female president was not able to control her people, whether it was the juvenile delinquents, the students, or the neo-Nazis. On the one hundredth-day anniversary of Bachelet's inauguration, the show took place outdoors in front of the Presidential Palace rather than in the studio to highlight the theme of the night, regarding how successful the president had been during her first one hundred days.

One would assume that Bachelet's losing presidential rival Piñera, as owner of *Chilevisión*, would have influence over the tone and content of the network's content and perspective. Del Río said that he and the show's producers received minimal pressure from Piñera. On the date of our interview in 2006, del Río had yet to meet him.

Regarding their choices of guests, del Río explained that it could be difficult for them when they invited "non-politically-correct" panelists. They sometimes received complaints and had to defend themselves. He acknowledged that some critics argued that allowing certain guests, for example, members of hate groups, onto the show is not appropriate because it allows these individuals a public, national forum. "But not inviting controversial guests is believing that the public is stupid, treating them like children." He argued that it was better to bring them on the show so that they could debate: "Whether the public is informed or not, they will still operate underground; it's better to know."

Del Río explained that the program was having the greatest success by concentrating on themes that the common citizen cared about—gas prices, education, and social and cultural problems. He explained that their ratings in 2006 were very good, reaching 6.9 percent.[1] He believed that the higher ratings could be attributed to covering topics people cared about at the expense of "almost abandoning the elite." Apparently, as the program achieved more status and recognition over the years, producers felt more freedom to cater to a wider audience—the upper class could be partially neglected in return for higher ratings.

In July 2006, the Bachelet government had criticized *Chilevisión* for concentrating almost exclusively on certain themes, especially delinquency, which, they argued, promoted a particular political agenda. Del Río responded, "The government thinks that Piñera controls our content, but it's not true. Journalists won't sell out for a higher salary. Piñera knows that top journalists would quit if they were feeling pressures. He wants the value of the network to grow. Guillier is the most respected journalist in the country and works for *Chilevisión*. The government is saying something that is not legitimate. This network does have an interest in delinquency and security, but it's a legitimate concern, and it was a concern before Piñera."

When asked about the selectiveness of the program's discussion of human rights, del Río responded, "We do cover human rights. The last two big cases were covered a lot by all media, including us. We did two shows on Patio 29 [the revelation that bodies of the disappeared buried in unmarked graves in Santiago's General Cemetery may have been misidentified], and we also addressed the Supreme Court report that Chilean jails were violating human rights. If the government says that we're not sensitive to human rights . . . Piñera was anti-Pinochet and anti-dictatorship, and *Chilevisión* journalists worked for publications that were anti-dictatorship and pro-human rights. If there's something going on, we'll cover it." Nonetheless, this coverage appears to be very selective, and the media plays a crucial role in predetermining what will get societal attention. Survivors and relatives of victims of the Pinochet regime have been living an eternal quest for truth and justice since the 1970s, and, most days, they do not receive any media coverage. We can only assume, then, that the likelihood of these themes getting any coverage is contingent upon factors such as a new event in the Tribunals of Justice, something else with sensational appeal, or, as previously mentioned, the level to which the story is international. Regarding their coverage of LGBTQ issues, del Río explained, "It's not because other media won't cover it, but they don't have the space to cover it . . . Maybe not channel 13 because they are associated with the Catholic Church, *La Red* has mostly foreign programs, and *Megavisión* is very conservative."

After a pause, del Río continued, "Any society that has had a dictatorship takes a while for people to express themselves. Not because it's prohibited, but because society, people, the media have been maturing. It's like the LGBTQ issues in Chile. Some people are in the closet, and some people are openly gay. Today there are a lot of organizations for LGBTQ people. The media is a reflection of society. Some societies are conservative, and the media is conservative. Other societies are more transparent, and the media is also more transparent." Journalists and media producers may characterize their work as merely illustrating what is happening in the larger culture, but this characterization neglects the powerful role that they have in choosing how to frame what is taking place in society—prioritizing what will get attention and what will not.

Del Río sees a progressive widening in societal and media discourses since the end of the dictatorship. Rather than mention institutional and legal changes (such as revisions to the Law of the Press), which have made it easier for journalists to broaden their discourses, including the fact the Pinochet was no longer a threat and had lost many of his faithful supporters by 2006, he focuses on internal, individual choices. "Probably after the dictatorship there was less expression, but that was our fault. We thought that we were still in a dictatorship and didn't want to offend the powerful. Today that doesn't happen. We all grew together—the people, media, etc. I have always had freedom of expression. What changes is the media, the context, society . . . Before we had freedom of expression, but perhaps we didn't all express ourselves. Perhaps we were self-regulated, self-contained. We had freedom, but we didn't take advantage of it. Today we have the same freedom of expression, but we feel more freedom to express ourselves."

El Termómetro was cancelled in 2007. Del Río is now the host of the late night show *Última Mirada* (*Last Look*), which airs Monday through Friday between midnight and 1:00 a.m. or 1:30 a.m., immediately after the late night news recap. On May 16, 2008, the program covered the news that the case of the detainment, torture, and execution of singer–songwriter Víctor Jara on September 15, 1973, in *Estadio Chile* (Chile Stadium, now called *Estadio Víctor Jara*) was suddenly cancelled on May 15. Del Río interviewed the prosecuting attorney Nelson Caucato. The lengthy interview was broadcast with a split screen—Caucato and del Río on the left, and film footage of Jara and the people and experiences he sang about on the right, including footage of soldiers and prisoners in Santiago's athletic stadiums that were converted into concentration camps, with the song "*El derecho de vivir en paz*" (The right to live in peace) playing softly in the background. Perhaps because Jara is such an internationally recognized figure of the Chilean *Nueva Canción* (New Song) movement and an emblem of the brutality of the Pinochet regime (his guitar-playing hands were cut off before he was shot forty-four times), and also due to the public call that Jara's widow and daughters made asking for more witnesses to step forward with information, the case was reopened on June 3, 2008. In December 2008, presidential candidates Eduardo Frei Ruiz-Tagle (December 24) and Sebastián Piñera (December 16) both appeared on Del Río's program.

Del Río is also a regular member (and sole representative of his generation) on the Sunday evening (10:00 p.m.) talk show *Tolerancia Cero* (*Zero Tolerance*), whose members (in December 2008) also included senior journalists and professionals Alejandro Guillier, Fernando Villegas, Fernando Paulsen, and Felipe Morandé. Guillier, however, has left *Chilevisión*; his last night on *Tolerancia Cero* was December 21. In January 2009, he has begun working at TVN's new cable network Canal 24 Horas. Piñera has appeared on both programs—*Última Mirada* and *Tolerancia Cero*. On most occasions, based on the material available to me through the Internet, I did not hear any acknowledgment that the guest also happened to be the owner of the network (despite the fact that most viewers would likely already know). Disclosure of such information is expected in such cases in the United States. However, when he appeared on *Última Mirada* in December 2008, del Río was able to raise the topic with Piñera since Piñera's presidential candidacy was being criticized by many as a conflict of interest with his ownership of multiple companies.

Boundaries in Action: Defining the Limits to Human Rights Discourses on Television

Perhaps the constraints imposed on *El Termómetro* and other network programming were never made more explicit than in another daring program on the same *Chilevisión* network called *Ciento*, which aired in 2002 on Monday nights from 10:00 to 11:00. The Spanish word *ciento* means one hundred, in the case of the TV show, signifying 100 percent since the show revealed statistics about the Chilean people (suggesting that 100 percent of the Chilean population counts; everyone is included—a controversial concept for such a segregated society). However, spelled with an "s," *siento* also means, "I feel," which is just as relevant for the show since it posed questions to the Chilean public through surveys as well as one-on-one interviews conducted by amateur videographers.

One episode of *Ciento* that aired in February 2002 was titled, "Who rules in Chile?" Among the individuals interviewed in this episode were *El Termómetro*'s host, Iván Núñez, and journalistic editor, Pablo Alvarado. When approached, Núñez initially turned his back on the camera and the questioner. When he finally agreed to comply with the questioner, he lightheartedly replied that Alejandro Guillier, then news anchor and news director for *Chilevisión's* nightly news, ruled. Alvarado, seated at his desk with a poster of revolutionary icon Ché Guevara plastered to the wall behind his computer, was more forthcoming. He identified Chile's powerful economic groups as ruling Chile.

In his 2002 interview, Guillier envisioned a moment in the future when human rights discourses would more rigorously be initiated again. He emphasized, "We need historical memory. People are tired of the theme now, but eventually it will arise again among younger generations." Alvarado declared, "This would be serious journalism—how the military plays games with relatives of the detained-disappeared, etc. There is no historical truth. We need more consciousness of the social role of journalism. To lose the fear. People are no longer afraid of Pinochet, but they're afraid of the economic groups. Lose the fear of those with power. If everyone plays games—politicians, journalists—who will address this?"

When asked if there was freedom of expression in Chilean media, Alvarado declared in 2002,

> No, there isn't. The media is controlled by only one class, one economic group; they're not interested in certain themes. We're trying to establish more. The written press is very strong. It's only controlled by the right. When you maintain a free market, there's inequality. No critical press. No investigative journalism. It's difficult to have freedom of expression if there is no free, liberal journalism. How do you define freedom of expression in the press? Truthful reporting. There is a social role of journalism; to raise consciousness. It's not clear to readers what perspectives you get in the news. For example, consider what has happened to Alejandra Matus[2] with her *El libro negro de la justicia chilena* (*The Black Book of Chilean Justice*). Serious investigations can only be written in books, but not in papers. If one goes to a press conference and asks critical questions, the respondent and other journalists will get angry.

Alvarado's description of conditions in 2002 appears prophetic in the context of six years later. On May 26, 2008, ninety-eight ex-agents of the DINA—Pinochet's secret repressive forces—were charged in the cases of detainment, torture, murder, and disappearance of forty-two victims, including Communist Party leader and father of Association of Relatives of the Detained-Disappeared (AFDD) leaders Viviana and Victoria Díaz, Víctor Díaz[3] and epic documentary *Battle of Chile* cinematographer Jorge Müller Silva. The victims had been detained at some of the most infamous torture centers in Chile—*José Domingo Cañas*, *Villa Grimaldi*, *Londres 38* (see Chapter 6), and *La Venda Sexy*. According to the newspaper *La Nación*, this was, to date, "the largest blow to the repression of the Augusto Pinochet dictatorship" (Escalante, May 27, 2008). Yet, scanning through the text and video links on the *Chilevisión* Web site during the last week of May and the first week of June, there was no information available on this case, and limited information available in other media outlets.

Television is expensive, limited, and tightly controlled. Sometimes the constraints imposed on journalists, TV producers, and networks seem insurmountable. Censorship and self-censorship are normally the rule. Nonetheless, certain discourses regarding crucial subjects normally considered taboo can sometimes maneuver their way into the mediated public sphere. It is what happens through these gaps and fissures in the television industry that offers hope in Chile, where, presently, the unspoken is often more pronounced than the spoken.

As divided as the Chilean people may be, they have all lived through some of the same experiences, especially during the dictatorship. While they may cling to different myths, or as Steve J. Stern would describe them, *emblematic memories*—whether they are the myth of Pinochet as savior of the fatherland, Allende as savior of the working poor, or something entirely different—they were all encouraged to accept *one* version of history during the military regime. It is that version of history, *already known* by those who survived the dictatorship, that now becomes, as the editors of *Cahiers du cinema* would describe it, the "factor of non-recognition" (Mast and Cohen 1979, 797).

The media's central role in structuring knowledge about history involves not only representation but also a lack of representation that ensures the strategic absence of certain topics. However, a lack of representation does not necessarily lead to a lack of consideration and even coded discussion of taboo subjects in the mainstream media. As Caldwell explains, "Televisuality is indeed a leaky system. Those who describe it as an inherently illusory, hegemonic, and deceptive system fail to see that it is also an instrumental system, one that can be used by the marginal as well as abused by the powerful" (1995, 330). Spigel and Curtin confirm the subversive potential of a medium that can sometimes challenge the very hegemonic structures that maintain it: "In short, it seems more productive to understand the ways in which powerful media institutions must transmit certain types of popular knowledge that ultimately disrupt the logic of their own functional requirements for economic stability" (1997, 9).

Those who wish to dismiss television as a tool that belongs exclusively to the controlling economic and political elite need to reconsider. As television personalities and audiences delicately dance around the sensitive themes of human rights, social justice, and political change, some significant dialogue is taking place through a medium to which an enormous number of Chilean people are exposed. Those who work within the industry, though, are quite aware of the constraints imposed on them. Guillier, acknowledging the restrictions imposed on television, proclaimed, "We need to make documentaries—if not for now, they need to be saved for later. For the moral and political responsibility." The next chapter will explore the role of documentaries in the reconstruction of historical memories and the quest for truth and justice.

CHAPTER 3

DOCUMENTARIES AND CONTESTED HISTORICAL MEMORIES

What is memory in a culture in which there is a general consensus to forget?

—Claudia Dreifus, "The New Battle of Chile: Keeping Memory Alive," *New York Times*, September 6, 1998

No medium seems more effective for informing and persuading audiences of specific historical perspectives than documentary film and video. Documentary has become a crucial tool in the articulation of various national consciousnesses: "Utilizing the capacities of sound recording and cinematography to reproduce the physical appearance of things, documentary film contributes to the formation of popular memory. It proposes perspectives on and interpretations of historic issues, processes, and events" (Nichols, ix). Hitler understood the power of documentaries and used the works of Leni Riefenstahl to convince non-Jewish Germans of his agenda. Michael Moore's *Fahrenheit 9/11* broke several box-office records for a documentary film in 2004, an election year, and triggered much critique and debate from all ends of the U.S. political spectrum because so many people realized the impact this film could have on Americans' understanding of what the United States should represent and who should be the nation's leader. In Cuba, Moore's film was broadcast on state-run television, suggesting the role such a film can play on a nation's consciousness when that nation's identity is understood in contrast to that of another powerful country like the United States.

For many, documentaries also take on a very personal role. They become a surrogate for family photos and home movies that were rarely taken or lost. Some viewers study the students in the street protests depicted in Patricio Guzmán's *The Battle of Chile* for a glimpse of a relative or the rallies supporting President Allende for an image of a friend. In this way, these national memory texts can also quite literally become family memory albums.

Documentaries have played a significant historical role in Latin America, where filmmakers from throughout the region have used them to highlight the poverty, exploitation, and state repression of the Latin American people. Documentaries have also been used to glorify the social movements and governments that have attempted to address these issues. As Julianne Burton argues, "Nowhere have the manifestations of documentary been as multiple and their impact so decisive as in Latin America. From its inception in the mid-1950s, the New Latin American Cinema movement accorded to documentary privileged status. Socially committed filmmakers embraced documentary approaches as their primary tool in the search to discover and define the submerged, denied, devalued realities of an intricate palimpsest of cultures and castes separated and conjoined by an arbitrary network of national boundaries" (6).

In 1967, the Department of Experimental Cinema at the University of Chile and the national film institute, Chile Films, hosted an international film festival for all of Latin America at Viña del Mar, Chile. It was at this conference and another one in 1969 that many Latin American filmmakers became aware of the work being done in other Latin American countries, including documentaries, feature films, and mixtures of both forms in one. Alliances were made and ideas were shared as the filmmakers realized that the only way their filmmaking could survive was if they worked together. These national cinemas merged into a pan–Latin American cinema or Latin American "New Cinema." Filmmakers, many who actually came from the "elite" class, from families with resources who could send their children to films schools abroad, strived to make films that spoke for, and sometimes spoke with, people from the most disadvantaged sectors of their societies.

Julianne Burton explains the significance of documentary films as a source of alternative media in the developing world: "Documentary provides: a source of 'counterinformation' for those without access to the hegemonic structures of world news and communications; a means of reconstructing historical events and challenging hegemonic and often elitist interpretations of the past; a mode of eliciting, preserving, and utilizing the testimony of individuals and groups who would otherwise have no means of recording their experience; an instrument for capturing cultural difference and exploring the complex relationship of self to other within as well as between societies; and finally, a means of consolidating cultural identifications, social cleavages, political belief systems, and ideological agendas" (Burton, 6).

For Chile, documentaries took on a significant role during the years of Popular Unity (1970–73). Emulating the role that cinema played in postrevolutionary Cuba with sponsorship from Fidel Castro, President Allende assigned and sponsored willing filmmakers to make films that depicted the current conditions in Chile and how Allende's government planned to address them. Documentaries assumed a much larger mission underground and in exile during the dictatorship (1973–90). Hundreds were produced inside and outside Chile by both Chilean and non-Chilean filmmakers, exposing the countless human rights violations that took place under Pinochet's regime. Many of these documentaries were made at great personal risk to those involved with production. Footage clandestinely shot inside Chile was frequently smuggled out to the rest of the world where it could be edited and screened for international audiences. Although fewer documentaries have been made since the end of the dictatorship—because a sense of urgency dwindled along with international funding sources when the dictatorship came to an end—production continues. Documentaries often have addressed the issues of state violence, repression, and traumatic memory in ways more forceful and poignant than are possible in other forms of media. I will discuss two short documentaries produced by two unlikely documentary filmmakers. Both films have played significant roles in the circulation of human rights discourses in contemporary Chile.

FERNANDO HAS RETURNED (TO GO MISSING AGAIN)

When I asked director Silvio Caiozzi to explain to me the conditions under which he made *Fernando ha vuelto (Fernando Is Back;*

1998), he shared, "I felt as if Fernando was directing" (personal interview, March 27, 2002). He claimed, "I didn't initially have any intention of making the documentary; I thought I was doing something bureaucratic for a friend." Indeed, Caiozzi had no background in making documentaries; he is known for his feature films. He also does not seem to have an easily identifiable political position in a country where many Chileans of his generation still hold, to a certain extent, to the militant political perspectives of the 1960s and 1970s. This does not suggest, however, that Caiozzi's films lack strong undertones of criticism toward Pinochet's regime. All of his films address the theme of human repression, and none more explicitly than *Fernando Is Back*.[1]

The structure of *Fernando* is divided into three parts. After introductory footage of a candlelight vigil, we begin in the Medical Legal Institute, in an office where the two female forensic scientists charged with Fernando's case explain what kinds of evidence they used to ensure that the skeleton belonged to that of Fernando. They demonstrate how family photographs of Fernando's head could be juxtaposed with the skull of the skeleton through computer software. They were able to match his dental structure, which, in the identification of skeletons, they say, is as unique as a fingerprint. The women also talk about the emotional toll that their jobs take on them, especially when they learn more about the victims through their family members.

Then Fernando's widow Agave and her family are led into the room where the skeleton is located. With sensitive dexterity, the women uncover the skeleton and slowly explain what evidence they found for Fernando's execution (gunshot wounds at the base of the skull) and prior torture and injury (dozens of fractures on the ribcage and gunshot wounds in the lower back and hip). Finally, the skeleton is covered, and the family is led back into the office to recover from their overwhelming emotions. One of the scientists explains, "For me, I can feel peace of mind when I can point to a skeleton and say here they killed him. Before we were talking about ghosts—not for us, but for them. Now we have proof. Although we know that probably nothing will come out of this. [Heads shake in agreement that justice will not be achieved.] But at least this can be useful for history. If not for now, then in the future."

With a look of emotional exhaustion, Agave proclaims, "If only he had had some mobility." (She has been told that Fernando was probably killed while kneeling.) She adds, "I can't get over the ability a human being has to do such things to another human being. It's incredible."[2] The family and the forensic scientists become key witnesses and historical interpreters in *Fernando*. Yet both sets of social actors can witness and interpret only so much material. Those who peer over the remains of the man they believe to be Fernando were not present during his detention and execution. They can deduce certain information from the physical evidence that is left on his skeleton, but they will never know exactly what he experienced during his torture and execution. Through the eyes of the camera, we absorb what is revealed but are left with a desire to learn what will never be known.

Agave becomes the moral conscience within the documentary. We in the audience identify with this woman of few words whose life has been overwhelmed by the loss and search for her husband. After this moment of deep sorrow and disbelief, we do not hear from her again. Rather, she becomes a silent participator and spectator in the funeral proceedings. As such, we are left with her exclamation of astonishment at the capacity for human cruelty. Her question becomes our own, and it crosses all boundaries within Chilean culture.

The one consistency in Chile has been its deeply segregated society. Since those who were victims of the human rights violations came primarily from certain sectors of the population (initially, the Socialist Party, Communist Party, and Leftist Revolutionary Movement but, later, others as well), those from the other end of the political spectrum frequently belittled and disregarded, systematically, the denunciations of violations, assuming that they were exaggerated and a necessary element of "saving" the country from "civil war." Yet Agave is not easy to ignore. Soft-spoken, stylishly dressed, not expressing the political Left's rhetorical explanations for the Chilean situation, and demonstrating deep love and loss for her husband, she does not fit the political Right's stereotype of the "human rights agitators." Instead, she poses a moral question that has no political boundaries that demonstrates the degree to which events in Chile have strayed from standard expectations for human behavior. The "human rights question" is removed from the realm of politics and becomes a humanitarian issue, one that blends with Christian doctrine with which many Chilean conservatives identify. In fact, when the documentary was first screened at the Film Festival of Valdivia, it won a prize "for the contribution to the diffusion of Christian values," given by the Catholic Organization of Cinema. By withholding voiceover commentary, Caiozzi accomplishes the same feat as Agave. Rather than espousing a specific interpretation, Caiozzi lets the stark images and voices speak for themselves.

In addition to the witnessing that is performed by Fernando's family and the professionals of the Medical Legal Institute, witnessing is also performed by the camera itself. Nichols explains how this technique—substituting the camera for the person controlling the camera—can be so effective in linking the viewers to the film, allowing them to witness the experience directly. "As in classical narrative fiction, our tendency to establish a repertoire of imaginary relationships with characters and situations prospers on condition of the filmmaker's presence as absence. Their unacknowledged, nonresponsive presence clears the way for the dynamics of empathetic identification, poetic immersion, or voyeuristic pleasure" (43–44). In *Fernando*, the camera plays a similar role, almost always staying in the same physical space as the remains, zooming in on the torture and bullet damage to the bones, standing in as another family member at the memorial service in the institute, the wake in Fernando's mother's home, the vigil in the cemetery, and the final burial at the memorial for those killed and disappeared during the dictatorship in the General Cemetery.

Another flashback leads to the candlelight vigil, where Fernando's son addresses the camera: "You know, my grandmother is another 'disappeared' who is not on the list. Go to her and try to understand her. She suffered her first stroke in 1973 when they took my father. She had her second stroke when they discovered the skeletons."

The visit to Fernando's mother is emotionally unbearable. No one represents the pain and suffering of the loved ones of the disappeared more than her. With the help of an interpreter, since her ability to speak is compromised by the effects of her strokes, we hear her stories through tears of anguish. We hear how the military denied knowing anything about Fernando and how they accepted the food and clothing that the family brought to the National Stadium when the family suspected that he was being held there along with thousands of others during the first few months of the dictatorship, even though the authorities did not offer any information about him. Most family members of the disappeared have had similar experiences. Relatives not only brought food and clothing, but they were also often swindled out of money, even life savings, because they were told that this would help them find and recover their relatives. For twenty-five years, Fernando's mother searched and waited for him to come home. Now, she exclaims, Fernando is finally back but not alive. At the time of this film's release, her family appeared to be one of the lucky ones, though, since most relatives of the disappeared were still waiting for the return of their loved ones.

During the wake, we hear from Fernando's brothers and sisters. One brother tells how he once spoke with a man from the military while enquiring about Fernando. The officer asked him with what political party Fernando had participated. The brother answered, "MIR," the extreme Left group, Revolutionary Leftist Movement (*Movimiento Izquierda Revolucionario*). In response, the officer exclaimed, "Oh, if he is MIR, then forget him." The brother explains, once Fernando's political affiliation was identified, he was no longer considered a person, just three letters. This, in fact, is how Pinochet's repressive forces were able to rationalize committing such acts of violence. The "leftist enemies" were effectively dehumanized by being relegated to a political affiliation. If the political affiliation was considered "hostile" toward the "fatherland," then the "problem" needed to be contained or eliminated.

The documentary ends with what we assume to be Fernando's burial at the Memorial for the Disappeared and Executed in the General Cemetery of Santiago. Also participating are other members of the Association of Relatives of the Detained-Disappeared (AFDD). The camera zooms in on their sad and tired faces and then scans down to the photos of their loved ones pinned to their chests. Caiozzi decided to identify Fernando only by his first name in the title of the documentary because he wanted this work to tell the story of all the disappeared "Fernandos." At the end of the film, a dedication is written on the screen to all mothers of the disappeared over an image of the tombs of the disappeared next to the memorial, most of which are still vacant and waiting for remains.

The story of what happened to *Fernando* after it was first screened in Chile at the film festival of Valdivia, only a couple months before Pinochet's arrest in London, is as gripping and intriguing as the documentary itself. *Fernando* was a surprise screening for participants in this annual domestic film festival. Caiozzi had been called at the last moment by the festival coordinator to participate as a judge, and he surprised her by mentioning that he had just finished making a documentary, which she immediately encouraged him to submit for the festival. She never asked for information about the content, and Caiozzi never gave it.

Caiozzi introduced the documentary but only said a few words. When the screening was over, Caiozzi describes the experience in the auditorium as magical. "You need to keep in mind," he says, "that many members of the audience were *Pinochetistas* [Pinochet supporters]." Many people were crying. Many stayed silent. As members of the audience started to move around, several approached Caiozzi and told him how moved they had been and how much they appreciated his film. He explains, "One woman, a *Pinochetista*, told me that she had always supported Pinochet, but now after watching this, she realized that he had gone too far—that this was unacceptable" (personal interview, March 27, 2002). The film also received glowing reviews by the various media outlets that were represented at the festival. Caiozzi's documentary appears to have been so effective with a diverse Chilean audience because it takes a humanist perspective rather than a political one and demonstrates, like Fernando's brother mentions in the wake scene, that "pain has no political colors."

In 2002, the video of *Fernando Is Back* was available in select video rental stores in Santiago, but mostly only in certain neighborhoods. The video could be purchased at the leading Chilean recorded music store, *Feria del disco*, but the store did not advertise that it was available, so most people did not know about it. Thus, four years after its release, most Chileans still had never seen it. As will be demonstrated shortly, the film seems to be attracting more attention with new video and DVD rental outlets available online.

I asked Gabriela Zuñiga, former public relations representative for the AFDD chapter in Santiago, whose husband disappeared, if she had seen this documentary and what she thought of it (personal interview, May 23, 2002): "I'm an aesthetic critic. *Fernando* serves the purpose of diffusion, but I prefer more subtle documentaries. For example, have you seen *La Venda* [refers to a torture center in Santiago where extreme sexual abuse was practiced]? It was made by women, about five or six women who were tortured. It's like a song to life, despite the weight of the tortures. Of course we [at the Association] know all of them [individuals in the documentary] . . . Caiozzi uses the camera well. But talking about the responsibility of the media . . . it was on TV *very* late at night."

Zuñiga is not your average Chilean media consumer or documentary viewer. For her, the subject matter of the documentary is lived on a daily basis, and has been for the past thirty-five years. She does, however, acknowledge the importance of Caiozzi's film as a source of education for the larger public and a potential tool for further support of her organization's mission.

An interesting source of viewer responses to *Fernando* is the DVD and VHS rental retail Web site, Bazuka.com. Here you can find a mix of reactions from what seem to be primarily Chilean viewers, keeping in mind that not everyone has access to the Internet or film rentals. The majority of responses (posted between August 2001 and April 2006) exhibit characteristics of historian Steve Stern's emblematic memories 2 (traumatic rupture) and 3 (a test of the nation's moral integrity and conscience). However, certain comments clearly fall under Stern's emblematic memories 1 (Pinochet's salvation) and 4 (closed box). Most comments concentrate on the subject matter of the documentary, not the documentary itself. However, some comments do pay attention to the role of the director and the construction of the documentary as a series of artistic choices.

On December 10, 2001 (exactly five years before Pinochet's death), someone named "A user" says, "At first it seems too explicit, but ultimately that is the reality . . . It's a film that reminds us again that in our country justice does not exist."[3] On February 4, 2002,

Ricardo García-Huidobro declares, "Now is the hour that these things are known, in order that they don't ever happen again." On October 28, 2002, a user naming oneself "Bart Simpson" states, "Without falling into the political disqualifications, seeing this documentary makes us reflect on the thousands that still have not been found and whose families wait without rest." On August 4, 2003, Pablo B. exclaims, "A copy of this video should exist in all the universities and high schools in order to show that these types of events cause amazing pain . . . so that they never occur again." On August 10, 2003, Alvaro Farias writes, "Seeing it is to take a step forward to the future, as contradictory as it may seem . . . In the end, it's one of those works, if we were able to call it such, that one can't not experience in the most profound way." On December 18, 2005, Pamela Gutierrez asks, "What do you do when you don't know how he died, you don't know when he died, who was with him, how much he suffered, what he was thinking? You don't know anything of the person whom you loved at the most dramatic moment of his life because you could not accompany him in his death."

Then there are the voices of Pinochet supporters. On September 21, 2001, Pedro writes, "Actually it seems to me deplorable that cinema is used in order to distort what really in Chile was the military government: the savior of our fatherland from diabolic Marxist hands." On February 7, 2002, Don Bertolucci writes, "It's again the cinema that erroneously shows us the military government (that saved this country from the Marxist-Leninist terrorism) as if they were dedicated to killing."

On February 12, 2002, Morphine, apparently from a younger generation, writes, "Please, no more! Carry your hatred to the tomb, cursed generation fixated on communists and rabid fascists, and don't give us more of the nuisance! Please!" Yet, María, another member of Morphine's generation, seems more appreciative of the documentary and points out that her only source of information on Chile's traumatic recent past is media. On August 31, 2004 (during the time when the narrative feature film *Machuca*, discussed in Chapter 4, would have been in theaters), she writes, "Since I didn't experience that era I've fed my knowledge by means of movies, books, and testimonies . . . and this movie seems to me almost like a real link with the era and saddens anyone."

The comments made about the film as a film were few but perhaps significant. In general, the film is praised for its "reflection of reality" and lack of artistic artifice. However, we need to keep in mind when reading these comments that all films are constructions. On August 21, 2001, "A user" writes, "Caiozzi with this not only contributes a grand delivery of the real but puts on its feet this genre (documentary), that in this country is not utilized, with the exception of Patricio Guzmán and some others." On February 14, 2002, Prestoopnik Chelloveck declares, "There has been lacking a documentary with the quality and professionalism like that which Caiozzi delivers to open the eyes of so many Chileans and show them with the harshness of these images the truth hidden for so many years, the truth behind a dictatorial regime sustained through cruel assassins and torturers." On January 9, 2004, Marco Canepa writes, "The documentary genre is difficult; it should move us without resorting to tricks or interventions, portraying reality with the perspective of the director. And here there is no room for doubt that this was achieved . . . It's from those few tapes from which one is incapable of opening one's mouth, aware that whatever comment will only trivialize the deep significance of what was seen."

Today in Chile, *Fernando Is Back* has attained further significance. Now it appears that Silvio Caiozzi, Fernando's family, and other members of the AFDD whose relatives were also supposedly identified from Patio 29, a mass grave in Santiago's General Cemetery created during the dictatorship, were deceived. In 2006, the AFDD was told that all investigations conducted by the national institute charged with criminal forensic evidence, *Servicio Medico Legal*, the Medical Legal Institute, may have been compromised. Relatives of the dozens of disappeared who, since the end of the dictatorship, were told that their missing loved ones had been positively identified and who had held funerals and burials with those remains, were informed that the remains they buried may not have been those of their relatives after all—the cruelest joke that could possibly be played on these families who have already endured such trauma. Along with these chronically traumatized families, a documentary critically acclaimed for its "truth" has fallen victim to the lies and deceit of the dictatorship and mismanagement of the postdictatorship era as well. Hence, on the Bazuka.com Web site, Xelpupla declares, "And actually everything appears to indicate that Fernando has gone missing again" (April 29, 2006). In June 2008, some of these remains, along with DNA evidence from relatives, were sent to the United States for scientific clarification.

The Day Pinochet Died

Documentaries can reach an even wider global audience thanks to the ability to post these films online. Although the Internet is not easily accessible to all Chileans, it does offer new opportunities for some groups, especially the exiles and children of exiles, to come together across geographic barriers.

When General Augusto Pinochet died on December 10, 2006—International Human Rights Day—blogger and filmmaker Nicole Senerman, using the alias "Rucia Sucia," documented reactions to the news of his death, creating *El día en que murió Pinochet* (*The Day Pinochet Died*), available worldwide on the Internet.[4]

The video begins its coverage on the afternoon of December 10, 2006, with Senerman approaching passersby and people sitting on benches and at outdoor cafés, asking them, their faces in close-ups, "Do you know what happened today?"

The first people who are approached do not know, including one foreigner who does not understand Spanish. "*Perdón; no entiendo*," she replies.

"In English?" asks Senerman.

"Yes."

"Do you know what happened today?"

"You mean, why everyone's beeping? No."

"Pinochet died."

"Who . . . who is Pinochet?" she says in unison with her companion, who Senerman catches through a pan across the table.

An elderly woman is walking toward the camera, which zooms in on her face. "Hello."

"Good afternoon." The camera zooms further in for a close-up.

"Do you know what happened today?"

"No."
"Pinochet died."
"No."
"He just died."
"Really? For sure?"

Then the camera observes people who already know and are starting to celebrate. "Adolph Hitler the Second has died!"

Two men shake hands and then embrace. "I never thought he would die. Congratulations."

An older man is waving his hands in celebration. "Did you find out what just happened?" Senerman asks. She zooms in on the man smoking, drinking, missing teeth.

"Yes. Now I can die in happiness!"
"The assassin dies!"

"He has fallen!" The rejoicers are skipping and trotting down the road, waving Chilean flags and red flags with the images of President Salvador Allende and Che Guevara, heading toward Plaza Italia, where a celebration is taking place. On Santiago's main avenue, Alameda, drivers and passengers go by honking, waving flags and T-shirts. People are holding up banners and posters, including one that reads, "You died. You old fuck." Others are throwing confetti. "Bravo!" They jump up and down, singing, "He died! He died!" and "Lucía! [Pinochet's widow] Don't weep! The people won't forgive!"

A woman in the passenger's seat of a car holds out a framed photograph of a young man, a victim of the dictatorship. Another woman standing at Plaza Italia holds a sign with another photograph of a man. The sign reads, "Justice. Why did you kill me, assassin Pinocho?" She also holds up a black T-shirt with the iconic image of a younger General Pinochet in uniform and wearing sunglasses, circled in red, with a red diagonal bar over it. The streets are a blizzard of confetti. We see a poster with photos of "los 119," the 119 victims of the Pinochet regime who were named in the press during the dictatorship as being killed in armed conflict among various members of the political Left outside of Chile. The stories were completely false. The poster is positioned in the midst of chanting and mayhem in the streets. Standing near the poster is a man wearing a red shirt, his fist in the air. Behind his shoulder we see what could be interpreted as a disapproving look from a man trying to pass by. A *carabinero*, a police officer, stands in the foreground, observing the crowd. A member of the crowd is shooting the scene with his camera phone.

Senerman continues to wander the streets with the camera. One person comments, "It's a pity that he wasn't tried." Senerman asks a young boy if he knew who Pinochet was. "Yes. He did the coup. He locked people in the stadiums. He killed everyone." Senerman enters a café with the news that some people are asking for an ex-president's funeral and national day of mourning. "She's going to hit the fan," responds one woman, thinking about President Bachelet's probable reaction. A little later, Senerman announces to passersby that Bachelet has announced that Pinochet will not be buried with presidential honors. The people to whom she tells this are pleased. "Criminals don't deserve any honors." The camera focuses on more graffiti. "Pinochet: Your death only confirms impunity."

A musical soundtrack—Gepe's "The Sickness of the Eyes"—begins to play as we watch the next section with only the moving images, no synchronous sound. We see more banners and graffiti. "Neither death nor burial will stop you from being a murderer." "Dictator, murderer, and forever thief." "No evil lasts a hundred years. You are screwed, old bastard." Occasionally, the camera tilts up to hovering helicopters in the sky—a foreshadowing of the events about to occur. In one brief instance of synchronous sound, Senerman stops a young woman holding a sign of a disappeared loved one that reads, "Where are they?" Senerman suggests, "Today is a day to smile, no?"

"Yes," the woman responds. "But where are they?"

A boy gives the camera the peace sign, holding up two fingers. The camera tilts up again to helicopters. In the foreground, we see a hand holding a bouquet of balloons; in the background, conflict builds as the sun begins to set.

We see thick black smoke over Alameda, Santiago's main avenue, beyond the San Francisco Church, near the University of Chile. Senerman drops the camera to her side, while it is still recording, and runs away from the antiriot police. Dozens of frantic feet, including her companion's feet in hot-pink pumps, are running away as the camera shakes wildly. We observe more helicopters. Then we witness people trying to escape from tear gas. We see close-ups of children and grandmothers affected by the gas. The camera is inside somewhere, observing the news broadcasting from a TV set mounted to the wall. Synchronous sound begins again. The news anchor is blaming the upheaval in the streets on juvenile delinquents who had allegedly planned the riots.

Senerman poses a new question to passersby: "What should the newspaper headlines be tomorrow?"

People give their responses. "Something positive. Let's think towards the future."

"The beast is dead."

"Someone who did the most damage has finally left this world."

"National celebration because the criminal is dead."

"Long live Pinochet. The jackass is dead."

"Merry Christmas to all Chileans."

"Finally he died. Long live Chile."

"Blind people are happy because the old bastard is dead."

While we hear these responses, we see the actual headlines: "The Last Day of Pinochet." "Over 60,000 people passed in front of coffin." "Augusto Pinochet dies." "Shocking image of Pinochet." "Justice wasn't done." "The end of an era."

Senerman asks a military guard, "What do you think of today?"

"I don't have any opinion."

"None?!"

One of the last respondents says, "The murderer is dead. The one who killed all the innocent beings."

The final person who Senerman records suggests that Pinochet continues to live as an Argentinean woman—Carla Sepúlveda. As this respondent's explanation becomes more and more bizarre, Senerman and the camera back away, literally and intellectually, while the respondent finishes with a "Sieg hiel!" The last image shows Senerman's arm with the words, "Registering history" scribbled on it.

While no mainstream commercial media outlet inside of Chile paid attention to the video, Senerman did receive tremendous informal feedback, especially through e-mail. She explains that the

Internet allows the user to create one's own programming grid. As a consequence, television networks are trying to reinvent themselves now that individuals can watch what they want, when they want, and without censorship. She remembers watching the 1988 Chilean plebiscite, which forced Pinochet to step down from power in 1990, from a television while living in the United States. She was struck by how much of what she considered most important about the event was not covered; there was simply an authoritative voice-over narration explaining the results. Through the power of the Internet, she and other media producers can document and exhibit events from a more inclusive, participatory, and active perspective (personal e-mail interview, May 17, 2007). In addition, documentaries that address human rights situations and violations are more accessible to wider audiences. Mainstream commercial media, especially television, will not show Senerman's video, but it is available for those who seek it out.

Conclusion

Elizabeth Jelin warns that traumatic history cannot be compartmentalized: "Today, some social and political actors believe that repression and abuses are phenomena of the dictatorial past. Others emphasize the ways that inequality and the mechanisms of domination in the present both reproduce and evoke the past. The recent dictatorial past is, nonetheless, a central part of the present. Social and political conflicts over how to understand and work through the recent repressive past remain active in the present and often are even intensified or deepened" (xvii).

Documentaries such as *Fernando Is Back* and *The Day Pinochet Died* address Chile's censored, recent history very explicitly. In the case of *Fernando*, we in the audience bear witness to the Pinochet regime's human rights violations through the remains of a victim of forced disappearance. In the case of *The Day Pinochet Died*, we observe huge crowds of Chileans celebrating the symbolic end of the Pinochet era. Both films offer layers of complexity. With *Fernando*, we can no longer be certain that the skeleton we see *is* that of Fernando, but it likely still belongs to one of the disappeared. Without intending to, Caiozzi managed to create a documentary that not only shows irrefutable evidence of the atrocities of the dictatorship but also illustrates, in hindsight, the ongoing traumas and uncertainties suffered by the families of the disappeared. With *The Day Pinochet Died*, Senerman not only captured valuable film footage of a significant day in Chilean history; she also demonstrated the mixed, bittersweet sentiments expressed by Chileans through their celebrations. Most would have preferred that Pinochet had been successfully prosecuted and punished for his crimes before his death. Those who opposed him are forced to celebrate his death because that day now will never come. Those who are religious hope that justice will be served in the afterlife. The scene in which we see how this story is being narrated on TV offers an ironic counterpoint to what we are witnessing more directly on the streets through Senerman's camera.

The development of new media outlets and their availability to a global audience allow narratives to be told from fresh and different points of view, including the perspectives of people whose voices have been marginalized and silenced in traditional media outlets. Parts of *Fernando Is Back* and *The Day Pinochet Died* are available on YouTube, with viewer comments included. A response to *Fernando* reads, "When the errors [in the forensic institute] were known, someone from this family interviewed on TV said that although it may not be their relative in the tomb that they care for, it was someone that they would still care about. This humanity gives one faith after so much inhumanity." Another respondent shared, "I have never cried before with any documentary or film. I saw this documentary today, by accident, in the university. I am ashamed of everything that has happened in my country. I am ashamed that I once defended the dictatorship." One response to *The Day Pinochet Died* reads, "I lived this afternoon in *el centro* [downtown Santiago]. I believe that this day, beer had the best flavor." Clips and links can also be found on many bloggers' pages. There is a global discussion taking place about these documentaries and the material they cover, whether the mainstream media chooses to engage with this discussion or not. While they are still effectively excluded from most mainstream media venues, the immediate and future impact that these two films have on human rights discourses in postrepressive Chile cannot be overlooked.

Chapter 4

The *Machuca* Phenomenon

> *When an image coincides with traumatic events of historical rupture, it plays a central role in the construction of national meaning.*
>
> —Marita Sturken, *Tangled Memories*

No Chilean filmic images have become more indelible than those of the bombing of *La Moneda*, the Presidential Palace, on September 11, 1973, at the start of the military coup that led to General Augusto Pinochet's seventeen-year dictatorship. Patricio Guzmán and his *Battle of Chile* (1975–79) film crew captured the live images from their television set on that decisive morning, and these pictures became the opening sequence to their epic documentary film. Guzmán featured the footage again at the start of his 1997 documentary, *Chile: Obstinate Memory*. In both instances, Guzmán used those moments of the Chilean Air Force bombings as a historical anchor point, capturing the audience's attention with these dramatic minutes frozen in time.

In *Twilight Memories: Marking Time in a Culture of Amnesia*, Andreas Huyssen discusses the role that museums can play in the preservation and erosion of selective historical memories: "Fundamentally dialectical, the museum serves both as burial chamber of the past—with all that entails in terms of decay, erosion, forgetting—and as site of possible resurrections, however mediated and contaminated, in the eyes of the beholder. No matter how much the museum, consciously or unconsciously, produces and affirms the symbolic order, there is always a surplus of meaning that exceeds set ideological boundaries, opening spaces for reflection and counter-hegemonic memory" (15).

Huyssen's words ring true for other elements of a national culture, including the media and larger public sphere. There are egregious absences in media discourses about recent Chilean history that circulate, for example, through television, but audiences can fill in the blanks and draw their own conclusions based on their own experiences. Many of the visible absences of Chilean television are very explicitly confronted in Chilean cinema; however, the Chilean public often needs to look in unauthorized spaces to find them. Completing a tour of the national history museum in Santiago will only give you a partial education. The museum, which glorifies the accomplishments of the conquistadors and wealthy elite and ends history on September 11, 1973, does do an excellent job of teaching the visitor what parts of Chile's history have been favored by the ruling class and what recent eras are too volatile for representation (namely, everything since September 11, 1973). President Salvador Allende's smashed glasses (a result of his death on this date of the coup) are enclosed in glass in the final small room of the museum's permanent exhibits. Purchasing and then viewing a pirated copy of *The Battle of Chile* from just outside the building (until recently, the only easy way to obtain a copy of this film inside Chile was on the black market) offers Chilean citizens a much more comprehensive and unintended (by the museum's designers) interpretation to their nation's history.

Our memories are a mix of personal experiences combined with collective experiences that we have as groups, nations, and cultures in specific historical contexts. These collective memories often get recirculated through representations in media texts, affecting and potentially changing our understanding of events. Visual media in particular play a crucial role in this circulation. As Sturken argues, "Images have the capacity to create, interfere with, and trouble the memories we hold as individuals and as a nation. They can lend shape to histories and personal stories, often providing the material evidence on which claims of truth are based, yet they also possess the capacity to capture the unattainable" (20). Sturken describes the historical authority as well as the potential for historical distortion of filmic images: "Camera images, whether photographs, films, or television footage, whether documentary, docudrama, or fiction, are central to the interpretation of the past. Photographs are often perceived to embody memory, and cinematic representations of the past have the capacity to entangle with personal and cultural memory. Just as memory is often thought of as an image, it is also produced by and through images" (11).

In Chilean cinema, these sensory properties of memory are useful to elicit since certain authorities and segments of the population are still attempting to deny and diminish the gravity of prior human rights violations. The repression of the dictatorship has *systematically* been "forgotten" under many circumstances by the postdictatorship elected governments, the public education system, and much mainstream media. It has sometimes even been suppressed by living survivors of torture and exile. Sturken refers to Freud's discourse on screen theory (with the double meaning intended) to highlight how the media, which we are exposed to, foreground, hide, and arrange our historical memories: "In Freud's formulation, forgetting is an *active* process of repression, one that demands vigilance and is designed to protect the subject from anxiety, fear, jealousy, and other difficult emotions. The concept of a screen memory is particularly useful in thinking about how a culture remembers. Cultural memory is produced through representation—in contemporary culture, often through photographic images, cinema, and television. These mnemonic aids are also screens, actively blocking out other memories that are more difficult to represent" (8).

Prior to, during, and after the dictatorship, the politics of Chile often were contested through competing media images. The fact that the *Battle of Chile* crew shot the film during the Popular Unity government's reign (1970–73) not only highlighted the massive support enjoyed by President Allende but also depicted the heated political debates among different sectors of the political Left. The filmmakers did not feature the more reasoned conservative voices of that era, but they did show in detail the right-wing extremists aligned with fascism. During the dictatorship, Chilean TV depicted General Pinochet as a strong but grandfatherly guardian of the country whose highest concern was the welfare of his fellow citizens. He was shown being honored by his soldiers and police forces during birthday celebrations and attending Catholic mass. However, documentaries shot secretly in Chile during the dictatorship showed how public protesters were sprayed with sewer water, beaten, and rounded up by police. None were able to expose what happened to citizens once they were detained and tortured, for obvious problems of access. The narratives of fiction films produced inside Chile during the dictatorship oftentimes took place during earlier periods of time; however, close reading of the film texts reveals the degree to which filmmakers were using allegory and metaphor to express veiled criticisms of the Pinochet regime. Now that the dictatorship has ended, media representations of conditions in Chile are much more diverse but still screened in various ways. The visibility of the Association of Relatives of the Detained-Disappeared (AFDD) and their cause has been much more prominent than representations and discourses of the much larger number of citizens who are survivors of torture (up to 400,000 victims). These representations and omissions all affect Chileans' and non-Chileans' understandings of the country's recent history.

Documentaries are the cinematic form through which Chilean human rights discourses circulate most directly, but narrative feature films play a significant role, too. The approach that filmmakers have taken to these themes in their fictional work is less direct. However, the potential that these filmmakers have to reach audiences is much greater. Chilean feature films make their way into Chilean theaters and homes, and they have an expanding national, as well as international, fan base. Packaged as entertainment that appeals to diverse audiences, these filmic texts include human rights discourses as well, and in recent years, those discourses have become more explicit.

Chilean cultural studies theorist Nelly Richard argues for more qualitative research and textual analysis to better understand current conditions in Chile. She explains,

> To give value to the theoretical benefits of [sign constructions'] furtive details, what is minor and off the track needs that small incision made by cultural analysis on the surface of utterances, which only then permits us to see—obliquely—its underside: the almost hidden textures formed by that which has no precise definition, sure explanation, or stable classification. To look beneath and between the principal codifications, to pursue lateral meanings and sinuosities of sense, allows us to see what has been set aside by the narratives of authority and its hegemonic

tales (what has been reduced, devalued, underrepresented by them) to throw into relief the loose and disparate fragments of ongoing experiences: fragments that lack a formal translation in the communicative language that dominates current sociology, and that would remain on the sidelines had certain readings not decided to incorporate the diffuse and precarious into their thought. (4)

Chilean narrative films are rich texts for the interpretation of polysemic discourses. It is precisely these films' potentiality for subjective and individually nuanced readings that lent a certain degree of protection to filmmakers during the dictatorship. Most frequently, coded messages were conveyed through the use of metaphor, a skill honed by Latin American artists of all kinds—musicians (especially Chilean groups such as Inti-Illimani), playwrights, poets, novelists (such as Isabel Allende and Gabriel García Márquez), painters, and filmmakers (especially in 1960s repressive Brazil).

According to Ascanio Cavallo, Pablo Douzet, and Cecilia Rodríguez in *Orphaned and Lost: Chilean Cinema of the Transition 1990–1999* (*Huérfanos y Perdidos: El cine chileno de la transición 1990–1999*): "If the cinema of the '90s replicates the phenomenon of the transition, that is to say, the passing from a society of police controls to one that is opening to public freedoms, it has been done gradually as this process would imply, vulnerable to the complex trauma of subjective and objective factors: the persistence of certain taboos, the evolution of historical justice, internalized censorship, and above all, the sensation of fragility in the transition from one environment to the other" (90). The authors' descriptions hold true for the beginning of the new millennium, too, despite that new events and proceedings in Chile in recent years may allow feature filmmakers to approach these sensitive themes with more assertiveness and intensity in the future. Previous Chilean film censorship laws were abolished in 2002, allowing many Chilean and international films to be screened for the first time in Chile, and giving more freedom of expression to filmmakers. Chile's current president, Michelle Bachelet, is a survivor herself of the Pinochet regime's human rights violations. She and her mother were tortured political prisoners. Her father, a general in the armed forces who disagreed with Pinochet, died as a result of the torture he received in prison. Most recently, General Pinochet's death on

December 10, 2006—International Human Rights Day—and the consequences of his dying without ultimately being punished for his crimes are yet to be fully determined.

Despite the new conditions, filmmakers still must operate through a series of constraints, both political and financial ones, which encourage self-censorship. In October 2004, a taxi driver who was a former political prisoner and about to testify against his torturer in court was found shot in the back of the head in his taxi, with his wallet and money intact beside him. Violent repression still occurs in Chile after nineteen years of renewed democracy. Filmmakers, who continue to be considered unpatriotic subversives by many in the military and on the political Right, must still fear for their safety. Many of them were once political prisoners themselves and had colleagues who were executed or disappeared. Famed filmmaker Miguel Littín, who narrowly escaped Chile after the coup because one soldier who was supposed to be involved in his execution was a fan of his 1968 film, *El Chacal de Nahueltoro* (*The Jackal of Nahueltoro*), secretly returned to Chile in 1985, disguised as a Uruguayan businessman, in order to shoot footage for a documentary on conditions in Chile under the dictatorship. These filmmakers have reasons to testify in the courts as well, but many prefer addressing these problems more generally in their films rather than acknowledge and discuss exactly what happened to themselves and their co-workers.[1]

Also, in order to produce their films, filmmakers need to apply for funding from various national and international sources. One source is Fondo Nacional de Desarrollo Cultural y las Artes (FONDART; National Fund of Cultural Development and the Arts), a state-run organization that provides money for Chilean artists. The foundation is run by a diverse board of directors who come from different backgrounds and do not necessarily maintain the same values and historical memories as those of the filmmakers, both older and younger. Another source is Ibermedia. Ibermedia, created in 1997, supports the production, distribution, and exhibition of its member countries' films. The organization also encourages collaboration across member countries. One consequence is that the proposed films that might be most appealing to this organization are those that offer narratives that cross national borders, resulting in a lack of geographical and historical specificity. Another consequence is that those involved in the creation of the film, including the actors, may not all be natives of the country in which the story is taking place. Furthermore, for a film to reap profits, it must be marketable to an international audience beyond Latin America and the Iberian Peninsula—an audience that likely may not be very knowledgeable or concerned about specific conditions and politics in a country such as Chile. Filmmakers need to be especially skilled to create something meaningful and palatable to such a heterogeneous group of viewers. Cavallo, Douzet, and Rodríguez describe the situation: "Feeling a heavy weight upon themselves, Chilean filmmakers live in an essentially abnormal state: each time that they make a movie, they activate a Russian roulette that could end their careers and their legacies. To film in this manner is a stimulus to pretensions, grandiloquence, and totalism" (248–49).

Themes that pervade Chilean narrative cinema include those of betrayal, redemption, repression, uncertainty, and innocence lost. These themes are conveyed through representations of religion, love and sex relationships, authoritarian parental figures, darkness, enclosed spaces, whispering, children, adolescence, the elderly, and contrasting depictions of excess and lack. Frequently, the (dysfunctional) family and the home can be read as a microcosm of Chilean society and its intransigent institutions.

Since the return to democracy, many once-exiled filmmakers, others who never left Chile but found their opportunities severely restricted during the years of Pinochet, and a younger generation of filmmakers who came of age after the dictatorship ended, contribute today to what is considered a new wave of Chilean cinema. In recent years, dozens of films have been produced annually, although usually only a handful get picked up by international distributors. Thanks in part to new opportunities available through new technologies, cinematic productivity inside of Chile has not been this high since the 1960s, and while films do not all get acquired by large distributors, these new technologies also offer alternative venues for distribution and exhibition. Although many of these films do not deal directly with the dictatorship and its aftermath, many of them do contain subtexts that approach the legacy of exile and disappearances in particular and violent repression more generally (i.e., Orlando Lübbert's 2001 film *Taxi para tres* [*Taxi for Three*]). A regular exception to this rule of narrative marginality for themes of Chile's recent traumatic history are Guzmán's documentaries (which most recently include *The Pinochet Case* [2001] and *Salvador Allende* [2004]), which are finally becoming accessible to a significant number of people within Chile, and a recent exception in the case of narrative fiction is Andrés Wood's feature film *Machuca* (2004), which will get further attention in this chapter.

Richard refers to the role that contemporary Chilean media play (and do not play) in discussions of historical memory:

> The word 'memory,' like many that insipidly circulate, without weight or gravity, through the communicative channels of the mediating politics of television, has erased from its public voice the untreatable, unsociable recollection of the nightmare that tortured and tormented its subjects in the past. Memory, dislodged even from the words that name it, now suffers from an emptiness with a lack of affective context that daily cancels its horrible past, increasingly separating and distancing the historical memory from an emotional network that previously resonated collectively. It would seem that the word 'memory,' thus recited by the mechanized discourse of the consensus, subjects the memory of its victims to a new offense: making the memory insignificant by letting it be spoken in words weakened by official routines, which work carefully to put the names at a safe distance from any kind of biographical investigations dealing with the convulsive and fractured elements of lived experience. (18)

The response to Pinochet's death in December 2006 is a reminder of how distinct and oppositional memories of Chile's recent history remain for various sectors of the population, depending on individuals' subjective experiences during significant moments in time, especially the years of Allende's Popular Unity government and then Pinochet's regime. Most often, these memories are suppressed and silenced. However, the moment of Pinochet's death, an example of what historian Steve Stern would call a "memory knot," brought these various feelings to the surface and manifested them in vocal and sometimes violent public demonstrations. As discussed in the previous chapter on documentaries, Nicole Senerman's documentary *The Day Pinochet Died* (*El día en que murió*

Pinochet), shot on December 10, 2006, and available for a global audience online, captures this memory knot and arranges the material in a significant manner.

Another instance of a Chilean "memory knot" occurred in the weeks following the release of Wood's *Machuca* in August 2004, when his film, which directly addresses Chile's traumatic history, broke all box-office records for a domestic film and became a "must-see" event for audiences from all sectors of the country's deeply divided population. In the remainder of this chapter, I will describe how this particular film—a Chilean, Spanish, French, and British coproduction[2]—works through posttraumatic Chilean memories that have been sanitized by other forms of media in a manner that is deeply affective yet also inclusive of a diverse and divergent audience. An investigation of the manner in which *Machuca* represents Chile's recent history and sparks audiences' memories is important because Wood's film managed to appeal to a mass audience in a deeply divided society and has received critical acclaim inside and outside Chile. In addition to analyzing the film text, I also consider the manner in which the film was received by significant public opinion influencers—Chilean and U.S. newspaper film critics, respondents on the Internet Movie Database, and members of the AFDD, the most consistently visible and vocal human rights organization in Chile.

Machuca Synopsis and Narrative Analysis

Machuca, according to its ads in the press, "dedicated to the children of yesterday," is the story of a friendship that develops between two boys—one privileged and one poor—in 1973 Chile, just prior to the military coup of September 11 that ended the democratically elected socialist government of President Salvador Allende and began the seventeen-year dictatorship of General Augusto Pinochet. The narrative, originally created as a 2002 novel called *Tres años para nacer* (*Three years to be born*) by author and poet Amante Eledín Parraguez, is told through the eyes of Gonzalo Infante (Matías Quer), the boy of privilege whose character attends St. Patrick—"An English School for Boys" based on the real coeducational school St. George's, which the author attended beginning in 1971 as a consequence of the integration experiment conducted by the priest and principal, Father Gerardo Whelan, a North American transplant. Director Wood also attended the school at that time as a student from a family with more resources, but he was only seven years old—younger than the characters represented in the film. The story begins with Gonzalo getting dressed for school—an indication that the story is being told through him and his memories—with somber, nostalgic music in the background. His sister and father are leaving the house for school and work. His mother remains in bed under the rumpled sheets, lying on her stomach, barely saying good-bye to her son, while the housekeeper makes sure he has had his breakfast and is prepared for his day. The colors are warm and soft—an indication of the filmmaker's childhood memories and a foreshadowing of the "romance" about to develop between the two main characters, as well as between these characters and the audience.

As Gonzalo arrives at school (actually shot at Catholic University in Santiago), the music turns more hopeful and upbeat. Through a shot from above, we see the boys in their identical uniforms entering the school courtyard as they rush to their classes. From his classroom window, Gonzalo looks down onto the same courtyard to discover his principal and priest, Father McEnroe (the fictional version of Eledín and Wood's Father Gerardo Whelan, who directed the school from 1969 to 1973, played by Ernesto Malbrán), leading a new group of boys in mismatched clothing into the school; they are his new classmates. One of the newly integrated students is Pedro Machuca (Ariel Mateluna), whose dark skin, tattered sweater, and indigenous name contrast with the pale skin, uniforms, and European names of the boys of privilege. According to Eledín, "Machuca is a metaphor. He doesn't represent one person; he doesn't represent me; he represents a figure which is the idea of 'the integrated'" (Pavez, 15). After school, Gonzalo's mother, María Luisa (Aline Küppenheim), picks him up and takes him with her on one of her regular rendezvous with her secret lover, Roberto (Argentine actor Federico Luppi), who offers more attention to Gonzalo's mother than her husband Patricio (Francisco Reyes), who appears busy and committed to Allende's government, despite the contradictions that it poses for his own lifestyle. On their way, they pass a wall with graffiti that reads, "No to civil war." Roberto bribes Gonzalo with black-market goods, including a book of *The Lone Ranger: Volume 1*. Later that evening, Gonzalo and his mother return home to find Gonzalo's father, sister Isabel (Andrea García-Huidobro), and Isabel's boyfriend, Pablo (Tiago Correa), watching the news in their living room. On the TV, President Allende is shown visiting the Soviet Union. In response, Pablo makes a snide, derogatory remark—"*Que huevón, éste*" (What a fucker)—an indication of the contempt for the president held by the upper class.

Next, we see the boys participating in more activities at the school. In the swimming pool, the boys of privilege make fun of the new boys who do not have proper bathing suits. In response, Father McEnroe shouts, "You will learn to respect each other, even if it's the only thing that you learn at this school!" Another day, Gonzalo is led to Pedro Machuca being restrained by Gonzalo's peers in the schoolyard who are pressuring him to punch Pedro. The lead bully shouts, "This is how we do things in Vitacura!" referring to the wealthy province of Santiago in which they are supposedly located. When Gonzalo refuses to hit Pedro, his peers call him a coward and wander off. Thus begins the friendship between Gonzalo and "Peter."

A whole new world opens up for Gonzalo beginning on this day when he accepts a ride offered by Peter from his neighbor with a beat-up pickup truck, Willi (Alejandro Trejo), who also happens to have a daughter, Silvana (Manuela Martelli), slightly older than Gonzalo and Peter, on whom Gonzalo quickly forms a crush. Willi and Silvana sell flags, and Gonzalo offers to help them out that afternoon at the demonstrations—anti- and then pro-Allende. At the anti-Allende rally, the demonstrators yell, "*Allende, Allende, la patria no se vende*" (Allende, Allende, the country/fatherland is not for sale). They jump in solidarity against Popular Unity. Silvana's father encourages the kids to jump, too, in order to blend in. Silvana refuses, and stands alone, a foreshadowing of her fate. At the pro-Allende rally, Gonzalo sees miners with their helmets on and one of the new integrated students, another foreshadowing of the fate of this student. "*Poder popular*" (Popular power), they yell. This time, "He who doesn't jump is a *momia* (mummy)." Gonzalo asks

Silvana, what is a mummy? "An ignorant rich person like you," she explains. Gonzalo freezes, hurt. She encourages him to jump, and he starts enjoying himself again. Jubilant music plays as they jump and we see beat-up pickup trucks filled to capacity with Allende supporters. The scenes of demonstrators in the streets look virtually identical to those in *Battle of Chile*; indeed, Wood studied *The Battle of Chile* in order to render these scenes accurate, only now the images are in color with music added. The power of these street scenes, already familiar to most viewers in another context, cannot be overstated. Wood has transformed visual representations of the Popular Unity era, which marked the rigid ideological divisions within Chilean society, into a scenario appealing to viewers of all backgrounds. We watch these moments through the eyes of an innocent child of privilege, and he is enchanted with what he witnesses. He allows audiences to reexamine the years of Popular Unity from a fresh perspective that is welcoming to everyone. The images of the trucks filled with Allende supporters are contrasted with the next scene in which we see Gonzalo and his mother driving into a dark, subterranean garage in order to visit her lover, Roberto. It is dark, quiet, and isolated.

One day Gonzalo offers to take Peter home on his bike. On their way, they pass a wall that reads, "Right wingers beware." Upon arrival at the *campamento*—the tent city or shantytown in which Peter lives—they encounter Peter's mother, Juana (Tamara Acosta), working the community garden. Inside Peter's humble home decorated with pro-Allende and pro-Popular Unity posters, Peter's mother serves tea. Silvana enters, helps to take care of Peter's baby sister, and continues her flirting with Gonzalo. Despite the rough conditions of poverty in which these families live, the atmosphere feels much warmer and more loving than the isolation and loneliness felt in Gonzalo's household.

Later in the narrative, we encounter Gonzalo's family intact during a rare instance of happiness. They have just dined at a fine restaurant and are in the car returning home when Gonzalo's father, who has to leave soon for a work-related trip to Italy, suggests, "Let's move to Italy. Socialism may be the best for Chile, but not for us." However, no one leaves the country except for Gonzalo's father. Conditions seem to be worsening in the city;

there is more tension in the air. During one of Gonzalo and his mother's afternoon visits to Roberto, Gonzalo looks down from Roberto's balcony to witness stray dogs being captured for food. (In the director's comments on the *Machuca* DVD, Wood explains that the rounding up of dogs is a metaphor for the rounding up of civilians in the near future.) Panicked, he bangs and shouts on Roberto's bedroom door, where he peeks at his naked mother lying on his bed—the moment when Gonzalo realizes how deeply his mother has betrayed his father and an indication of the betrayal about to come in the form of the military coup. "Everything's okay. Go watch TV. Your mother will be out soon," says Roberto. They are safe, sheltered above the chaos in the streets, and can live happily in their self-contained bubble. On their way home, they pass the wall that used to read, "No to civil war," but the "No" has been painted over.

Gonzalo is back in the *campamento* visiting Peter and Silvana. Peter's drunken father, Ismael (Luís Dubó), shows up. He ridicules Peter for having a friend like Gonzalo. He asks Peter, "Do you know where your friend will be in five years? He'll be in the university; you'll be cleaning toilets. Do you know where he'll be in ten years? He'll be working in business with his father; you'll be cleaning toilets. Do you know where he'll be in fifteen years? He'll be the owner of his father's business; you'll still be cleaning toilets." After he wanders off, Silvana says to Gonzalo, "Kids and drunks don't lie, do they?"

Tensions continue to grow. The St. Patrick School, represented as a microcosm of Chilean society, is in turmoil. The wealthy parents complain that they are subsidizing the tuition of the poor boys. They call the priest a communist. "You're trying to brainwash our children by mixing them," one parent complains. Gonzalo's mother asks, "What's the whole idea of mixing pears with apples?" Peter's mother proclaims, "I grew up on a farm; we were blamed for everything. We still are blamed for everything." Further tension is evident in the streets of Santiago. Gonzalo gets scared when he accidentally holds up a red, Socialist Party flag at an anti-Allende demonstration and quickly tosses it to the ground and steps on it, to hide the evidence. Gonzalo's mother and his sister's boyfriend, a member of the extreme right-wing fascist organization *Patria y Libertad* (Fatherland and Liberty), march against the Allende government shouting, "Communists, Bastards, living off the state!" Gonzalo's mother gets into a confrontation with the flag-selling Silvana after Pablo has refused to pay her for a cigarette and shouts, "Go back to your shantytown, fucking lowlife!" A close-up of Gonzalo's face reveals his shock. He runs back to Willi's truck, where he meets Peter and Silvana, all seeking refuge in the back. An aerial view shows their three bodies forming a triangle, suggesting their special connections with one another and the unit that they create. Silvana discovers that the woman with whom she was having the confrontation is Gonzalo's mother. A close-up of her face reveals her disgust and anger as she tells Gonzalo, "She is a shit, whore, mummy, *huevón*!"

They drive home in the rain. There is chaos and fire in the streets. The images outside the truck are out of focus. The music is sad. A close-up of Gonzalo shows him observing what is taking place outside and inside the truck. The camera pans across the front seat to show Peter and Silvana sleeping and Willi driving with a look of concern on his face. The anti-Allende women demonstrators are banging their *caceroles*, their empty casserole dishes, on the curbs. Back at St. Patrick's, the pigs, the representation of Father McEnroe's social experiment in which he had the boys working together on the school farm, are dead and are set on fire.

Gonzalo's relationship with Peter and Silvana is also in jeopardy. When Gonzalo gets angry with them for taking away his bike in jest, he parrots the members of his own social class, "*Rotos de mierda! Hijos de puta!*" (Shitty hicks! Children of whores!). When Peter confronts him, Gonzalo implores, "Go on. Hit me!" But Peter simply walks away, leaving Gonzalo standing alone. As tensions soar within Chilean society, Gonzalo's friendship with Peter and Silvana appears to be crumbling. Gonzalo is crying in his bed. His mother approaches and he embraces her, "I don't want you to be with that shit [Roberto]."

Next we see Gonzalo's bike leaning up against the wall in his house, trembling. We first assume that it's an earthquake, but then we realize that we have arrived at the moment we all were expecting—the start of the coup. The trembling is coming from the Air Force planes flying overhead on their way to *La Moneda*. In contrast to the filmic images of the actual bombing of *La Moneda* Palace, we see instead what would have been witnessed by the wealthy and middle class living in eastern Santiago—the Air Force planes flying from their base east of the city toward downtown Santiago on their way to bomb the palace. A close-up of Gonzalo's face shows him watching from his rooftop with a look of happy anticipation on his face, which quickly changes expression. His sister steps up next to him so that her face is also silhouetted in the close-up. Next, we see them from behind in a medium close-up. Here is the younger generation bearing witness to this historical event, as they can hear neighbors singing from adjacent rooftops.

School is cancelled. Gonzalo watches the TV footage with his housekeeper Lucy (Gabriela Medina) and sister. His mother is absent, possibly out celebrating with Roberto and her peers. We overhear the generals on TV describing the "Marxist cancer" that they needed to stop. We see Pinochet on the screen. The next day, Gonzalo arrives at school to find a very different environment. The school is teeming with military men in uniforms. As the boys enter the building, they are segregated according to hair length. All boys with long hair are forced to get it cut. As soldiers bark their orders, the music turns funereal. From above in Gonzalo's classroom, we witness the largest and probably oldest of the poor boys whom we saw earlier in the film in the pro-Allende demonstration, shouting from the center of the courtyard, "Army bastards! Go back to the barracks!" He is quickly escorted away by the men in uniform, never to be seen again. Soldiers enter Gonzalo's classroom and hand his teacher, Miss Gilda (María Olga Matte), a poster of the members of the junta that she left behind in the teachers' room. "Strange things have been going on here at this school. Students who don't pay will not be attending anymore—we don't want lazy students," proclaims Colonel Sotomayor (Pablo Krögh).

The soldiers escort the children to a mass with a new priest. Father McEnroe enters in the middle of the service. Somber music plays and the camera zooms in as he goes to a cabinet and proceeds to eat all of the communion hosts and then extinguishes the adjacent flame. "This place is not sacred anymore," he proclaims. "The Lord is no longer here." As he leaves the chapel, Peter stands up from his pew to say, "Good-bye, Father McEnroe," in English.

"Good-bye, Machuca," responds the priest solemnly, his image adjacent to that of Jesus hanging on the chapel wall behind his shoulder. The rest of the congregation, except for the soldiers, takes Peter's lead and stands up to bid Father McEnroe good-bye. Colonel Sotomayor approaches Peter's pew. Without words, Peter follows him out of the chapel.

According to author Eledín, "I didn't live the tragic finale of the movie, but that doesn't mean that it wasn't like that. There were integrated *compañeros* who ended up in jail or tortured. Others who were 'arrested' when they were in school. In this there is no exaggeration" (Pavez, 16). Eledín was forced to leave St. George two months after the coup, and Father Gerardo was replaced on October 9, 1973, by Commander Verdugo, the principal under the Pinochet regime. Father Gerardo was imprisoned in 1974 for protecting former student Andrés Pascal Allende, then leader of the persecuted extreme Left group MIR. He returned to teach at St. George in 1992 and died on October 31, 2003.

When school is dismissed, Gonzalo cannot find Peter anywhere. He exits the school, passing the soldiers with rifles standing at the doorways and goes home. No one is there except Lucy, knitting and soaking her feet. Gonzalo lies on his bed, a Lone Ranger poster visible on the wall behind him. He decides to ride his bike to the *campamento*. This is the first of two significant scenes in which Gonzalo, the unpersecuted, bears witness to what happens to his friend and the rest of the vulnerable underclass.

Wood portrays this violent scene in an eerie light—the colors are washed out; the footage is nearly in black and white. The silhouettes of soldiers with rifles are visible on top of the surrounding hills. Gonzalo finds the soldiers storming the homes of the community, shouting, "Get out here, you fucking communists!" Inhabitants are lined up against the outside walls. Piles of books and papers are burning in the roads. The camera tracks alongside Gonzalo, walking through the community with his bike. He freezes when he sees Peter, his family, Silvana, and her dad. Eerie orchestral music surges. The soldiers are terrorizing them. Soldiers are kicking Silvana's father. "You like flags? Go on, eat them!" They stuff his flags down his throat, trying to choke him. Dogs are barking at the soldiers. Silvana intervenes to save her father.

She positions herself between him and the soldiers, screaming and fighting back. Suddenly a gunshot is heard and soon we see a limp, dead Silvana. The music stops. Peter approaches Silvana and stands over her. The film cuts to a close-up of Gonzalo, standing at a distance, tearful and silent. We cut back to Gonzalo's perspective—Peter, his mother, her baby, and Willi hovering over Silvana.

Gonzalo's observation is interrupted by a soldier who starts shouting at him to line up with the other residents to be driven off. Panicked by the switching of his role from outside observer to potential victim, Gonzalo yells, "I don't live here! Look at me!" The soldier scans his body from head to toe, noticing his red hair, fair skin, and nice clothes and sneakers. He looks equally panicked that he almost misidentified Gonzalo. "Then, beat it!" Peter stares through his tears at Gonzalo, and then down at Silvana, as if he has been betrayed. Gonzalo, terrified, turns away on his bike. Somber music swells as we watch Gonzalo ride toward the camera, out of the *campamento*, through fire and fumes. Cut to black.

Next, we see a bicycle wheel and hear whistling from a child's toy. The camera tilts up to reveal Gonzalo riding down the street, passing a group of children who pretend to shoot him. "You are supposed to die!" they yell. He drops his bike at the front door of his home. We see that Gonzalo has moved into a nicer house. His father is absent; Roberto is there. Gonzalo looks disgusted by what he observes—his mother, Roberto, and another woman chatting outside on their patio. Gonzalo travels to school, accompanied by Roberto, presumably driven by a chauffeur. The wall that formerly read "No to civil war" and then "civil war" has been whitewashed. In Gonzalo's classroom, there is a new taller, blonder teacher, and the poster of the generals in the military junta stands alone against the back wall. Gonzalo's class is taking a quiz. The blond bully who once picked on Peter asks Gonzalo for help on the quiz. Gonzalo grabs the quiz, writes "ASSHOLE" on it, and returns it. He heads to the front of the classroom where he turns in his quiz, dated October 5, 1973, and leaves the room. The teacher looks at the quiz to see that he has left it blank.

The music that played at the beginning of the film starts again. We cut to an image of the open sky; Gonzalo steps into the frame. He looks down at a tin can, a reminder of his previous exploits with Silvana and Peter. We watch him from behind, looking across the soccer field to an empty space where the *campamento* had been located. Cut to a close-up of Gonzalo's face, bearing witness for the second time. Gonzalo's expression reveals an emptiness—an unspeakable sadness. Cut to our watching Gonzalo from behind; the audience is now bearing witness along with him. He turns to leave, we watch him from behind as he walks away from the field and camera, and the image goes out of focus. Fade to black.

Wood's conclusion reiterates that we are seeing this memory through the eyes of someone who was *not* a target of the Pinochet regime. All Chileans can mourn the disappearance of Peter, his family, and his neighbors through an innocent person of privilege. The conclusion is ambiguous as we are left to wonder how this experience is going to influence Gonzalo. He was present to bear witness to the experience of Peter. Will he now suppress the memory and conform to the expectations of his sheltered life of material wealth and superficialities, as represented by his endearing but shallow mother, whose last words in the film to the furniture movers are "Don't walk over the carpet!"? Or, rather, will this experience transform Gonzalo into a man of deep humanity who will honor Pinochet's victims and work for truth and justice? Only by being aware that the film is autobiographical for the director do we lean toward the second conclusion.

Andrés Wood's Description of *Machuca*

After a screening of *Machuca* at the Latin American Bureau in London, Gus Alvarez of *6degreesfilm* asked Wood why it had taken so long for a film like *Machuca* to be made in Chile. Wood responded,

> I don't know . . . self-censorship? It's still something that really divides the country. There is an impulse that you want to turn over the page, keep walking, keep moving, you know? And of course there is also a big powerful Right that didn't want to go back. I am an optimist with my country right now, but if we want to keep walking and taking care of the future problems and challenges, it's very important to know who we are. And we are who we *were*. That's why it was very important to do this movie . . . One thing that I am proud of is that the film provoked debate and conversations between the generations. It has created a link between the generations. (Alvarez)

Wood's description of his own hesitation to confront Chile's recent history so directly stands in as well for the nation as a whole. Responses to the release of *Machuca* in Chile suggest that the nation breathed a great sigh of relief and gratification for Wood's finally breaking the taboo of remembering and doing it in such a way that it does not alienate different sectors of the population. "We are who we *were*," emphasizes Wood. He refutes the claims of others who say that there is no use in stirring up these traumatic memories. He legitimates for a mainstream Chilean audience the need to reengage with the years of Popular Unity and the Pinochet dictatorship in order to heal the nation. In an interview with the online journal *nuestro.cl*, Wood also emphasizes the timeliness of the subject matter in contemporary Chile. "Classism today is more exacerbated than it was in those days" (Mena). Just as filmmakers, such as Silvio Caiozzi, created earlier period films during the dictatorship in order to make veiled criticisms of their contemporary era, Wood uses the early 1970s to highlight the problems that still exist today.

Chilean Press Reception of *Machuca*

After the film's release in Chile in August 2004 (the film was first released in Spain in June 2004), journalists were unanimous in their description of the film as a heart-wrenching narrative that all Chileans should see and an opportunity for more open dialogue about the legacy of Chile's dictatorship. Through these positive reviews and, perhaps, most importantly, word of mouth, the film proceeded to break box-office records. During the first weekend of its release, 60,250 spectators attended the film, beating the previous record held by Boris Quercia's 2003 *Sexo con amor* (*Sex with Love*) record of 58,750 spectators for its first weekend (Bustos B., *La Nación*, August 10, 2004). The manager of the only movie theater in the city of Osorno was forced to resign from her position after extreme public outrage by her decision not to show the film, finding it "not profitable and politicized" ("Renunció Administradora de Cine en Osorno," *La Nación*, August 10, 2004). Testimony from the already acclaimed filmmaker (and New York University film school graduate) Andrés Wood may have led to further public interest in the film. In an interview that he gave to *La Nación*, he admitted, "I'm embarrassed to say it, but I have cried with *Machuca*, and more than once." He also stresses the impact that it had on a young Wood to have been a part of "that Chile and that experiment. It was very impressionable" (Fernández, *La Nación Domingo*, August 8–14, 2004).

Ernesto Ayala of *El Mercurio* commends the film with reservations, giving it four out of five stars.

> It's certain that the film works over a base of stereotypes, that which does something explicit. But where a film more primitive would have remained in simple parallel between the microcosms (the school) and the macrocosms (the Chile of *Unidad Popular*), 'Machuca' is able to move beyond the sociological view and tries to tell a story with individual and ambivalent, possible and probable characters . . . the great achievements of Wood are in the tone: more nostalgia than denouncement; more melancholy than bitterness or resentment; orange, beige, and brown tones dominate the screen and envelope you in this state of calm, gloomy, and beautiful spirit of memories. The only moment when the movie breaks this tone—in the fierce rounding up of the people in Peter's shantytown—the narration leads to censure and lacks a strong, less explicit resolution.

Lidice Varas A. from *La Nación Domingo* (August 8–14, 2004) describes the film in this way:

> Rarely are the times that seated in a theater with the lights out, we feel with every fiber the brilliance of a film so gentle, violent, and irrevocably lighting paths which until now were closed. "Machuca" not only puts in perspective an epoch that has been treated by all the artists: social, political, and artistic; it opens paths also for all those who today are found with camera in hand asking oneself what new story do I want to tell, what is there which is new to say. In "Machuca" there aren't discourses, there are only voices without sides, voices which want to say something, something that still is impossible to say. "Machuca" is the journey on bicycle as a space of reflection in movement, with the wind in one's face, the cold in one's hands, with the body rigid, and the legs weak. "Machuca" moves as move the children who thinking of everything and nothing cross from the asphalt to the field, feeling in the wheels the differences of the landscape . . .
>
> "Machuca" will be praised for its technical sparkles, for its brilliant performances, for the cinematography, for the music. But these are not the main reasons to adore the film. "Machuca" puts in perspective those which

are the true reasons for leaving the cinema hopeful. There are films which are perfect technically without a gram of vitality. "Machuca" surprises precisely for being an unexpected glimmer, a story without borders that certainly is placed in the space reserved in the memory for those experiences that are difficult to define for beauty, for the indescribable.

As Fernando Zavala of *El Mercurio* describes it, after mentioning *Machuca*'s breaking of all previous box-office records in Chile, "It's official. *Machuca* can be described as a phenomenon" (August 10, 2004).

In general, Chilean press reviews emphasize the historical significance of the narrative of *Machuca* as a memory text to be consumed by Chileans. The sentiment is essentially unanimous that this film serves a higher purpose than sheer entertainment; it is a significant tool for recovering traumatic national memory and, through its sensitivity and use of innocent children as central characters, nation-building.

Eugenio Tironi, a former student of St. George, wrote in *La Tercera*, "The echoes of the historic event had been silenced, until now . . . *Machuca*, by Andrés Wood, put an end to this silence . . . It appears that a torrent of emotions that were buried in the darkest zones of our memory will begin to slowly revive. And to recognize that, crouching [in our memory], we may return in order to reconcile with ourselves" (Tironi, 19).

Writers emphasized the verisimilitude of the experiences represented in the film, including in the new millennium. Andrea Lagos G. of *The Clinic* revealed that Ariel Mateluna, the actor who played Machuca, was living an experience even more desperate than his fictitious character before he participated in the making of the film—not attending school and eating leaves and twigs. "In his house there is no bread or toilet paper. They don't have money. Never. And like a drawing of Japanese animé, his eyes shine. Of hunger" (12). With the money he earned from the film, he bought his mother a refrigerator and an oven.

U.S. Press Reception of *Machuca*

Just as Wood's sympathetic upper-class characters ensure that Chileans of all ends of the socioeconomic spectrum can identify with the film, *Machuca* also was clearly not only envisioned with a domestic audience in mind. Wood managed to tell the story with little reference to the larger forces at play in the events leading up to, during, and after the coup. The United States, a key player in the sabotaging of the Popular Unity reforms and the coup itself, is never mentioned. The only subtle reference to the United States is through the selection of pop music that plays at Gonzalo's sister's birthday party. This lack of geopolitical specificity helps to make the film appealing to a global audience who may not want to feel implicated in the events that they witness. Of course, the fact that the story is told through the eyes of a child also encourages these details to be overlooked since the child only knows what he has experienced directly. The simplicity of the narrative encourages a global audience to connect with the universal themes brought forth from the innocent relationship fostered between two such disparate characters.

International responses to the film shed light on the global marketplace that filmmakers such as Wood must consider while making their films. When *Machuca* was released at art house theaters in the United States, press reviews were relatively positive, but responses were mixed. Some reviewers were more critical of the film as a narrative, stylistic text, and many did not seem to fully understand the significance of this film's release and popularity in Chile as a key cultural marker and unifier in the postdictatorship nation. Rather, they attempted to draw out the universal themes that would appeal to a non-Chilean audience:

> The bullying and violence that Wood portrays is in contrast with the coming-of-age moments that Pedro, Gonzalo and Silvana enjoy while Allende is in power. "Machuca" isn't preachy. It's a sensitively wrought work that reveals a time in Chile when class differences were both ignored and emphasized, depending on your perspective. (Curiel)

> A story of national violence and guilt seen through innocent eyes, "Machuca" communicates the moral crises of Allende's fall with so much dramatic force that I think it can be enjoyed by people of many political persuasions, who simply like humanity and a good story. (Wilmington)

"Machuca" is a quiet film, moving sadly toward its inevitable climax, the final scenes a lesson in the methods by which the military restores order to a divided country. (White)

Wood was 8 years old when the coup that brought Gen. Augusto Pinochet to power took place, and, he's written, "Nobody has ever touched the loss of the democracy in Chile from this innocent perspective. Children experience events, but they do not judge. They simply live, and bear witness." (Turan)

The final moments of the film are both moving and strangely muted. As [Matías] Quer plays him, Gonzalo is not so much a character as a placid observer, a receptor through which Wood can come to grips with his country's past and his own feelings of guilt. This is the trap presented by all memory tales, and the filmmaker hasn't found his way out of it. "Machuca" is an important act of bearing witness, but there's a hollow spot at its core where there needs to be a human being. (Burr)

Selling it to the cheap seats, Wood keeps the dynamics Ron Howard-iconic: The upper-middle-class families are vain and arrogant gargoyles, the poor are lively and soulful über-peasants. As if we're in danger of missing something, Gonzalo has an appetite for *The Lone Ranger* comics. ("White men and Indians are never friends!" someone yelps. "Sure they are!" is the reply, summing up the film's philosophy.) Every scene leads up to a class-war exclamation point. Given this particular social storm, attaining a realist texture would've been a substantial achievement; Wood settles for clichés and spotlighting . . . Even amid the military crackdown, Wood's plot mechanics are formulaic; someone'll take a bullet, and you knew in the first half-hour who it would be. In the end, *Machuca* (the film named after Pedro and his Syd Field-doomed family) feels dismayingly solipsistic—Wood seems to think that of all the tragedies and dramas that the Pinochet putsch produced, none are as profound as his own, riding home from the war zone on his bike, plagued by a guilty memory. (Atkinson)

[*Machuca's*] point is not to settle scores or reopen old wounds, but rather to explore, after a long period of repression, the possibility of grief. The youthful condition it evokes most strongly is not innocence but impotence—the discovery that you are powerless to protect the people you care about from harm, and also powerless to protect yourself against the shame of your own failure. (Scott)

Apparently, some American reviewers also had trouble understanding the details of the narrative, as several claimed that Silvana was Peter's cousin when in fact she was not. When we are first introduced to Silvana's father, Peter calls him *tío* (uncle), but this name is used as a term of endearment and respect. Peter does further clarify this relationship to Gonzalo when he explains that Silvana's father is his neighbor. (This also suggests that some reviewers may be borrowing ideas from other printed reviews without carefully watching the film themselves.) This erroneous description of Silvana as Peter's cousin upset some viewer respondents on the Internet Movie Database who pointed out the reviewers' mistake. American reviewers were also more likely to make comparisons to other films and national cinemas. Louis Malle's *Au Revoir Les Enfants* (1987) was frequently referenced.

Some American reviewers' responses were insightful. A. O. Scott's interpretation of the main theme as not innocence lost but impotence is significant. In the film, we are encouraged to see through the eyes of Gonzalo, the boy of privilege who betrays Peter and the other residents of Peter's *campamento* by illustrating to a soldier his social class position in order to save his own life. The final moments of the film depict Gonzalo returning to the area of the *campamento* to find hardly a trace of evidence that it, along with its residents, ever existed. All viewers, alive to view the scene along with Gonzalo, must deal with survivor guilt.

Comments from the Internet Movie Database

> I believe that this is one of the best Chilean films ever made. The director chose excellent actors, and his idea for his movie was very creative. I don't normally feel emotional after watching movies, but at the end, when the director played the song "Mira Niñita" from Los Jaivas, I almost cried . . . The movie gave a very well balanced view of each side of social class. Giving one a better understanding of why things happened how they happened . . . I have to say, most movies with kid actor[s] are major garbage in my opinion, but Machuca was a great film, with a great plot. (inakiligu2 from the United States)[3]

Observing responses on the Internet Movie Database is useful as this Web site is free of cultural and intellectual gatekeepers. Anyone can post a response, and most responses suggest that these amateur film reviewers are young people—those who feel most comfortable using Internet technology. Young Chileans (and other global respondents) appear to appreciate all Chilean films, including *Machuca*, which confront Chile's recent past. Younger generations of Chileans have grown up with historical censorship in their schools and silences at home. As is suggested in what follows, young people may also have used this film text as a source of inspiration for their protests against the current education system.

Interpretation of Members of the Association of Relatives of the Detained-Disappeared (AFDD)

When asked to describe what importance *Machuca* had in helping to spread the theme of human rights and the legacy of the dictatorship throughout Chilean society, members of the AFDD had much to say.

Mónica Pilquil, whose spouse disappeared, responds,

> The movie showed some of the history of Chile. The political right began the black market. I remember students being active in Popular Unity. We went out in groups to protest against the right. Many on the right were paid to hit us . . . The right began to arm itself. *Machuca* explains why there was a military coup. There were organizations that supported Popular Unity and powerful unions. Workers, housewives . . . The government had a milk program. There were donations of sugar from Cuba and other countries . . . The economy shut down from outside Chile, most notably the United States. We wanted to defend the government. The movie also shows the protests. Upper class women went out with pots and pans. I knew a woman who protested against the upper class women. I warned her that she might get beat up. It brings back memories. Also, the integrated schools. I never went to one; the movie taught me about this. It also shows the time of the coup. That's important for people who didn't see that. They realize why everything happened. (personal interview, July 14, 2006)

Mireya Rivera, whose spouse disappeared, adds,

> The movie shows discrimination between the poor and upper classes. People's lives were difficult. The powerful caused that. Often one gets scared. Like what's happening with the truckers' strike right now. And delinquency . . . People got scared back before the coup, and now the

same thing is happening. Some things in the movie were not true. Poor families did not send their kids to school looking that rough. They wanted to dress the kids up. The way the movie dresses the kids wasn't true. The movie is good for the youth of Chile. The schools screened the movie for the kids. They analyzed it with the kids. It brings back memories . . . and hopefully that will never happen again. Except that some things are happening, like what's happening with the severe weather [causing the flooding of homes in poor communities]. That's the reality of the people of Chile. Chilean people are too aggressive and don't show respect to authority. What President can solve all the problems in four months [referring to the challenges of the newly elected Michelle Bachelet]? People want everything solved immediately. (personal interview, July 14, 2006)

Victoria Díaz, whose father disappeared, says,

The movie is important for new generations. What happened . . . It's a very difficult theme because Chile is still divided. *Chile is still divided!* After the dictatorship, the divisions, the deaths, brutal repression . . . this country remained divided. So a divided country like ours, that sees this movie . . . the director of the movie wanted to show the dream that Popular Unity had. And that is what is most important to me. The ideal of Popular Unity—educate everyone. To unify despite everyone's differences. The moment when the child sees all the repression and doesn't know what to do so he leaves. He didn't want to get involved. But at the same time, the implication is that they have a friendship that won't break. There's hope. This can't be in vain. Like the child, one day we will bring about a more equal society, like the dream of Popular Unity. Today there are ghettos, in contrast to the Popular Unity dream. The movie ends with the hope of a possible unified country. A sign of hope—that it's possible to understand what it was like during Popular Unity. I'm interested in the youth, because they will always be idealistic. Kids from the upper classes that have been able to see this film will have seen another form of thinking. (personal interview, July 14, 2006)

Rivera adds, "After the dictatorship, all the development was erased. Now there are so many private schools, which are very isolated. And a lot of illnesses. This is what the dictatorship left." Pilquil responds, "But the *Concertación* is also to blame. I think that the school kids who protested [massive demonstrations taking place in 2006, and subsequently, 2007 and 2008] likely watched *Machuca*. They're giving the government some time to respond, and if nothing happens, they'll come out and protest again."

Individuals whose families are victims and survivors of the Pinochet regime interpret the film as validation for their experiences, as a narrative that tells their story in a manner that is accessible to the upper and middle class families that supported and benefited from the coup and subsequent dictatorship. They also interpret the film as an educational text for the younger generations—an important historical document from which lessons can be learned and inspiration can be drawn. In 2006, when students from all walks of life across the country barricaded their schools and took to the streets, they were teaching their parents that diverse sectors of their divided society could come together for a common cause. This is a lesson that they did not learn from their parents' generation. Indeed, women of the AFDD may be right that *Machuca* served as a source of mobilization.

Perhaps most disturbing are Mireya Rivera's observations that a lot of what is depicted in the film is actually occurring in Chile again and, in some cases, has never ceased to occur since the period of time represented in the film. Abject poverty and unsafe living conditions, transportation strikes, violence in the streets, the dehumanizing of various groups of people through stereotypes and name-calling, and a call for "an iron fist" with which to control delinquency and petty crime—*Machuca* is not only a story of the past; it is also a reflection of the present. As another former student of St. George, Claudio Orrego, wrote in *La Tercera*, "*Machuca* is more than a personal experience or memory of the coup. It serves as a shout which should be interpreted by all who observe the irritating social contrasts of Chile today . . . Today it's not strange to know youths of the upper classes who have never known how the majority of their poorest compatriots live . . . Will it be possible to build the bridges which will allow the construction of socially integrated *comunas* without hateful differences?" (Orrego, 3)

Conclusion

As the preceding discussion has demonstrated, the very same film text, while it may have a tendency for certain emotions to be elicited from many different viewers in similar ways, can also produce very different interpretations of meaning. Thus, memory and forgetting are inexorably linked to one's particular life experiences in any historic context. In order for us to preserve an understanding of ourselves within these given contexts, we select memories that help us to feel comfortable with our situation and ignore or "forget" those that make us uncomfortable. Hence, a Chilean journalist from a commercial newspaper writing for "the masses" describes *Machuca* as apolitical while a member of the AFDD whose disappeared father was a leader in the Chilean Communist Party interprets the film as a glorification of Allende's Popular Unity government. An American film critic notices the universal themes and overreliance on narrative film conventions, and Chilean youths embrace the film as a positive memory text worthy of defending and emulating in their own lives.

More importantly, *Machuca* and its release in theaters in 2004 offered a unique opportunity for all Chileans to reconnect emotionally with their traumatic past and see the relevance of that past in contemporary Chile. In hindsight, August 2004, the time of the film's release in Chilean theaters (as well as the time in which Chileans united in celebration for their Olympic medal-winning tennis players), could be considered a significant *memory knot*, in Steve J. Stern's terms, or turning point, in relation to the nation's approach to addressing its collective memories of the Popular Unity and dictatorship eras. Andrés Wood accomplished something that had previously only been imagined—he created a commercially successful narrative film that was appealing to a heterogeneous, mainstream audience *and* explicitly approached the most controversial moment in Chile's recent history.

Film directors edit for a certain form (or lack) of closure to the narrative by the end of the film. At the conclusion of *Machuca*, we do not know what happens to Peter—is he alive or dead? We also do not know what happens to Gonzalo. Will his adolescent friendship with children from a different socioeconomic class allow him to remain compassionate and sensitive to the lives of the less advantaged when he becomes an adult? Or will his forced separation from those friends lead to his complete absorption back into the bubble of the upper class? One could surmise either way. The burden is placed on the viewer to enact the life that they wish for Gonzalo.

Sturken explains, "Camera images—photographic, cinematic, televisual, documentary, and docudrama—play a vital role in the development of national meaning by creating a sense of shared participation and experience in the nation" (24). In the case of Chile, there will never be one shared national meaning—as responses to Pinochet's death indicate, progress still needs to be made in relation to the negotiation of competing historical memories. However, individuals who found themselves on opposing sides at the time of Pinochet's death in December 2006, shouting and spitting at each other, may have been sitting next to each other in a dark movie theater in August 2004. *Machuca* not only fosters a sense of the traumatized nation, but it also instills a sense of the healing nation. More, however, needs to take place outside of the realm of cinema for true healing to occur.

Indeed, nowhere may Chile's current situation of extreme inequality be more apparent than on the very pages where *El Mercurio* printed an article on *Machuca* (Sepúlveda, 8). Juxtaposed with the article on the social experiment of St. George and the plight of all Machucas is an ad for Sheraton Santiago Hotel and Convention Center. Pictured in the ad are a mother and son, the boy close to the ages of Gonzalo and Peter, wearing a crown with the Sheraton logo. The text reads, "This Sunday, I will be the king. And I want my parents to take me to lunch at the Sheraton. Adults $21,500 pesos (US$43 dollars), children $12,000 pesos (US$24)."

CHAPTER 5

PRINT MEDIA

SIGNIFICANT DISCOURSES IF YOU KNOW WHERE TO LOOK

In communication, credibility is fundamental.
—Claudio DeNegri, personal interview, March 1, 2002

The agenda of the country is determined by the media.
—Guillermo Hormazábal, personal interview, February 12, 2002

The newspapers of a nation play a significant role in shaping the consciousness of its citizens. Indeed, Benedict Anderson has described how a sense of "nation" was not really even conceived until after the development of the printing press (1983, 1991). Through print media, citizens read and respond to stories about their community, their country, and their country's relationship with the rest of the world. Journalists and editors determine which stories get to be told and how those stories get told. In the process, they offer their readers certain windows on the world, while keeping many more windows shut.

The decisions that these journalists and editors make are often very practical and do not necessarily have anything to do with personal or ideological agendas; rather, these workers are constrained by the pressure to get a paper completed within a limited amount of time, to do stories that can be researched and written with limited financial and human resources, *and* to offer stories that will not prevent further obstacles to completion and publication—those that will be accepted by their bosses and their advertisers. Nonetheless, these practical concerns yield significant consequences for how readers interpret their nation. As Marita Sturken describes in *Tangled Memories*, "The writing of a historical narrative necessarily involves the elimination of certain elements . . . The desire for narrative closure thus forces upon historical events the limits of narrative form and enables forgetting" (8). What versions of recent history are Chileans obtaining in their papers? How are human rights violations discussed, and through what types of narrative conventions? Are various papers enabling the forgetting of certain versions of history and certain experiences within that history?

While it is understandable and recognizable that severe restrictions exist in the Chilean media in relation to discourses of human rights violations that resulted from Pinochet's regime, there are also remarkable instances of significant discussion. Memory is not linear and transparent for anyone, but it is even more fragmented when you live and work within a posttraumatic nation. Journalists who try to engage with these combustible themes are battling several demons—personal, familial, political, institutional, and commercial—that, in most cases, encourage suppression. Former *La Nación* (*The Nation*) director and editor Guillermo Hormazábal rejoiced, "There is a climate now in Chile for freedom of expression" (personal interview, February 12, 2002). Others offer a bleaker picture, though. According to former director and editor of *El Siglo* (*The Century*) Claudio DeNegri, "There are poor possibilities for expression in our society. No paper is independent. In this country, we have democracy, but it's only formal democracy. It's not in the press, Congress, etc. We have no ads in our paper. Most papers in Santiago are free; they're financed by ads—like *El metro* [available at subway stations]. Sponsors don't like what we do. There was more media for democracy during the dictatorship than now—*Hoy, Análisis* . . . They renounced the dictatorship. Now there is more concentration of ownership" (personal interview, March 1, 2002).

Former director and editor of *The Clinic* Patricio Fernández remarked in 2002 that

> The situation is still very traumatic; people are afraid to speak . . . An example of the problem was demonstrated when the media covered Pinochet's detainment in London. It was ridiculous. Most of the media

supported Pinochet; they're very right wing. There was hardly any criticism. In almost all other countries, they were covering the story critically. The media have a lamentable manner of dealing with Pinochet; they mostly protect him. But when Pinochet was in London, it was the first time that Chileans started to realize that he was someone who could be judged. Chile changed after his detainment in London. There was more freedom of expression. But when he returned to Chile, it was tightly controlled again. (personal interview, February 20, 2002)

In *State Repression and the Labors of Memory*, Elizabeth Jelin quotes Brazilian journalist Zuenir Ventura describing the climate in postdictatorship Brazil:

In 1978 the country was still living under what was called the 'residual' authoritarianism—the brunt of the unhealthy legacy of the dictatorship—and this involved a heavy burden of fear and impulses of self-censorship. Censorship had already been officially eliminated from pressrooms, theaters, films, etc. But it had left something behind that, from my point of view as a journalist, was perhaps more pernicious than censorship itself. We had internalized all the paranoia and all the censorship. You did not need to have anyone beside you to inhibit or repress you . . . and this lasted a long time. For a long time we lived with this ghost, this shadow, this thing that hovered above us when it was time to write or to speak. (quoted in Jelin, 100–101)

This "ghost" is still hovering in the Chilean press, but its presence seems stronger in some newspapers more than others. As Chile moves further away from the years of the dictatorship, and now that Pinochet is gone, the censorial and self-censorial pressures imposed by this legacy are loosening, albeit gradually. At the same time, certain types of censorial and self-censorial pressures are not relaxing—specifically, those imposed through a capitalist media institution.

Political economic media scholars who bemoan the effects of capitalist globalization on local and national media industries argue that investigating the corporate sponsors, along with noting patterns of ownership, will illustrate the specific constraints imposed on discourses that circulate within that media. Viewing Chilean newspapers, as well as listening to the editors of some of these papers, may lead you to the same conclusion. As former *La Nación* editor Hormazábal explained, "The problem today is how will you finance the media? The only way is with publicity. Ads represent the [political] right" (personal interview, February 12, 2002). As Fernández described it, "Business men are fascist; they control the other papers" (February 20, 2002). While his comments may sound extreme, they are not far from the truth. The Chilean print media duopoly, consisting of *El Mercurio*'s Edwards conglomerate and *La Tercera*'s Consorcio Periodístico de Chile S.A. (COPESA; Journalistic Consortium of Chile S.A.) conglomerate, is owned by men who supported the dictatorship. Nonetheless, my research has found that in the Chilean case, globalization blended with unique local and national situations allow for the circulation of a more diverse spectrum of discourses than these comments would otherwise indicate.

With the press, too, there are nuanced ways through which the global has a positive impact on human rights coverage at the local level. Globalization is not inherently evil or benevolent, not enormously supportive of the powerful or the powerless, the "First World" or the "Third World." As stated in Chapter 1, Annabelle Sreberny-Mohammadi argues, "Modernity has created a paradoxical global unity (Berman, 1988:15) which remains deeply problematic in its patterns of inequality and domination. Yet it may also hold some opportunity. A recognition of the many inextricable linkages that bind us is part of an emergent global consciousness that might just do some good" (68).

Globalization allows for tremendous diversity of opportunity, while at the same time, the institutional structures that organize these opportunities impose enormous constraints. The marketplace of Chilean print media is similar to that found in the United States and the rest of Latin America. Capitalist globalization, while it does engender some freedom, also imposes similar restrictions on the media industries of many different countries. Political economic media scholars, such as Edward Herman and Robert McChesney, argue that

> Private systems of media control pose a threat to the public sphere for several reasons: first, they rest on ownership control and therefore will tend to represent a narrow class interest; and because of increasing economies of scale and scope, and other benefits of large size, media ownership tends to become more concentrated over time, aligning the

media more closely with larger corporate interests. Second, privately owned media depend on advertising revenue and must therefore compete for advertiser attention and serve advertiser interests to prosper. Owner and advertiser domination give the commercial media a dual bias threatening the public sphere: they tend to be politically conservative and hostile to criticism of a status quo in which they are major beneficiaries; and they are concerned to provide a congenial media environment for advertising goods. (6)

Despite the fact that every newspaper director or editor whom I interviewed was involved in a journal or newspaper that offers an alternative to the two corporate giants, which will be mentioned in the following pages, they resorted to this bleak description, which denies their own agency to express significant discourses through and outside of the institutional structures that exist in the Chilean media industry.

The Chilean printed press offers many options for purchase at the local kiosks. A rich variety of newspapers and magazines seem to exist for consumers. However, closer analysis reveals that many newspapers and magazines belong to the same owners, and, consequently, the editorial and ideological perspectives of many are similar. The two printed press empires in Chile are that of *El Mercurio* (*The Mercury*[1]) and *La Tercera* (*The Third*). Most mainstream commercial newspapers and magazines are owned by one of these two Chilean corporate giants. As professor, editor, and journalist,[2] Abraham Santibáñez[3] described the situation, "They lack a counterpoint . . . There is no independent press" (personal interview, May 8, 2002). Fernández claims, "There is no press; only a couple of newspapers" (February 20, 2002). DeNegri says, "There is no independent or objective media. There is discrimination. Human rights are not given much importance. The point of view is commercial" (personal interview, March 1, 2002).

Contrary to these individuals' impressions, however, there are several varieties of alternative printed press that do offer more comprehensive human rights discourses. In particular, there is *La Nación*, funded through a mix of state subsidy and commercial advertising. Then there are papers historically linked with the political Left, such as *El Siglo*, funded mainly through newsstand sales with a little support from international solidarity groups. Finally, there are alternative papers, such as *The Clinic*, first established during Pinochet's detention in London in 1999. The composition and financing for this paper has gone through a series of changes over the past ten years and will be discussed in further detail later in this chapter.

When I began my research in 2002, coverage of human rights in the commercial papers of the two big franchises was sparse.[4] Frequently, when a human rights violations theme was addressed, it was done simply with a photograph and a caption—no article included. In addition, when there was an article, there was often no journalist's name attached to the piece.[5] Most of the time, the topic of human rights, when it was covered, was limited to the issues of the detained-disappeared and politically executed; in particular, articles did not discuss the much higher number of torture survivors.

By contrast, the alternative papers that are not part of the *El Mercurio* and *La Tercera* duopolies are some of the main media sources for human rights information in Chile. Along with other Chileans whom I interviewed, including filmmakers and television producers, these editors often delineate a distinction between the electronic media, such as television, and the printed press.[6] They were reluctant to use the terms "media" (*los medios de comunicación*) and "press" (*la prensa*) interchangeably, as they caught me doing occasionally during my interviews. When asked a question regarding the responsibility of the media to educate new generations of Chileans, Santibáñez stated, "It's not the mission of the media. TV is media of entertainment, not information. But the press should be part of the mission" (personal interview, May 8, 2002). While a critical media scholar must challenge the assumptions that a medium of entertainment cannot also be educational and that a serious newspaper cannot also be entertaining (in addition to the fact that there is serious, journalistic programming on television and sensational, entertaining "news" in newspapers), the fact that Chileans make this delineation is significant. It suggests that they hold much higher standards for print journalism; therefore, the way a human rights story gets covered or avoided in a newspaper takes on extra significance.

The various newspapers that I investigate take different approaches to the coverage of this material. Although a diachronic analysis of the Chilean press from 2002 to 2008 suggests that many patterns have remained the same, the press has broadened its human rights discourses since 2002 as a response to the *Valech Report* on torture survivors released in 2004 by the Chilean government, constitutional reforms in 2005, the 2006 election and inauguration of President Michelle Bachelet, and the death of former dictator General Augusto Pinochet in December 2006.

The Chilean Press and the Dictatorship

Print media (and radio, too) had a particularly important history during the times of the dictatorship as it often offered subtle and not so subtle critiques of the regime. By the late 1980s, several newspapers and magazines had emerged that opposed the dictatorship.[7] These sources covered stories that the more censored press would not, called for Pinochet to step down, and urged a return to democracy. Many of these journals were funded with international support—a combination of solidarity groups and commercial advertisers, especially from Europe. One of these opposition publications was the magazine *Hoy*. In the late 1970s, *Hoy* played a crucial role in the circulation of human rights discourses. When Abraham Santibáñez, current professor of journalism studies at the University of Diego Portales and current president of the Association of Journalists, was assistant director of the magazine in 1978, he was asked by clergy of the Catholic Church to join a team of investigators who went to investigate a rumor that bodies had been found in abandoned limestone ovens in Lonquén, south of Santiago. The team discovered that the rumor was true when they made the gruesome discovery of the remains of fifteen people who had been arrested in October 1973. Forensic scientists concluded that the fifteen boys and men were placed in the ovens while still alive, since there was no evidence of bullet shots or other means of execution. Santibáñez undoubtedly would have been affected by this experience. The story was eventually covered in almost all Chilean media.

Having lived and worked as a journalist and editor throughout the entire period of the dictatorship, as well as during the transition to democracy up to the present, Santibáñez offers unique insights into the trajectory of Chilean journalism during the past several decades. He was a colleague of former *Chilevisión* news director and anchor Alejandro Guillier throughout the dictatorship. They worked together at *Ercilla* and *Hoy*. Their affiliation with the Christian Democrats allowed them a certain level of protection under the regime, even though many of the journalists working for these magazines did receive threats and were detained by Pinochet's repressive forces.[8]

Santibáñez describes how Pinochet was not consistent with the degree of censorship he imposed over the Chilean media during his regime:

> We had a closure for eight months. There had been a kidnapping and murder of a child. Mrs. Pinochet took a stance. Emilio Felippi, from our magazine, writes commentary about her concern—how it doesn't flow to others, like the relatives of the detained and disappeared. Felippi put $100 in his wallet in case he had to flee the country. He received anonymous death threats. An animal's head appeared in Felippi's yard. The censorship was arbitrary, difficult. (personal interview, May 8, 2002)

Some times were more restrictive and dangerous for journalists than others. For example, after the election in the United States of President Jimmy Carter, Santibáñez and his colleagues enjoyed more freedom of expression. Carter withdrew support, while at the same time, a U.S. congressional committee led by Senator Ted Kennedy was probing the actions of Pinochet and his secret police force, the Directorate of National Information (DINA). In addition, the assassination of Chilean Orlando Letelier and his American colleague, Ronni Moffitt, in Washington, DC, on September 21, 1976, as well as other assassinations and assassination attempts committed outside Chilean borders and orchestrated by Pinochet, lost Pinochet international supporters and increased international criticism of him and his regime, while offering Chilean journalists more freedom to cover the crimes of the regime under the cover of an "international" story.

Pinochet was forced to eliminate the DINA, although he replaced it with a different organization with essentially the same responsibilities and criminal activities—the Center for National Information (CNI)—and granted amnesty to his soldiers and security officers for all human rights violations that had taken place under his watch between 1973 and 1978.[9] The U.S. election of President Ronald Reagan in 1980 reduced the international pressures on Pinochet and again increased the censorship restrictions on journalists, as well as increased the violence committed against them.[10] Repression was especially severe after mass protests began on September 11, 1983, on the ten-year anniversary of the coup, which resulted in monthly demonstrations thereafter. Another brutal crackdown took place in 1986 after an assassination attempt on Pinochet.

Restrictions on Chilean journalists eased again in 1987 with the visit of Pope John Paul II.[11] Through his visit and his comments, journalists were able to expand their own discourses by using him as a springboard to talk about social issues. The pope raised concerns about human rights violations, and the press dutifully covered his concerns.

Santibáñez offers multiple reasons for why most of the opposition magazines of the 1970s and 1980s no longer exist—one being that the urgency for an opposition press demanding a return to democracy no longer exists and another being that international funding for these opposition magazines has stopped. He conceded that most of the Chilean press is owned by large media oligopolies and that Chilean society needs more media diversity.

When asked what responsibility the media have to address issues such as human rights violations of the dictatorship era, Santibáñez suggested that the weight of the responsibility should not all lie on the media's shoulders; rather, the media should help to facilitate dialogues when possible. He gave an example of a meeting held in the south of Chile among Mapuche Indians,[12] government leaders, members of the university, and the media, in which land disputes were discussed. Clearly, the media alone are not responsible for addressing significant issues in contemporary Chile, but they do play a crucial agenda-setting function in the circulation of public dialogue. Without their leadership, human rights issues may receive minimal discussion at the societal level. This is precisely why the activists of the organization Funa, who denounce those who perpetrated the state-sanctioned violence of the dictatorship, feel compelled to loudly take up their mission of "truth and justice" for human rights violators in the streets. They seek to reach the public directly, since they are overlooked by the media.

CORPORATE GIANTS OF THE CHILEAN PRESS: *EL MERCURIO* AND *LA TERCERA*

Before any discussion of the alternative printed press in Chile, the two big corporate franchise papers, *El Mercurio* and *La Tercera*, must be addressed, albeit briefly. I emphasize that I am not attempting an exhaustive analysis of these papers—a project that would exceed the boundaries of this chapter. Rather, I sample various issues of these sources to try to identify consistent patterns of coverage of human rights, as well as any discourses suggestive of certain editorial perspectives or reluctance to cover this topic—perhaps as a result of fear of censorship or disapproval from employers and, in some cases, as a result of having to fear for their lives and the lives of their families, as was the case for *El Mercurio* writer Mónica Guerra in 2004 (Carmona, "Amenazan de muerte a dos periodistas"). In a lot of cases, it is more likely that these journalists are censoring themselves in order to preserve their own jobs, and if self-censorship is not sufficient, editors take care of the rest. Individual journalists and editors are expendable; someone else can easily be hired to replace an employee who causes trouble for the editorial line. Especially at the commercial papers, journalists have very little power to implement change.

El Mercurio is Chile's equivalent (in style and appeal to a higher socioeconomic class) of the *New York Times*. It is a prestigious paper that portrays itself as more serious and assumes a more educated and elite readership than its commercial competition as well as its own other newspapers, such as *Las Últimas Noticias* (*The Latest News*). For many decades, it has been owned by the powerful and politically conservative Edwards family of Chile. During the years of Allende's government, from 1970 to 1973, this paper blatantly expressed disdain and hatred for the Allende government and its policies. It also deliberately distorted factual information to demonize the political Left and sanitize the political Right. During the dictatorship, it played a crucial role in supporting Pinochet's repressive regime, often publishing false stories about what had happened to the victims of the repression—suggesting that they had fled the country with their illicit lovers or had been killed in an armed conflict that they had instigated, or that they had died in neighboring countries in gun battles with others on the political Left.

El Mercurio and its affiliated Santiago and regional papers are funded through advertising (especially for high-end consumer goods) and newsstand sales. Compared to coverage of human rights issues in alternative papers and even *La Tercera*, coverage in *El Mercurio* tends to be the sparsest. When I began my research in 2002, any mention of human rights in *El Mercurio* was frequently just a photograph with a caption. For instance, on March 22, 2002, there was a photograph of Michelle Bachelet, then minister of defense, pinning an honor badge onto the uniform of a member of the military during a ceremony celebrating the seventy-second anniversary of the Air Force. This image is rich with layers of meaning since Bachelet's own father, who was a general in the military, was killed as a consequence of the torture that he received from his peers during the early years of the dictatorship. There was no article or name attached to the photograph. It was placed in the middle of the paper between an article about tourists canceling their trips to Easter Island due to fear of dengue fever and a senate vote on an education bill (p. C7). Likewise, on February 10, 2002, there was a photograph (in black and white, whereas the previously mentioned military photo was in color[13]) of members of the Association of Relatives of the Detained-Disappeared (AFDD) burying the identified remains[14] of nineteen-year-old Jorge Torres Aránguiz at the Memorial for the Detained Disappeared and Politically Executed in the General Cemetery of Santiago. Again, there is no article or name attached. It is positioned in the middle of the paper between articles on a kidnapping in Brazil and the murder of a boy by gang members in the south of Chile (p. C9). Noting the inclusion of photographs in newspapers is important because a photographic image grabs a reader's attention and offers a sense of emotional immediacy in ways that are not available through written articles. Sturken suggests that "camera images—photographic, cinematic, televisual, documentary, and docudrama—play a vital role in the development of national meaning by creating a sense of shared participation and experience in the nation" (24).

La Tercera is the more popular alternative to *El Mercurio*, roughly equivalent to *USA Today* in the United States. It is also funded by extensive advertising and newsstand sales. Perhaps in its quest for more "human interest" rather than marketplace and political news, the paper offers more coverage of human rights than does *El Mercurio*. Indeed, it might be safer to publish a human rights story as a personal anecdote, rather than as a political and judicial case, while still possibly having a political and judicial result. If enough readers are moved through empathy to engage more concretely with these issues (and I would argue that they are more likely to be affected through a melodramatic narrative rather than through political rhetoric), then they could form enough of a critical mass to call for change in Chilean society.

During Pinochet's detention in London, *La Tercera* offered an online chat room for Pinochet-related discussions that was popular with Chileans both inside and outside the country. Eliza Tanner's research, in which she studied 1,670 letters posted online, shows that such an electronic forum can serve as a public space (2001). She argues that individuals' responses contributed to a collective sense of national history that plays an important role in the reconciliation process. Despite opportunities for the circulation of human rights discourses that are offered through a paper such as *La Tercera*, this coverage pales in comparison to the other papers I will discuss later in this chapter. Issues of *La Tercera* published in 2002 showed that their human rights articles were usually short and perfunctory. These articles frequently had no authors' names attached.

One article on judicial investigations into the DINA's role in several cases of the detained and disappeared, published on February 14, 2002, was sandwiched under an article on new leadership in the Christian Democrat Party and the imminent trip to Europe of President Ricardo Lagos (p. 5). On February 27, 2002, there was a full-page article on former U.S. Secretary of State Henry Kissinger's cancellation of a visit to Brazil due to fears of human rights protests against him (p. 16). A human rights story that has an international dimension (even if it is inextricably linked to Chile) is often afforded more space, dialogue, and apparently safety (from censorship) than a story that is specifically Chilean. On April 3,

2002, *La Tercera* included a tiny article with a photograph attached on the forced expulsion from the senate of a group of protestors who had been dismissed from their jobs for political reasons during the dictatorship and were demanding the compensation that had been promised them by the government (p. 5). This article was positioned under an article on the United Kingdom's aggressive attempt to repair relations with Chile since Pinochet's detention in London in order to sell Chile naval frigates. Underneath was an article on the minister of the interior's criticism of the conservative National Renovation Party's position regarding the continuation of "designated senators"—lifelong senators appointed by Pinochet who were not democratically elected.

In 2002 issues of *El Mercurio* and *La Tercera*, articles and photographs that connected to themes of human rights violations in Chile appeared to be deliberately hidden. Employees at these franchises were clearly working under censorial and self-censorial restrictions; that this subject matter was still able to sneak through at all is worthy of appreciation. Despite the convoluted manners in which these themes were presented in the papers, readers could still interpret this material in complex ways. Fortunately for Chileans, though, they also can engage with these themes more directly in other newspapers with fewer restrictions.

Viewing *El Mercurio* and *La Tercera* up to 2008 suggests that not too much has changed in relation to these papers' coverage of dictatorship-era human rights abuses, although the coverage has clearly expanded and diversified as would be expected due to the larger changes taking place in Chilean society. An interesting phenomenon occurred in July 2008 when the Association of Journalists, *el Colegio de Periodistas*, formally apologized to families of dictatorship victims for which the stories of how they had died were fabricated by journalists working in collusion with the DINA. In addition, some of these relatives were seeking justice in the courts. Implicated in these cases were ex-media director Fernando Díaz Palma of *Las Últimas Noticias*,[15] ex-media director Alberto Guerrero Espinoza of *La Tercera*, and journalist Beatriz Undurraga Gómez of *El Mercurio*, among others. According to Ernesto Carmona, writing for *El Siglo*,[16] the online version of *El Mercurio* published information that was omitted in the newsstand version of the paper: the act of apology from the Association of Journalists and the role that this newspaper played in assisting the Pinochet regime with the fabrication and distribution of stories, inside and outside of Chile, to explain what happened to the 125 victims of "Maipú Corner" (*"Rinconada de Maipú"*) and "Operation Colombo" (*"Operación Colombo"*).[17] Carmona indicated, however, that this online story was an exception; both *El Mercurio* and *La Tercera* were proceeding to omit and hide information about their papers' roles in the censorship and distortion of information during the dictatorship, and their ongoing omissions were a continuation of this legacy.

Alternatives to the Corporate Mainstream and the Case of *The Clinic*

Most significant discussions of human rights take place in the alternative press—both in printed papers, many of which also have Web sites, and through exclusively online outlets. All of these outlets, including, among others, *Plan B* and *Punto Final*, deserve attention. However, an investigation of these outlets is beyond the scope of this chapter.

One example of an alternative to the two corporate giants, which resembles them most closely, is *La Nación*. At the newsstand, *La Nación* looks a lot like *La Tercera*—both have clear and bold headlines, both have many full-color photographs (and their online versions contain the obligatory photos of naked women), and both have extensive sports sections. Upon closer inspection, though, *La Nación* has fewer ads,[18] and Chile's legacy of human rights violations is given fuller coverage in a more visible section of the paper. Since *La Nación* is less reliant on commercial advertising, it is shielded to a large extent from the market pressures faced by *El Mercurio* and *La Tercera*. Since *La Nación* is a daily paper, unlike most of the other alternative papers, it offers the most consistent coverage of human rights issues. For example, on February 7, 2002, an article with a photograph of the interior of the Tribunals of Justice was positioned on page two, regarding an appeals court decision to keep a major in the police force in prison for the September 1973 disappearance of two men. On page three of this same edition, an article discussed the prosecution of a leader of the Air Force for the kidnapping, detention, torture, and disappearance of a Communist leader in September 1975. The article mentioned other current human rights judicial cases as well. No author's name was attached to either article. On February 22, 2002, all of pages two and three were dedicated to human rights. On page two, there were two articles written by Jorge Escalante about an attempt by members of the U.S. Congress to prosecute Pinochet for the assassination of Orlando Letelier and Ronni Moffitt in Washington, DC, in 1976. Included was a photograph of individuals placing bouquets of flowers on the spot where the two were killed by a car bomb. On page three, there was an article by C. Montecinos and V. Mondaca about the Chilean government's reaction to the letter they received from members of the U.S. Congress. On the same page, under a large color photograph of General Pinochet sitting in full military attire, with a stern expression, sunglasses, and a weapon that appears to be an encased knife held in his lap, there was an article by Quintin Oyarzo L. on the official changing of military rank titles to what they used to be before Pinochet's dictatorship, during which Pinochet had created a new name for himself, "Captain General."

On April 29, 2002, the cover headline of *La Nación* was about a document from the CNI, Pinochet's secret military intelligence service, signed by a military general, which gave the orders for the assassination of a labor union leader in 1982. The story, also by Jorge Escalante, was on page three and revealed that this newspaper obtained the original document, signed by a deceased general who had denied any involvement in the death of the labor leader. Included were photographs of the murdered Tucapel Jiménez and the original documents.

On May 2, 2002, the cover story of *La Nación* was an article on the failed attempts of the Chilean police to find and capture Paul Schäfer, the Nazi German leader of the German commune in Chile, *Colonia Dignidad*, who was wanted for child rape.[19] During the dictatorship, *Colonia Dignidad* supported Pinochet's regime and allowed Pinochet's repressive forces to bring political prisoners to their grounds, where they were tortured in underground caves and chambers and sometimes disappeared. The article, again written by Jorge Escalante, featured photographs of the wanted poster for the commune leader and the extensive surveillance equipment and underground caverns that allowed Schäfer to hide when he knew that someone was approaching the grounds. On page thirty-five of the same edition, there was a feature article in the culture section by Nancy Arancibia on the upcoming release of the autobiography of Gladys Marín, the former leader of the Communist Party[20] whose husband was detained and disappeared during the dictatorship.

Former director and editor of *La Nación*, Guillermo Hormazábal, pointed out how human rights stories were usually covered on the first pages of the newspaper (often pages two and three). Indeed, given the amount and location of human rights coverage, this theme has clearly been a priority for the various editors and directors of *La Nación*. The degree to which Chileans engage with the articles that *La Nación* offers, however, is questionable because the paper does not get the same readership as *El Mercurio* and *La Tercera*. As Hormazábal explained, "Our readers are middle class, upper-middle class. People who work for the state. Center-left readers. More intellectual people. And younger, university types" (personal interview, February 12, 2002). The fact that the paper receives a significant portion of its funding from the state probably prevents a larger readership due to the negative connotation that "the government's newspaper" could have, suggesting a lack of journalistic freedom.[21] Nonetheless, the paper remains an important outlet for regular human rights coverage—for example, the colorful, photographic coverage the paper gave to Chile's first LGBTQ pride parade, held on July 2, 2006, featured in *La Nación* on July 3. One of the several photos featured a scantily clad participant holding a rainbow flag, standing next to street graffiti that read, "No to military service. Don't train to kill." The potential that this paper has to reach an audience that may be lucrative to advertisers also has not been overlooked—in evidence, a full-page ad found in the same July 3, 2006, edition of the paper from the *Chilevisión* network for the primetime investigative journalism program *"En la mira"* (In Sight), with the caption, "We show the problems that they want to hide."

El Siglo, published weekly and also funded almost exclusively from newsstand sales, frequently has a cover story on human rights, and always includes human rights stories in their paper in a section dedicated exclusively to human rights. This paper's cover page usually presents the headlines superimposed over large, vibrant photographs that fill the page. On April 4, 2002, the cover read, "Human Rights: The Conspiracy against the Special Judges," over an artistically composed photograph of the Tribunals of Justice imbued with an orange hue, as if they were on fire. On February 7, 2002, the headline read, "The School of 'Mamo' Contreras[22]: The Torturers of *Tejas Verdes*." The full-page photograph was of General Manuel Contreras in military uniform with medals posing with the men who worked under him in the *Tejas Verdes* detention facility, all wearing military uniform or suits and ties and beaming at the camera. Included inside this edition were unedited testimonies of former political prisoners who were tortured at *Tejas Verdes*.[23] On March 21, 2002, the full-page color photo was of Juan Emilio Cheyre, then commander of the armed forces, and the headline read, "Violations of Human Rights: The Participation of Cheyre." Inside the paper were detailed articles on Cheyre's role in the "Caravan of Death,"[24] children who were killed under his supervision, and the testimony of a former political prisoner who was tortured in Cheyre's presence.

In *El Siglo*'s June 23, 2006, edition, an article in the *Verdad y Justicia* (Truth and Justice) section addressed the case of "*el Príncipe*" (the Prince), the nickname for the notorious soldier at *Estadio Chile* (Chile Stadium)—used as a concentration camp after the coup—who was in charge when folk singer and composer Víctor Jara was tortured and killed (Ascencio D., 16–17). Underneath this article was positioned a demand from the National Association of Public Employees (*Agrupación Nacional de Empleados Fiscales* [ANEF]) for the dismissal of Edwin Dimter Bianchi—an ex-army lieutenant who has been recognized as the man who killed Jara—from his position as chief of the Department of Control of Institutions in the public sector. Underneath both of these articles were two announcements—one for a tribute and remembrance ceremony for all Chileans who were "executed in false confrontations or died in the legitimate act of fighting for democracy," ("Combatientes por la vida, constructores de la libertad," *El Siglo*, June 23, 2006, p. 16) hosted by the Association of Relatives of the Politically Executed, and the other for a pilgrimage from the memorial of the detained and disappeared and politically executed to the family members' tombs in honor of three relatives who were killed by police officers in 1986, and whose killers had been recognized but not punished.

Former director and editor DeNegri was proud of the human rights violations coverage in *El Siglo*. He realized that *El Siglo* offers more extensive coverage than any other paper. It is quite logical that *El Siglo* would offer the most extensive coverage because many of its writers, editors, and readers are survivors of Pinochet's repression. In the 1980s, DeNegri's teenage nephew and a female companion were burned alive by Chilean security forces during the crackdown of a neighborhood street demonstration in Santiago. That incident became an emblem of the barbarity of Pinochet's repressive forces for the opposition movement in Chile. Despite the extensive, very comprehensive coverage that *El Siglo* gives to human rights, the degree to which the paper manages to affect a large readership must be questioned. Especially given the paper's historical links to the Communist Party, effectively demonized before, during, and after the dictatorship, many members of the general public will choose not to purchase the paper. The result is that the paper primarily caters to, and is consumed by, a preselected group of readers with relatively homogenous perspectives and experiences.

One alternative paper that does get consumed and discussed voraciously by a diverse group of readers is *The Clinic*. *The Clinic* was created by a group of Chilean generation Xers during Pinochet's detention in the United Kingdom. The paper's title, printed in English, is named after the hospital in London called "The Clinic," where Pinochet was recovering from surgery when he was placed under arrest. According to the paper's original director and editor, Patricio Fernández, "With time, we realized that beyond the old man and all his resplendence, in Chile, as in all countries, or at least many others, there were permanent absurdities" (Mena).

The Clinic, initially funded almost exclusively from newsstand sales, and now that it has become so popular and arguably mainstream, receiving much more financial support from advertising, including from Chile's main TV networks, is primarily a newspaper of satire with many inside jokes for Chileans who keep up with current events, politics, and pop culture. Communication scholars have pointed out how the jokester or trickster is given unique authority to criticize the existing social order with relative safety (Carlson 1988; Conquergood 1989; Johnson 1998). Any serious newspaper that so explicitly refers to Pinochet's legacy with its title would not have been so freely available and popular at the kiosks at the time of the paper's inception.

According to Rosario Mena, *The Clinic* "revives an extinguished tradition of Chilean satirical press which has had notable examples such as *El Clarín*, from which they take their slogan 'solidly joined with the people' [*firme junto al pueblo*]" (Mena, "Los herederos de la prensa satírica"). Patricio Fernández was the first director of *The Clinic*. Young, cynical, and apparently nonpartisan, he explained in 2002, "When it started, we had no intentions of being a newspaper. It was more like a pamphlet. There were eight issues. We distributed them hand to hand. We were a group of friends. After ten months, we were selling them in kiosks. It was very limited; we had little capital and no plan. Now it's more of a business . . . We have a young audience—people who don't identify with other newspapers. It's sold in rich sectors and poor sectors. Some read it just for the jokes; some for the intellectual vigor" (personal interview, February 20, 2002).

"It was as if we lifted the lid off a pot. Not in the sense of revealing something that no one else knows, but we began to speak in a loose tone about things that until then had been taboo," Fernández explained in his 2003 interview for *nuestro.cl* (Mena).

Not mentioned by Fernández is the large amount of nudity and semipornography, especially of women but also of men, depicted through photographs and cartoons, which must also help to attract consumers, especially a younger audience that feels alienated and disenfranchised from the existing political and power structures in Chile. What brought my attention to this paper in 2002 was an image on the cover page of one of the issues of the Chilean Air Force bombing of *La Moneda* Presidential Palace on September 11, 1973, an iconic image for the exile community and frequently shown in documentaries on the dictatorship, but an image that was still essentially taboo in public spaces, such as newspaper kiosks in

Chile. In this case, the image was used to attract readers' attention to a story on the controversial purchase of new air force jets. The question of that time that was circulating in various media was why it was considered necessary to buy such expensive new jets when Chile did not have any perceived external enemies. The suggestion made by *The Clinic* through the juxtaposition of this image with the headlines was that they were being purchased so that the military could continue to battle its imagined internal enemies, perhaps through a second coup. At this time in *The Clinic* was also a regular section (that no longer exists) dedicated to the detained and disappeared and a feature story in one issue about the School of the Americas in the U.S. state of Georgia (now called the Western Hemisphere Institute for Security Cooperation), which trains Latin American military members in "antisubversive" measures, a.k.a. torture. This article demonstrated again the trend for more Chilean media coverage of human rights issues if the story has an international angle, but it was exceptional in that the discussion of the role of the United States in the 1973 coup and subsequent repression was made very detailed and explicit for a wide variety of Chilean media consumers.

The regular section on the detained-disappeared, positioned on one of the last pages of the paper, was written by family members of disappeared victims. Every issue featured a specific disappeared person and contained an essay written by a family member. Issue after issue, familial memories were offered up to *The Clinic*'s readers as national memories, strengthened through their consistency and repetition. This was the one regular section of the paper that was not satirical. The format stayed the same in each paper. Covering a half-length of the page, the article featured the title "Detained-Disappeared" over a snapshot of the person spread across the page (sometimes doubled or tripled to fill the space). Under the title, the nickname of the victim was typed. The author of each of these articles was usually the mother, wife, or daughter of the victim. Here, again, we see the circulation of human rights violations discourses through their framing as human-interest stories. Indeed, the personalizing of the narrative through the use of family photographs, victims' nicknames, and the telling of the story by a relative or loved one offered the reader a feeling of intimacy and connection with the victim and the victim's family. The insertion of these narratives among satirical stories and jokes was effective, for their authenticity stood out when they were juxtaposed with nothing else that was overtly serious. In addition, *The Clinic* is purchased and read by a diverse array of readers, many of whom would never dream of picking up a paper like *El Siglo* at the kiosk. They might not go out of their way to find material on Chile's human rights violations, but they may end up reading human rights stories and having their perceptions changed by them while reading the jokes and looking at the silly pictures.

While the section on the detained and disappeared is gone, *The Clinic* still intersperses serious human rights-themed features, sandwiched between its pages of jokes. One example is the feature story printed on June 29, 2006, titled, "Do you want to end delinquency? Legalize abortion" (M.R., 34–35). Especially since the March 2006 inauguration of President Bachelet, the commercial media in Chile appears obsessed with the topic of juvenile delinquency, alluding to Bachelet's perceived weakness in addressing the matter. *The Clinic* is engaging with this dialogue by raising another subject that is essentially taboo in the mainstream media of this nation with strong historical connections to the Catholic Church and the rise of Evangelical Christianity. The article offers credibility to a Chilean public through its citing of research conducted by Steven Levitt, prized economist from the University of Chicago, home of Pinochet's "economic miracle" "Chicago Boys," whose research indicates that a decrease in delinquency in the United States in the 1990s can be attributed to the legalization of abortion in the United States in 1973. This was not the first time that the topic of illegal abortion in Chile has been raised by *The Clinic*. The theme has been covered before in op-ed articles; the significance of this coverage cannot be overstated given the climate for such discussion in this patriarchal, chauvinistic society.[25]

The April 5, 2007, edition contained a feature article on the uncompleted 1973 film by Raúl Ruiz about Father Raúl Hasbún's role in the March 1973 murder of Jorge Tomás Henríquez, who had been responsible for taking care of the interference equipment that was allowing the Allende government to block transmissions of *Canal 13* (Channel 13) to the south of Chile in Concepción.

On Septmeber 11, 1973, the official first day of shooting, Father Hasbún was a powerful figure at *Canal 13*, the Catholic University's television network, and a strong supporter of the coup. The film, titled *Interferences*, was never completed (Torres López, 18–19).

In the May 31, 2007, edition, *The Clinic* featured an article on María Paz Santibáñez, the piano player who was shot in the head by a police officer outside of the Municipal Theater of Santiago, where she had been protesting against the Pinochet regime, on September 24, 1987 (Pizarro, 34–35). Chilean Cecilia Bolocco, crowned Miss Universe on May 26, 1987, and later married to former Argentine president Carlos Menem, declared after Santibáñez was shot that Santibáñez had known what she was doing, implying that it was her own fault that she was shot. Bolocco then supported Pinochet by telling young people that they should go study in the university and stop protesting. Writer Claudio Pizarro highlights this anecdote for the readers to remind them that "the *farándula* [celebrity, gossip culture] and its personalities are usually a weapon of the right used to distract the people from worrying about problems that are really important" (34). Explaining why she chooses to live in France and not in Chile, Santibáñez explains, "I have every right to be afraid to return to my country if the [police officer] who almost killed me from behind still walks the streets a free man" (35). Through the voice of Santibáñez, Pizarro manages to accomplish what few Chilean journalists dare—confront the primary problem that remains in contemporary Chile—the impunity with which most individuals who committed the state-sanctioned violence of the dictatorship continue to live their lives and the consequent ongoing trauma that the survivors of the violence experience without the resolution of truth and justice.

The Clinic, amid its jokes, consistently offers scathing, in-depth analyses of subjects that other wide-reaching media does not touch. In a further example, in 2008, a feature article addressed the ten-year anniversary of the firing of police officers for the only reason that their wives had conducted a public protest regarding the salaries of their spouses and how what had been promised with raises had not been fulfilled. *The Clinic* described how "after ten years a demand in the Inter-American Commission promises to lay bare the irregularities of one of the most shameful processes which has occurred during democracy" ("Las mujeres que desafían a carabineros"). Women and children often get more attention in *The Clinic* than in other media. A recent example is the feature article on schoolgirls being sexually abused by their male peers—with the apparent ignorance of their teachers who were often in the same room—in a Santiago area school ("El salvaje 'Wena N' en un colegio de La Pintana"). The headline read, "Read here a brutal story about solitude and about something very grave which some children are not learning . . . self respect and respect for others. Human rights."

In January 2006, the cover of *The Clinic* showed the iconic image of the face of a young Pinochet with sunglasses, taken in 1973, on top of another man's body, with tattoos and tank top, in what appeared to be a mug shot, holding a sign that would normally show a prisoner name or number, reading, "Happy new year" (*Feliz año nuevo*). Now, this image from *The Clinic* has become almost as iconic as the original image in which Pinochet was posing with the other leaders of the junta in 1973, thanks in part to the availability of the image on T-shirts available through *The Clinic*'s merchandise store.

In August 2008, *The Clinic* offered an extensive article on a dramatic story that received scant coverage in the mainstream press. On July 16, 2008, a woman's decapitated body was discovered in the desert near Arica in northern Chile. Due to the arid conditions, the body, clothed in jeans, poncho, and a package of cigarettes with a price tag dating from 1973 still in her pocket, had been mummified; forensic scientists were able to rehydrate her fingertips and then match her fingerprints to those of Monique Cristin Benaroyo Pencu, a Romanian-Uruguayan woman who had received a Chilean identity card while working in Arica in 1973. According to a response that the woman's brother received from Chilean authorities in 1974 upon his inquiry into her whereabouts, Benaroyo had been detained briefly at the National Stadium in Santiago, over a thousand miles away from Arica, and then released. However, the discovery of her body, with a nine-millimeter bullet nearby, suggests that the story given by Admiral José Toribio Merino was a lie. The significance of this story is high. Not only does it illustrate the international coordination of intelligence services and repressive forces and offer evidence—through the letter written and sent to Benaroyo's brother that the leaders of Chile's military junta were involved in the fabrication of false stories explaining what had happened to the victims—but it also highlights the fact that many of the disappeared are not on any official lists, suggesting that the actual number of people who disappeared could be much higher than what the official data demonstrate. *The Clinic* does not hold back in what it exposes to its huge readership.

Despite Fernández's characterization of the capitalist media system as fascist, in recent years *The Clinic* has successfully and creatively taken advantage of this free-market system in order to sustain itself. While the paper is still primarily funded through its own sales at the kiosks, revenue is supplemented through advertising. The types of ads that are now found in the paper run the gamut. For example, the following have all placed ads in the paper: *Televisión Nacional de Chile*, the Cultural Center of *La Moneda* Palace, Oxfam International, Samsung, Paris (department store), *Universidad Arcis* (the University of Arts and Social Sciences), and the Chilean government's Ministry of Health (promoting the flu shot). *The Clinic* advertises its own advertising potential with classified ads: "Classified ads. Publish your classified ads in *The Clinic*. More than 300,000 people will read you." The paper's ultimate countercultural, capitalist coup is undoubtedly its aforementioned own merchandise store, *The Clinic: El Bazar*, in downtown Santiago located at *José Miguel de la Barra 459*; much of the merchandise is also available through its online store.

In addition to his agreement with the other newspaper editors that the marketplace constrains the discourses that circulate in the Chilean press, Fernández further blames the Chilean people for being too complacent and passive under these circumstances: "I would like to see more people develop other media. There is not enough political will. There isn't censorship, but a lack of action" (personal interview, February 20, 2002). Since his 2002 statement, Chilean bloggers have proliferated, which must offer some comfort to Fernández despite the questionable reach that bloggers have for a general reading public. In addition to his other activities,

Fernández was a regular panelist on *Chilevisión*'s debate show *El Termómetro* (discussed in Chapter 2).

Chileans take their newspapers seriously, and journalists and editors mentioned in this chapter judged the popular commercial papers harshly by emphasizing the restrictions imposed on newspaper publishers due to the institutional, corporate structures through which they must operate. Their depiction of the institutional constraints is accurate, but they disregard the fact that the papers they criticize do include coverage of human rights, even if it is sparse and carefully encoded, and they also underestimate the potential that the very newspapers for which they themselves have worked have to create richer, more diverse dialogues about significant issues, including human rights, in the public sphere.

In an investigation of the Chilean press, one also must seriously consider the role of the Internet. The papers discussed in this chapter are not just significant for Chileans inside of Chile; they are read widely on the Internet as well by an extensive global Chilean community. The availability of these papers on the Internet brings in a huge global readership that is distinct in many ways from that situated inside Chile, especially when we consider the Chilean exile community. Many letters to the editor published in these papers come from foreign lands, and, on most of these papers' Web sites, reader responses are not limited to traditional letters to the editor; oftentimes, there is a way to respond immediately to any specific article, eliminating the gatekeeping effect of an editor.

Viewing the newspapers mentioned in this chapter in 2008, it becomes clear that while patterns have remained the same in relation to the comparisons of the different periodicals discussed, quantity and diversity of topics in all of the newspapers has expanded. Torture, a subject that formerly was essentially forbidden from discussion in media coverage,[26] is now mentioned slightly more frequently. This must be due in part to the release, in November 2004, of the *Valech Report*, mentioned previously, which detailed the cases of at least 27,153 recipients of torture under Pinochet's regime (and this number only includes those former political prisoners who were tracked down and willing to talk to investigators). In addition, constitutional reforms in 2005, Bachelet's presidency, and Pinochet's 2006 death, along with the more general passing of time since the end of the dictatorship, have allowed for greater discussion. Chile is progressing in the societal task of seeking truth and justice, but there still are obstacles to overcome, and at least some of the press is covering every step forward and every step back. Arguably, one of the obstacles is the attitude of the readers. According to Abraham Santibáñez, "We had a strong sense of freedom of expression before the coup. The military government renounced the right to freedom of expression. People feel comfortable with only good, light news. They were happy when the dictatorship said, 'Now there will be only good news' . . . The public attitude is more important and problematic" (personal interview, May 8, 2002).

Filmmaker Pablo Larraín reiterates this concern with public attitude: "To decide over the life of others is the darkest part of the human being, but by far the most violent is the indifference that there is in Chile with many people that died and are disappeared. No one talks about this. For me . . . it's very strong that everything continues functioning as if nothing happened" (Alvarado E., accessed July 20, 2008).

This perception by media producers of apathy for human rights issues among the general public is dangerous because it can lead to avoidance of the topics in the media, which now, more than ever—especially with the ability to track the number of hits that each article receives in a paper's online version—cater to the assumed interests of consumers (Enrique Mujica, 134).

Another obstacle is that journalists and photographers are not protected in terms of job security and personal safety. Editors are under enormous pressure to offer only a limited window on the world that is palatable to owners and advertisers; journalists and photographers may often find their story ideas, articles, and images discouraged, cut, or buried. Media professionals not only receive threats of violence but also sometimes get attacked. A case in point is that of Víctor Salas, a photographer who was attacked by a Special Forces *carabinero* while covering a public demonstration in Valparaíso on May 21, 2008. His eye was seriously injured, and he is required to have multiple surgeries (Moraga L.).

Despite the grim descriptions offered by political-economic media scholars and Chilean journalists themselves, consideration of Chilean newspapers' discourses of human rights violations suggests that there is much reason for optimism in the globalized capitalist economic order of media institutions. A global corporate media structure does not entirely determine the realm of possibilities and constraints for journalists, and sometimes it offers unique opportunities. The Chilean printed press offers the most consistent, comprehensive coverage of human rights discourses in Chile, and some of these media outlets are covering these subjects with more freedom of expression than at any time since the end of the dictatorship.

Nonetheless, there are plenty of opportunities for further development in the printed press and other forms of media. According to DeNegri, "Human rights are not given much importance. The point of view is commercial . . . Human rights themes are bothersome; it's more than just not being interested. The Viña del Mar music festival is more important. Entertainment. The mechanisms of control are economic, political, cultural . . . There are no legal freedoms for public information" (personal interview, March 1, 2002).

According to Fernández,

> Changes are needed. There is no press; only a couple of newspapers. I don't want the traditional ones to change. I want to see more variety of newspapers and media that are independent. There needs to be less fear to speak. We need to be more friendly and open. TV is important; people spend the most time watching TV. It gives a false sense of reality. It hasn't changed much since the end of the dictatorship . . . In general, it's very dangerous, Pinochetista, and conservative. Cable is bad, but better. The cinema is politically compromised. Some of it is starting to incorporate important themes. For example *Chacotero Sentimental* (*The Sentimental Jokester*), *Fernando ha vuelto* (*Fernando Is Back*), *Estadio Nacional* (*National Stadium*). They're dealing with painful themes. But cinema needs money, so it needs to serve everyone. The Law of National Security was altered recently. There were certain categories, such as the judges of the Supreme Court, which you couldn't discuss. It was considered an attack; certain people were protected. That's why there was such a scandal with Alejandra Matus's *The Black Book of Chilean Justice*.[27] There are more restrictions than there should be, but there is freedom of expression. Chile needs to advance more, but not like before. We are missing media and people who say things. What we're doing is a small thing. We're just a group of friends who wanted to offer something different. We need more

people participating. They can do things if they want to. The media are fundamental to how people live. TV is much more important than a senator. (personal interview, February 20, 2002)

As we will see in the following chapter, some people are responding to the voids in media discourses by taking their voices to the streets.

CHAPTER 6

PUBLIC PROTESTS

RESPONDING TO SILENCES AND OMISSIONS

¡Verdad! ¡Justicia! ¡No a la impunidad! (Truth! Justice! No to impunity!)
—Frequently shouted at human rights demonstrations

Chile has a rich history of public demonstrations and protests. One need look no further than Patricio Guzmán's *The Battle of Chile* (1975–79), reconstructed in Andrés Wood's *Machuca* (2004), to witness the frequency and magnitude with which Chileans from all ends of the political spectrum took to the streets. The 1973 coup effectively ended the era of massive demonstrations for ten years until the pro-democracy movement managed to begin them again, on a monthly basis, in 1983. In contemporary Chile, it is the high school and college students protesting the state of Chilean education who are carrying on the tradition of large-scale public protests. This chapter, however, is concerned with smaller-scale demonstrations that explicitly denounce the human rights violations of the Pinochet regime; they consistently offer a three-dimensional public venue for discourses that are still repressed in the mainstream media.

Small-scale demonstrations, as well as individual acts of bravery,[1] performed at great personal risk, were conducted throughout the dictatorship by members of human rights organizations. Most recognizable throughout this era were members of the Association of Relatives of the Detained Disappeared (*Agrupación de Familiares de los Detenidos-Desaparecidos; AFDD*), primarily women who appropriated Pinochet's traditional patriarchal rhetoric regarding the proper role of women to be serving as wives and mothers for their own ends—marching with placards that carried photographs of their missing loved ones with the question, "*¿Dónde están?*" (Where are they?). These courageous individuals subverted (while appearing to conform to) the dictatorship's paradigm in order to highlight that they could not fulfill their traditional roles with their spouses and family members missing. Their protests were creative and perpetual throughout the entire Pinochet regime, including, among other activities, chaining themselves to the fences of the Supreme Court building, a United Nations building, and the ex-Congress building; dressing in black on anniversary dates significant to Pinochet, such as September 11, which the regime celebrated as the date of "national salvation"; and hunger strikes. While many of these individuals are now elderly or deceased, those who are able continue to demonstrate, especially through the creation and exhibition of *arpilleras*[2] and the organization's folk music *conjunto*, in which a subversion of Chile's national partner dance, *la cueca*, was transformed into a visible embodiment of members' missing dance partners through *la cueca sola*.[3]

In *Postmemories of Terror*, Susana Kaiser explains how many Argentines condemn the violence committed by the repressive forces of their 1976 to 1983 dictatorship, but they passively accept the lack of justice served to the perpetrators of that violence if their own families were not affected directly by the violence. In contrast, the Mothers of the Plaza de Mayo represent themselves as the symbolic mothers of all estimated 30,000 Argentines who disappeared, not just their own children and relatives (129). A parallel can be drawn to the situation in Chile. Many Chileans not directly affected by the state-sanctioned violence of their own dictatorship believe that it is not their job to demand truth and justice. The mission of human rights activists, including the AFDD and the newer groups of demonstrators described next, is also very similar to that of parallel groups in Argentina. These groups challenge "the reinforcement and encouragement of a bystander role for society" (Kaiser, 129), reinforced and encouraged in no small part with the collaboration of the media, "key sources and referents in the memory construction process" (Kaiser, 146).

The Cases of Funa and Londres 38

A younger generation of protesters, primarily HIJOS-Chile—the organization of children of people who were tortured, killed, or disappeared during the dictatorship—and their peers participate in Funa. *Funar* is Chilean slang for stirring up or causing a ruckus. Inspired by a similar group of children of the disappeared in Argentina (HIJOS-Argentina) who perform *los escraches*[4] (*Escrachar* is an Argentine slang term meaning "to uncover"), Funa began in Chile in 1999 during Pinochet's detention in the United Kingdom.

On random days and nights on an almost weekly basis, an alert will be advertised among sympathetic circles of the next Funa event in which protestors will congregate at a specified time outside of the home or workplace of a member of the military, security forces, or civilian leaders who worked in collusion with Pinochet and who was involved—directly or indirectly—in the violent repression of political dissidents during Pinochet's regime. At the designated time and place, demonstrators beat drums, distribute flyers, and recite information about the role that the target of the particular event played in the torture, murder, and/or disappearance of people. Then they march throughout the local neighborhood to distribute more flyers and alert those in the area that someone who committed human rights violations lives or works nearby while chanting, "*¡Si no hay justicia, hay Funa!*" (If there is no justice, there is Funa!). Some of these moments of confrontation are available for viewing on the Internet, including the Funa confrontation on May 25, 2006, with legendary folksinger and songwriter Víctor Jara's assassin,[5] "El Príncipe."

Participants in Funa demonstrations must continually stand up to threats of violence. Demonstrators, mostly in their teens, twenties, and thirties, are usually always monitored and confronted by police forces, *los carabineros*, in full riot gear.[6] One unusual occasion on which the ever-vigilant *carabineros* were nowhere to be found was at the Funa demonstration on January 10, 2007, which targeted ex-CNI (Centro Nacional de Información/Center of National Information, the second version of Pinochet's secret police after he eliminated the DINA) agent Enrique Sandoval Arancibia, in which members of Funa were confronted by neo-Nazi gangs.

Journalists attempting to cover Funa activities have also been repressed or threatened. In a denouncement presented by Ernesto Carmona on August 20, 2007, he explained how he received a threat over the telephone and how Argentine journalist Benjamín Ávila and his Chilean technical support team were illegally and arbitrarily arrested and detained with the charge of "public disorder" when they were trying to cover a Funa demonstration targeting Héctor Bustamante Gómez, the ex-*carabinero* who shot and killed Argentine cameraman Leonardo Henrichsen on June 29, 1973.[7] Carmona requested that the Association of Journalists make "some gesture expressing concern," since the event had taken place in complete secrecy without any media coverage "with the notable exception of Radio Bío Bío and very few other independent media" (autor Colaboradores).

A special element of the Funa demonstrations is that the perpetrators of state-sanctioned violence are aware that, any day, this organization could decide to visit them at their home or place of work, in essence, offering the offenders a small taste of what it felt like for many former detainees who were suddenly apprehended at home, work, school, or on the streets. Members of Funa have done their research, and when they choose a target, they have the evidence to support the claims they make about what these individuals have done. The targets, who are used to living their lives with impunity, and who may falsely believe that their histories are not known, are hit with the fact that not only are their past crimes known, this information is being shared with those closest to them—family members, friends, neighbors, and co-workers. The unpredictability of date, time, and location are a crucial component in this organization's method of denouncement.

Since Funa rarely gets mainstream media coverage, and reporters are often intimidated or censored when they do try to cover these events, members of Funa bring their own bevy of media technology to ensure that there is a historical record of their event. Footage is frequently then uploaded to the Internet, available through the organization's own official Web sites and Web sites of other human rights organizations, blogs, and YouTube. There is no escaping Funa—if you are their target, it is likely that how you receive the protesters will be perpetually available for observation online. In the demonstration considered in the following section, the effectiveness lies elsewhere—in the ritualistic predictability of a gathering at a fixed geographical location, but methods for media coverage and distribution are similar to those used by members of Funa.

Every Thursday night in Santiago until 2008, a group of torture survivors, relatives of the disappeared and executed, and allies congregated outside of the former torture center in Santiago, named after its street address: *Londres 38* (London 38), whose address was changed to *Londres 40* during the dictatorship in an attempt to "disappear" the remains of the former center of tortures and killings. Slowly and peacefully, demonstrators plastered the front of the building with graffiti that read, "Here they tortured and killed," and pasted posters of the dead and disappeared to the walls. They lit candles, which they affixed to the windows, the security bars, the entranceway, and the cobblestones in front of the building. They sang songs, recited poetry, and gave testimonials, while the *carabineros*, the Chilean police, stood by. The entire procedure took about sixty to ninety minutes. Then, with hugs and words of encouragement, they disbursed.

If you walked by the building again on Friday morning, you would not notice that any event took place the night before. The evidence had been erased. However, if you investigated the walls closely, you would detect the graffiti and posters underneath a fresh coat of beige paint.

Londres 38, prior to the coup, a building belonging to the Socialist Party, was not the only torture center in Santiago, nor is it the only site of a former torture center where there are regular demonstrations. However, some of the other detention centers have been torn down—such as *Villa Grimaldi*—and while many of these locations now contain memorials and are sites of demonstrations and remembrance events, most of the physical evidence of what once took place is gone.

Visiting *Londres 38*, one is struck by a variety of information that leads one to wonder how anyone who lived through the early years of the dictatorship in which this building was used by the DINA, Pinochet's secret police, could claim ignorance of what was happening. To begin, this building is located in the heart of downtown

Santiago, footsteps away from the main avenue—*la Alameda*—and the San Francisco Church, and directly across a narrow cobblestone street from a small hotel. Survivors from *Londres 38* say that they could hear the church bell—hence, the name that they gave it—*Casa de la Campanas* (House of the Bells). Even with an evening curfew and the use of music to drown out the screams of prisoners, how could passersby, and especially the staff and guests of the neighboring hotel, not be aware that something sinister was taking place inside? Those who lived, worked, or commuted near any of these detention centers must have trained themselves not to pay attention—to not hear and not see what was in front of them; the fear of violence silenced them. Diana Taylor describes this phenomenon as "dangerous seeing"—"illicit or unwilling witnessing that spectators want to avoid because it puts them at risk" (213). She elaborates, "Like an obedient audience, some members of the population can remain passive in the face of the most extreme brutality. Their leaders, after all, assure them that everything is under control . . . The witnesses were reluctant witnesses; they didn't know and they didn't want to know, for not knowing became the source of their sense of well-being" (Disappearing Acts).

This posture of ignorance or apathy continued until 2008 as one observed the behaviors of Chileans passing by the weekly Thursday night demonstrations on their way home from work. Aside from the people participating in the event and the *carabineros* monitoring from a distance, the only ones who stopped were usually international visitors. Demonstrators were aware of this phenomenon and often made a special effort to reach out to these foreigners—speaking with them individually and catering their performances to an international crowd, including guests at the neighboring hotel.

Each Thursday night demonstration had its own unique feel—depending on who attended, any current events that needed to be discussed, such as the plight of Mapuche indigenous activists who are classified and treated as terrorists by the Chilean state apparatus (a legacy of the Pinochet regime), and special anniversaries on different dates for people who disappeared or were executed. Oftentimes, relatives of the disappeared and killed participated hand in hand with ex-prisoners who may have witnessed the missing relatives' last known days alive. Entire families attended together—the lighting of the candles, the performance of music, the reciting of poetry, speeches about departed loved ones, and the shouts for truth and justice appeared to serve several purposes—healing for those who have most directly been affected by the state-sanctioned violence, an educational lesson for those they encounter in the street who are not familiar with recent Chilean history, and a reminder to the Chilean public that truth and justice have not been achieved, despite a lack of attention given to this subject in the media and other institutions.

Perhaps the most compelling facet of the *Londres 38* demonstrations was their persistent reconstruction every week despite the erasure of what participants left behind on the building within twelve hours of their events. Those demanding historical memory and justice performed a ritualized, choreographed dance with those charged with the deconstruction and obliteration of their work and the memories embodied in that work (presumably a custodian employed by the military organization that owned the building—the O'Higgins Institute). Countless layers of paint have been applied to the façade of the building. However, due to carelessness or perhaps a secret shred of solidarity with the demonstrators, the "destroyers" were not always that meticulous with their duties—perceiving what was underneath the paint was often quite easy.

In 2006, the O'Higgins Institute put the building up for sale. Most likely as a result of the regular protests and vigils conducted by demonstrators as well as the government declaration of the building as a historical monument in 2005, there were no buyers. Today, with slowgoing support from the Bachelet government, *Londres 38* is being transformed into a memorial. Two significant parts of the project are taking place in the public area outside of the building. One is that the number for the original address—38—is being reinstalled. However, it is being placed over the "40" on a transparent acrylic plaque as a visual reminder of the attempt to "disappear" the building. The other part of the project that demands the attention of passersby is that black-and-white bricks made of granite and marble have replaced some of the gray cobblestones and bricks on the sidewalk and road in front of the house. Survivors of *Londres 38* described how they were able to see from underneath their duct tape blindfolds that the floor consisted of square black-and-white tiles that reminded them of a chessboard. Also embedded in the ground are ninety-four iron plaques; each contains the name of someone who was disappeared or executed during the regime and was known to have spent time in *Londres 38*.

Today, the faithful still congregate at *Londres 38* every Thursday evening, but they can sometimes take their meetings inside since it is now open to them and, indeed, is dedicated to them and their deceased and disappeared loved ones. While they are relieved that the building has become a national house of memory that honors those who were detained at this location—including those who died here or passed through here on their way to other sinister torture centers, and for some, whose destinies ended with their bodies being transported in refrigerated trucks to the Bay of Quintero and then tied to pieces of railroad tracks to ensure that they would sink, tossed into the Pacific Ocean from military helicopters—their struggle is not over. They will not rest until complete truth and justice have been achieved.

The Internet has a plethora of information and photographs of *Londres 38* and its recent demonstrations as well. While some people associated with the site and its demonstrations have their own Web sites and blogs, many tourists and foreigners who stopped to observe and chat with the demonstrators have posted material as well. Again, we see the role of the global in covering and distributing human rights discourses in Chile, in this case (as in many others), depending on the grassroots organizing and educating of Chileans.

In a postrepressive society where media, education, and the government are still marked by the absence of significant representations of the state-sponsored violence of former dictator Pinochet's regime, citizens have created alternative venues for visible representations of taboo topics of national significance. Quite explicitly, many of these public demonstrators demand the formations and reformations of visible memories by their choices of locations for demonstrations and the chants that they shout. Preferred locations for demonstrations include spaces that were used as secret detention centers during Pinochet's regime, the sites of discovered remains of the disappeared as well as the workplaces and homes of individuals who committed the violence and have not been prosecuted.

Oftentimes, the spirits of the dead are evoked when the names of those who were killed and disappeared are shouted, and others respond with the chorus, "*¡Presente!*" (Present!) or "*¡Viva la memoria!*" (The memory lives!).

Chilean demonstrators strategically construct events that allow for the manifestation of three-dimensional historical memories. When the majority of society, with support from government, the educational system, and the media, calls for putting the past behind them and looking toward the future, the advocates for confronting Chile's recent past in order to establish truth and justice emphasize that a country without memory has no future.

As Susana Kaiser warns when characterizing the context of a post-repressive regime society, "Attitudes toward the human rights violations committed and the perpetrators of those crimes would be key in either reinforcing a culture of impunity or developing a culture of accountability" (Kaiser, 129). Activists such as the members of Funa and the demonstrators at Londres 38 are instrumental in shifting these attitudes. Without these individuals, Chile will likely remain a society of deliberate forgetting, indifference, and impunity.

Chapter 7

Conclusion

I began this research in 2002 under the grim assumption that upon arrival in Chile, I would not find very many discourses about the human rights violations of Pinochet's regime circulating either in the media or the larger cultural and public sphere. My perceptions of Chile were formed primarily through watching the documentaries of Patricio Guzmán, especially *Chile: Obstinate Memory* (1997), in which you see members of a traumatized nation remain silent except for occasional bursts of intense emotion. What I found, though, in many cases, was a compulsion of many Chileans and their media outlets to address the themes of the dictatorship's violent legacy, even if the manner in which they addressed those themes was hesitant and indirect.

The memories that we and our media choose to express reveal our identities in relation to concepts of community, nation, and the global public sphere. Our "memory remains," as Sturken describes them, which are often largely determined and dispersed by the media, offer different versions of the past. But when memories from various sources contain certain consistencies, they increase in significance, suggesting an element of the national consciousness that a critical mass of citizens considers important. Since we cannot travel back in time, we depend heavily on the articulation of that time through our media in order to make sense of that past and see its relationship with our present and future. As Sturken explains, "The original experiences of memory are irretrievable; we can only 'know' them through memory remains—images, objects, texts, stories. Saying that memory is changeable does not imply that it is only constructed through the agendas of the present. Rather, it shifts the discussion of memory, in particular cultural memory, away from questions of truth and toward questions of political intent . . . What memories tell us, more than anything, is the stakes held by individuals and institutions in attributing meaning to the past" (*Tangled Memories*, 9).

The stakes are high for a more comprehensive retrieval of historical memory in Chile, and the media need to play a larger role in this memory retrieval. Those who were directly affected by the violent repression are aging and dying. Not only is it important that their voices are heard and they directly experience full truth and justice, but their children, grandchildren, and great-grandchildren also need it. To know that a parent or close relative was tortured, killed, or disappeared and that those responsible were not held accountable can leave a person with such tremendous feelings of rage and sadness that one loses all personal investment in a society perceived to be broken. Likewise, it is equally crucial for children of the torturers and assassins to know that their parents were held accountable. It is also important for children to be able to confront and talk with their parents and grandparents now while they are still alive rather than to be filled with confusion and doubt later in life when they can no longer ask the significant questions. The media's ignoring of sensitive, troubling themes may seem like the safer route at the moment, but it is only making the situation worse. Many media professionals *do* want to address these themes more comprehensively, but they feel enormous pressure not to. The solution is for media professionals to build stronger networks of solidarity with one another so that they can stand up to those imposing the constraints. Those implementing the restrictions may yield if they feel that they have no other option. Media professionals also need to be better protected from violence and threats of violence, and the more that these themes are addressed in the media, the safer they will be.

In the case of Chile, certain images and sounds, circulated with the assistance of the media, have withstood time to become "memory knots," as Steve Stern describes them, in the nation's consciousness. Examples of this include the bombing of *La Moneda*, the Presidential Palace, on September 11, 1973; the four commanders of the military junta, including an austere General Pinochet in uniform and sunglasses, who pronounced on TV later that same day that they were compelled to enact the coup for the sake of the fatherland; the mothers, wives, daughters, and sisters of the detained disappeared with photographs of their loved ones pinned to their chests, holding signs that read, "*¿Dónde están?*" In recent years, these mediated memory remains have been joined with new ones: a frail Pinochet in his wheelchair in London and then standing up victoriously upon his return to Chile; Judge Juan Guzmán Tapia uncovering graves of the disappeared throughout north, south, and central Chile; military commanders being flanked by journalists as they enter and leave the Tribunals of Justice; Pinochet's face visible through the glass of his coffin. How do these shifting emblems of national memory suggest appropriate actions for the nation's leaders, activists, and media producers to take in the process of achieving truth, justice, and reconciliation?

Just as memories, especially traumatic memories, operate in convoluted and unexpected ways—keeping certain themes submerged at times and releasing them at various moments for reflection and articulation—so, too, does the media, reacting to what is happening in the larger culture and responding to it through direct address, tangential mentions, or structured absences. In our modern world, we can no longer distinguish between our "authentic" memories and those offered through our media. Whether we are conscious of it or not, our sense of ourselves, our nation, and our history is entwined with the images and words offered to us through our media.

For this reason, various sources of media, such as *Chilevisión*'s "El Termómetro," the documentaries and features of filmmakers, such as Andrés Wood, Silvio Caiozzi, and Nicole Senerman, and the headlines, photographs, and articles available in papers, such as *La Nación*, *The Clinic*, and *El Siglo*, have played a crucial role in the articulation of national memory and in pushing themes of human rights violations into the nation's consciousness. In addition, public demonstrations have served as a voice for uncensored truth and demands for accountability when the media have failed. Events in Chile in recent years have demonstrated that once these issues are at the forefront of the nation's consciousness, social and political change is possible, although oftentimes frustratingly slow.

Citizens of the globe are now more connected than at any time before, and news spreads with tremendous speed. At the end of his life, Pinochet could no longer rely on the support of some of his staunchest allies; many of them were incensed to learn that the general had been involved in embezzlement and money laundering through a complex web of globalized banking.[1] In the case of Pinochet, the local and national were inextricably tied to the international. While many of these international connections have been extremely detrimental (i.e., CIA involvement and Operation Condor), he was asked to account for his actions to a concerned global community, linked through the Internet, television, radio, newspapers, and word of mouth. As cases continue against those who committed human rights violations under his leadership, the individuals involved in these crimes are finding their options for escaping prosecution narrowing, especially if they choose to leave the relative safety of Chile to travel abroad.[2]

With the assistance of the media, Chile is not only responding to events occurring at the international level, but the world is also responding to Chile. U.S.-based Riggs Bank agreed to put $9 million into a fund for the victims of Chile's human rights violations as a result of charges brought against the bank by Spanish lawyer Joan Garcés. Garcés acted on behalf of Chilean exiles and Spanish citizens whose testimony was used by Spanish Judge Baltasar Garzón in his attempt to have Pinochet extradited from the United Kingdom to Spain. These actions have been held up by some (such as Saul Landau and Sarah Anderson of the Institute for Policy Studies in Washington, DC) as a beacon of hope and model behavior at a time when other powerful leaders, institutions, and governments in the contemporary world, including the United States, are not being held accountable for violations of human rights and refuse to honor international human rights agreements or cooperate with the International Criminal Court. Even former U.S. Secretary of State Henry Kissinger is no longer immune to interrogation and prosecution; he has been forced to cancel and cut short several visits to other countries in response to protestors and prosecutors concerned about, among other issues, his role in the support of repressive Latin American regimes during the cold war, perhaps in part due to the wide release of the book by Christopher Hitchens, *The Trial of Henry Kissinger*, that was turned into a documentary, *The Trials of Henry Kissinger*.

As it is produced through particular institutions, I do not intend, however, to paint an overly optimistic picture of the capacity of the media to promote social and political change. In Chile, rarely do the mainstream media pay particular attention to the country's legacy of human rights violations. One exception to this was *El Termómetro*, which, perhaps tellingly, is no longer on the air. Even when Chilean TV does address these issues, ratings for these programs are often quite low. It is not enough for the media to offer human rights discourses; the media audiences and consumers must be willing to engage with them. In a media environment that offers consumers so many choices, individuals are not obligated to pay heed to particular media outlets or programming if they have no desire to do so. However, over time and through repetition, the media can help to cultivate these desires.

Perhaps we need to consider again the power of structuring absences, since this still appears to be the representation of choice for sensitive issues in mainstream Chilean media. Likewise, it may be the only mode of discourse acceptable for certain Chilean audiences who feel resistant to a direct address of human rights issues. Cultural studies scholar John Storey explains the importance of interpreting these structural absences: "The task of a fully competent critical practice is not to make a whisper audible, nor to complete what the text leaves unsaid, but to produce a new knowledge of the text: one that explains the ideological necessity of its silences, its absences, its structuring incompleteness—the *staging* of that which it cannot speak" (119). Storey quotes literary theorist Pierre Macherey: "The act of knowing is not like listening to a discourse already constituted, a mere fiction which we have simply to translate. It is rather the elaboration of a new discourse, the articulation of a silence. Knowledge is not the discovery or reconstruction of a latent meaning, forgotten or concealed. It is something newly raised up, an addition to the reality from which it begins" (quoted in Storey, 120).

As I have discussed in previous chapters, there are multiple reasons for individual media journalists and producers to operate through the encoding of structured absences rather than direct language. One significant reason is the need to preserve one's job in a work environment that is not friendly to workers' rights and where individual employees are expendable and easy to replace. And media editors and directors must concern themselves not only with the knowledge that most Chilean media is owned by individuals who are very conservative and supported the dictatorship but also with the bottom line—the funds they receive from advertisers who favor a conservative ideological agenda and "light" entertainment that audiences will not find disturbing. Another reason is that the staff at these media institutions may find these themes too traumatic and divisive. While it is reasonable to assume that at a media outlet like *El Siglo*, the staff may all share a certain ideology and may all come from families and communities that have experienced similar versions of history, at a mainstream television network or commercial newspaper, the staff is probably much more diverse, having friends and relatives that run the gamut, from being involved in the violent repression to being complacent about the situation as it existed for so many years, to being victims and survivors of the violence. Maintaining a collegial work environment, as well as harmonious relationships with friends and family, could get complicated if one were to pursue these stories more directly. A commercial media institution, especially in Chile where the concentration of ownership of the media, as well as other significant industries, is so extreme, does impose significant constraints on the discourses that circulate through it; at the same time, the largest, most engaged venues for public discourse are these commercial media institutions—they influence larger numbers than the alternative media, as well as any public event. Thus, we need to take seriously the role that these institutions play in the shaping of our identities, our consciousness, and our priorities. As Nancy Fraser explains, "In this public sphere the media that constitute the material support for the circulation of views are privately owned and operated for profit. Consequently, subordinated social groups usually lack equal access to the material means of equal participation. Thus political economy enforces structurally what culture accomplishes informally" (525–26).

Fraser's words support the concerns expressed by many of the media professionals whom I interviewed in this project. While the repression and absolute censorship of the dictatorship is gone in Chile, the society's hyperliberalized market system, first developed during the dictatorship, along with the high degree of media ownership concentration, continues to exist and undoubtedly will remain as a force that exerts tremendous influence on cultural discourse. Again, I quote Fraser: "This is the shift from a repressive mode of domination to a hegemonic one, from rule based primarily on acquiescence to superior force to rule based primarily on consent supplemented with some measure of repression. The important point is that this new mode of political domination, like the older one, secures the ability of one stratum of society to rule the rest. The official public sphere, then, was, and indeed is, the prime institutional site for the construction of the consent that defines the new, hegemonic mode of domination" (523).

If we consider the official public sphere to be what includes the most people in a society, then we have to recognize that to be the commercial media. However, hegemony is not static—it is in constant struggle as competing groups and ideologies vie for power. Thus, multiple smaller public spheres engage with the "official" public sphere, and, in the case of Chile, the alternative media that I have discussed, as well as alternative discourses available through the arts, blogs, and public protests, serve that function. They raise key issues that often trigger some sort of response in commercial mainstream media; they guarantee that significant themes cannot be entirely forgotten. We can use the example of *The Clinic* as an example of an alternative media that has become mainstream—if we consider its huge readership and popularity with advertisers. *The Clinic* fulfilled a need that was not being satisfied by the other commercial papers. The paper has forced its competitors to expand their discourses and topics.

Observing the dialogues, political reforms, and judicial procedures—all influenced by the circulation of media discourses—that have taken place in Chile from 1998 to 2008 suggests that, despite the enormous constraints imposed on a postrepressive society and its globalized, capitalist media system, there are many ways through which significant topics, such as the violation of human rights, can circulate. I hope that this project has served to highlight the crucial role that the media plays in the articulation of a nation's historical memories, as well as the promotion of social and political change.

Chileans have a rich history of using the media to promote cultural change. Media professionals need to reconnect with this media history to find sources of inspiration because there is so much that needs to be further addressed in the media today. Beyond the violent legacy of the dictatorship, Chile faces other grave human rights situations that also usually receive limited coverage in the mainstream media. The smog of Santiago is deadly. Farm workers are exposed to toxic pesticides. Poor children are being deprived of a good education. Senior citizens are not getting sufficient pensions. Thousands of women get dangerous illegal abortions. Women and children are not adequately protected from domestic violence. Children are working in the streets. Members of the LGBTQ community are victims of hate crimes. Indigenous people are treated as second-class citizens and characterized as terrorists. According to the 2008 *Annual Report on Human Rights* released by Diego Portales University Law Department's Center for Human Rights, the Chilean government and Chilean state exhibit a "mistaken and profoundly conservative conviction that authority should not give reasons for exercising its power" and "while the Chilean State exhibits an excessive diligence for ratifying commercial treaties, the same does not happen with diverse basic essential instruments for the human rights of thousands of people" (quoted in Escalante, "Informe de derechos humanos critica al Gobierno y al Estado"). Perhaps part of this mistaken conviction is derived from being accustomed to an absence of media demands for accountability.

Media studies need to take a more holistic approach that acknowledges media's integration with the larger surrounding cultures and societies in which it circulates. Conditions of media production and distribution should be considered along with conditions of media reception. Local and national media should be considered along with international media. The role of media institutions needs to be considered in conjunction with educational, governmental, and financial institutions. Also, more attention should be given to the media and surrounding cultures of "developing" nations in general. Just as the most powerful media institutions tend to come from "developed" nations, there is also an imbalance in media research that favors the parts of the world that have the highest concentration of media scholars.

Research on new media needs to consider its integration with more traditional media systems. Not only is the Internet an increasingly powerful new source of media, but it is also an additional outlet for older media networks and institutions. Most TV stations, radio stations, and publications have Web sites. Many documentaries and feature films can be watched on the Internet. How does the Internet expand audiences, allow for more audience feedback, and provide new ways for audiences to engage with their media? In the case of Chile, the impact has been tremendous, with Internet users being able to access Chilean news instantaneously from anywhere in the world (as well as people in Chile finding less censored media from abroad available online) and consumers being able to post comments and responses to stories and articles right on the very pages of these traditional network news' spaces, oftentimes without editorial censorship. How does the circulation of local and national discourses change when they are internationalized via the Internet? Access to the Internet varies greatly across the globe. How does the Internet serve to mitigate or further fracture social inequalities? How can the Internet and other new media, such as camera phones, be used by activists to empower the disenfranchised and bring people together to promote social change? These questions are worthy of investigation in the future.

In closing, I wish to acknowledge my own subjective position in relation to this research. I am not Chilean, but I have friends and relatives who are, and I have witnessed, firsthand, the consequences of a society's denial to adequately address its violent legacy—the wounds run deep throughout generations of families and communities. As someone who is not Chilean, perhaps my distance from what I attempt to describe allows me to notice and mention certain elements of Chilean media and culture more easily. I am also aware, though, that my position as an outsider might lead me to neglect consideration of crucial factors known only to a native. I look forward to further discussion of the issues raised in this project, with both Chileans and non-Chileans.

This study is also not just about Chile. Many of the patterns that I observed in this context apply to other national contexts as well, including the United States, where the mainstream media have done a terrific job of entirely avoiding the investigation and discussion of U.S. involvement in human rights violations across the globe.

NOTES

CHAPTER 1

1. In the early 1990s, it was discovered that the army had written checks for General Pinochet's son—$3 million U.S. dollars were paid to him for the purchase of a munitions supplier that never appeared in the armed forces inventory. After the newspaper *La Nación* published the headline, "Case of Pinochet son's checks reopened," General Pinochet sent black beret special forces to the Presidential Palace with rocket launchers (León-Dermota, 70).
2. An interview that he gave on November 23, 2003, to reporter María Elvira Salazar at Miami-based television station WDLP-22 demonstrated that he was mentally fit to stand trial, and the U.S. Congress, as a result of the U.S. government's increased ability through the 2001 U.S. Patriot Act to investigate personal bank accounts, revealed that Pinochet held millions of dollars in secret bank accounts under false names at Riggs Bank in Washington, DC, as well as other international financial institutions.
3. The Valech Report is available at http://www.comisiontortura.cl/listado_informes.html.
4. I refer in particular to the following authors: Oppenheim (1993, 2007), Borzutzky and Oppenheim (2006), Petras and Leíva (1994), Collins and Lear (1995), Drake and Jaksic (1995), Agger and Buus Jensen (1996), Siavelis (1997), Castillo and Piper (1998), Human Rights Watch (1998), Chilean Commission of Human Rights (1999), Roniger and Sznajder (1999), Loveman (2001), Jelin (2003), Richard (2004), Wright (2007), and Stern (2004, 2006).
5. These authors include Pablo Vildósola, Ken León-Dermota, Robert Buckman, Rosalind Bresnahan, Stephen B. Crofts Wiley, Patricio Bernedo, Abraham Santibáñez, Eliana Rozas, John Dinges, Peter Kornbluh, Juan Poblete, Eliza Tanner Hawkins, Guillermo Sunkel, Ernesto Muñoz, Darío Burotto, Ernesto Carmona, Ascanio Cavallo, Virginia Herrera, Carlos Ossa Coo, Ana López, Zuzana Pick, Jacqueline Mouesca, Carlos Orellana, and Michael Chanan.
6. These commentators include Steve J. Stern, Nelly Richard, Macarena Gómez-Barris, Antonio Skármeta, Isabel Allende, Ariel Dorfman, and Elizabeth Jelin, among others.
7. I should mention that there is plenty of Right-leaning, even fascist, alternative media as well. One need look no further than the Internet to see the large numbers of pro-Pinochet blogs and fan sites.
8. Kandell did play a crucial role during the dictatorship in working with human rights organizations inside Chile to get information about the repression out to a global audience.
9. Today, much of this information is available on the Internet through the declassified CIA documents of the National Security Archive.

10. See Steve Randall's "*Missing* the Chile Story at the *New York Times*."
11. See Peter Kornbluh's "The *El Mercurio* File: Secret Documents Shine New Light on How the CIA Used a Newspaper to Foment a Coup."
12. During the Popular Unity Government, Agustín Edwards V, owner of *El Mercurio*, went to the United States to seek support. He met with U.S. National Security Adviser Henry Kissinger, who had already been involved in attempts to prevent Allende from winning the election. Other supporters for the destabilization and disruption of the Popular Unity Government were ITT, Chase Manhattan Bank, and the Pepsi-Cola Company, the latter at which Edwards later served as a company vice president (León-Dermota, 15–16).
13. The Catholic Church gave refuge to families of the disappeared in their basements and other locations. Oftentimes, the surviving relatives of the disappeared needed an income since their missing loved ones had been the wage earners. The church would pay these women for the craftwork they would sew with scraps of cloth attached to a piece of burlap, and then the church would smuggle these *arpilleras* abroad where they could be bought by others. In this fashion, these *arpilleras*, which told stories about what was happening in Chile under Pinochet's regime, helped to circulate information to a concerned global community.
14. Ethnoscapes refer to the movement of people.
15. Mediascapes are "image-centered, narrative-based accounts of strips of reality . . . out of which scripts can be formed of imagined lives" ("Disjuncture and Difference in the Global Cultural Economy," 224).
16. Technoscapes refer to the movement of technology.
17. Finanscapes refer to the movement of global capital.
18. Ideoscapes describe the movement of frames of thinking including terms such as "freedom," "welfare," "rights," "sovereignty," "representation," and "democracy" ("Disjuncture and Difference in the Global Cultural Economy," 224).
19. Censorship laws did exist in Chile's previous Constitution as well; those restrictions were maintained and developed further in the 1980 Constitution.
20. Marita Sturken, Andreas Huyssen, Tamar Ashuri, Nelly Richard, Elizabeth Jelin, Diana Taylor, Susana Kaiser, Macarena Gómez-Barris and Steve J. Stern are scholars whose ideas I find useful in analyzing the current situation in Chile.
21. These authors include David Morley, Tony Bennett, Annette Kuhn, Janet Staiger, Barbara Klinger, and Jostein Gripsrud, among others.
22. Pinochet is remembered as the savior from the "catastrophe" of 1964 to 1973 in Chile.
23. The open wound is the physical and psychological trauma inflicted on victims of Pinochet's repression.
24. This is a memory held by those who attempt to hold a more distanced, analytical, and philosophical perspective on the dictatorship.
25. This is the memory of amnesia or forgetting, which Stern describes as actually full of memory (2000, 17).
26. According to Charles Horman and Frank Teruggi's friend and colleague Steven Volk, Purdy initially denied him access to the morgue where Teruggi's and Horman's bodies were located, and when he finally did allow access, he did not reveal to Volk that Horman's body was there as well (Volk).
27. In the early 1990s, after Pinochet sent his black beret special forces to the Presidential Palace in response to *La Nación* publishing the headline about

the $3 million in checks that had been written out to Pinochet's son, the newspaper was forced to amend the previous headline with a new one, "Army acted within the law in checks case." However, the headline was juxtaposed with a photograph of the black berets; one can easily interpret an alternative meaning (León-Dermota, 70).

28. Due to present knowledge that many of these remains were misidentified due to inconsistencies and irregularities at the forensic institute, *Servicio Medico Legal*, it is possible that the victim to which these remains belong was not positively identified.
29. As told in Abraham Santibáñez's *Entre el Horror y la Esperanza* (Santiago: Editorial Don Bosco, 2003), 221–40, Rodrigo Rojas Denegri initially survived his burns. He and Carmen Gloria Quintana were dumped in the road on the outskirts of Santiago near the airport, where they were eventually picked up and taken to a local hospital.

CHAPTER 2

1. The rating is the percentage of households with TV sets watching a specific show, versus a share, which is the percentage of households with TV sets turned on at a particular time that are watching a specific show. The show's rating on July 15, 2003, was 5.2 percent.
2. Alejandra Matus is a journalist and professor who was temporarily exiled from Chile after the release of her book that critiqued the Chilean justice system. She has been a panelist on *El Termómetro*.
3. Víctor Díaz was asphyxiated with a plastic bag held over his head and injected with cyanide.

CHAPTER 3

1. For further discussion of *Fernando Is Back*, see Macarena Gómez-Barris's *Where Memory Dwells*, 103–31. Gómez-Barris also interviewed Silvio Caiozzi in 2002.
2. In the words of Gladys Díaz, describing the experience of torture,

"We were prepared to be arrested, yes, but no one is ever prepared for the torture, because torture is just an intellectual concept until you experience it. The worst part of torture is not the physical pain that you suffer—I think that the worst part of torture is to have to realize in such a brutal way that human beings are capable of doing something so aberrant to another person as torturing them. For me, I think that was the most terrible part. It shows that human beings are capable of lowering themselves on the human scale to such a level. In order for this to happen . . . It's impossible, because I could have the greatest enemy in the world, and I couldn't do it. And I couldn't be with anyone of any ideology–or even who shared my ideology–if that man were hurting another to make that person talk, even to the point of killing him or her. I really think that civilization has made great strides, but it has not progressed enough if human beings are still capable of doing this" (Wright and Oñate, 81).

3. See http://www.bazuca.com/cgi-bin/ncommerce3/ExecMacro/Bazuca/GetComent.d2w/report.
4. See http://www.ics.cl/icsweb/movs/El_dia_en_que_murio_Pinochet.mov.

Chapter 4

1. Here, I am struck by my interview with director Silvio Caiozzi, who never mentioned during the thick description of his filmic career that his cameraman for his 1974 film, *A la sombra del sol* [*In the Sun's Shadow*], Jorge Müller, who also operated the camera for Guzmán in *Battle of Chile*, along with his girlfriend, Carmen Bueno, who acted in Caiozzi's film, disappeared the morning after the film's first public screening in November 1974. Müller and Bueno are two of the victims whose perpetrators are charged in the prosecution of ninety-eight members of the armed forces in 2008.
2. *Machuca* was produced for $1.7 million with support from Ibermedia, FONDART (Chile), and CORFO (Chile) by Andrés Wood Producciones (Chile), Tornasol Films (Spain), Mamoun Hassan (United Kingdom), and Paraiso (France) "in association with Chilefilms" and "with participation of Canal Plus Spain and Televisión Española." *Machuca* is cowritten by Roberto Brodsky, Mamoun Hassan, and Wood, directed by Wood, shot by Miguel Joan Littín (son of Miguel Littín), edited by Fernando Pardo, with music by Miguel Angel Miranda and José Miguel Tobar and sound by Miguel Hormazabal and Marcos Maldasky.
3. Comment retrieved from http://www.imdb.com/title/tt0378284/usercomments.

Chapter 5

1. Mercury is the Roman god of commerce, thievery, eloquence, and science, and messenger to the other gods (*Random House Webster's College Dictionary*, 1999).
2. Abraham Santibáñez contributes regularly to many periodicals, including *El Sur* of Concepción and another significant alternative paper not discussed in this chapter, *Punto Final* (*The Final Point*).
3. Abraham Santibáñez is former director and editor of several periodicals, including *Ercilla*, *Hoy* [*Today*], the antidictatorship magazine permitted by Pinochet, and *La Nación*.
4. The editors of these papers also did not respond to my requests for an interview.
5. This tendency to omit authors' names is still prevalent at all of the daily papers. This practice may be part of the branding of all articles as belonging to the paper and not individual writers but it could also serve a protective function for writers who are addressing sensitive topics.
6. Maintaining this bifurcation today would be especially challenging considering that virtually all printed press outlets now have electronic versions online.
7. Of note are *Fortín Mapocho*, *La Epoca*, *Apsi*, and *Análisis*, as well as the Jesuit journal *Mensaje*, which was first published in 1951, and *Solidaridad*, published under the relative protection of the Catholic Church.

8. The Christian Democrats had initially supported the military coup, but quickly withdrew their support of Pinochet when it became clear that he did not intend to return the country swiftly to democracy and as human rights violations became evident.
 9. Special Judge Juan Guzmán Tapia would later be able to argue that forced disappearances were not covered under this amnesty. If a body had not been found, then the crime was active—an ongoing kidnapping that had not ended by 1978, the final year of the amnesty.
 10. Ernesto Carmona's book *Morir es la noticia (To die is the news)* documents the lives and deaths of hundreds of journalists and media professionals who lost their lives during the dictatorship.
 11. The pope had an ambiguous position on human rights violations in Latin America. He chastised Latin American priests who preached "liberation theology" to their congregations and tried to protect victims of repression who had been fighting for better livelihoods through socialist movements. In 1987, however, he had the power to do good in Chile, for, after all, Pinochet considered himself a devout Catholic and, consequently, would be expected to pay heed to the concerns of the pope.
 12. The Mapuche are fighting to protect their tribal lands from transnational timber companies and hydroelectric energy projects.
 13. In *El Mercurio*, color photographs stand out on the page because so much of the paper is in black and white. A photograph in black and white remains more camouflaged.
 14. In light of revelations in recent years that many remains of the disappeared may have been erroneously identified due to irregularities at the forensic institute *Servicio Medico Legal*, this could be one of those cases of misidentification.
 15. *Las Últimas Noticias* is part of the *El Mercurio* chain.
 16. "Y los periodistas chilenos pidieron perdón," http://www.elsiglo.cl/noticia.php?id=3717&sec=0&subsec=0&area=agencia (accessed July 3, 2008). His article was also available through numerous online media outlets.
 17. Maipú Corner and Operation Colombo refer to programs implemented by the secret police and repressive forces in collusion with media professionals to explain the secret detainments, tortures, deaths, and disappearances of individuals as a consequence of armed conflicts between feuding sectors of the political Left and the police. In some cases, fictitious street fights were staged for television cameras.
 18. The paper is funded 30 percent from advertising and 70 percent from state subsidy and newsstand sales.
 19. Paul Schäfer was captured in Argentina on March 10, 2005, and returned to Chile to face charges. This event received extensive media attention in the Chilean press.
 20. Gladys Marín died from a malignant brain tumor on March 6, 2005. Thousands of Chileans mourned her loss in the streets of Chile. This news received extensive media coverage at the national and international levels.
 21. Alejandra Matus and Marcela Ramos suggest the same in their article "Spiniak B" when they explain that the creation of their paper *Plan B* was a response to censorship experienced from the Sunday version of *La Nación*, *La Nación Domingo* (Santibáñez and Vildósola, 28).
 22. "Mamo" refers to Manuel Contreras, leader of Pinochet's repressive secret police force, the DINA.

23. See *Tejas Verdes: Diario de un Campo de Concentratción en Chile* by Hernán Valdés.
24. In the months following the coup in 1973, an elite troop of military men flew by helicopter to cities in the south of Chile and then in the north, rounding up and murdering individuals, especially key labor and political leaders who were considered a threat to the new military regime (Escalante, *La mission era matar*).
25. For more information on the dangers and consequences of illegal abortion in Chile, see Claudia Lagos Lira's *Aborto en Chile*.
26. For further analysis of the taboos of discussing torture, see *De la tortura no se habla: Agüero versus Meneses*, edited by Patricia Verdugo.
27. Former court reporter Alejandra Matus was forced to leave Chile in temporary exile after publishing her book on the secrets of the corrupt Chilean justice system and judges, *El libro negro de la justicia chilena* (Buenos Aires: Editorial Planeta Argentina S.A.I.C., 1999).

Chapter 6

1. An example is when working in downtown Santiago as a hotel maid, Inelia Hermosilla learned that General Pinochet was walking down the street with his entourage. She rushed out of the building and ran up to him, shouting, "General, give me a Christmas gift . . . Tell me what you have done with my son!" She was immediately escorted away and detained (as told to the author by Hermosilla).
2. See Marjorie Agosín's *Tapestries of Hope, Threads of Love: The Arpillera Movement in Chile, 1974–1994*. Albuquerque: University of New Mexico Press, 1996.
3. See Ramón Bannister's "*The AFDD Conjunto: Commemoration, Pain, and Memory*." Master's thesis. Indiana University, 2004.
4. Kaiser, 184.
5. "El Príncipe" ("The Prince"), Edwin Dimter Bianchi, was the commander in charge at Chile Stadium who ordered Jara's torture and murder.
6. In a Funa demonstration attended by the author in 2002, participants were also confronted by military guards holding machine guns at the entrance to the office building on Avenida Bernardo O'Higgins where General Juan Emilio Cheyre, then commander of the army and the target of this particular demonstration, worked.
7. The footage of Henrichsen capturing his own murder on film—Bustamante aiming his gun at Henrichsen, shooting, and then the camera falling down as Henrichsen collapses—is included in Patricio Guzmán's *The Battle of Chile*.

Chapter 7

1. A U.S. Senate investigation revealed that Pinochet and his family used secret bank accounts for at least twenty-five years that included the Riggs Bank, Bank of America, Coutts, and Citigroup.
2. A case in point, as of August 2008, is that of an ex-military official of Temuco, Adolfo Podlech Michaud, who was arrested in Spain and extradited to Italy to face trial for the disappearance of Italian priest Omar Venturelli in 1973.

BIBLIOGRAPHY

A. G., J. "El cine de los 60 nos lleva a un momento muy dura de nuestra historia." *The Clinic*, April 5, 2007.
Agger, Inger, and Søren Buus Jensen. *Trauma and Healing Under State Terrorism*. London: Zed Books, 1996.
Agosín, Marjorie. *Scraps of Life: Chilean Arpilleras, Chilean Women and the Pinochet Dictatorship*. Trenton, NJ: Red Sea Press, 1989.
———. *Tapestries of Hope, Threads of Love: The Arpillera Movement in Chile, 1974–1994*. Albuquerque: University of New Mexico Press, 1996.
"Agrupaciones de familiares: 'Rechazamos la presencia de Lagos en funeral de Banzer.'" *El Siglo*, May 10, 2002, 20.
Aguilera Jara, Julia (mother). "Detenido desaparecido: Alberto puertas afuera." *The Clinic*, May 2, 2002, 24.
Allen, Tom. "Coup de Cinema." *The Village Voice*, 23, no. 3 (1978, January).
Alvarado, Pablo. Personal interview. Santiago, April 4, 2002.
Alvarado E., Rodrigo. "'Me violenta la indiferencia con los desaparecidos.'" *La Nación*, July 20, 2008. http://www.lanacion.cl/prontus_noticias_v2/site/artic/20080719/pags/20080719185150.html.
Alvaray, Luisela. "National, Regional, and Global: New Waves of Latin American Cinema." *Cinema Journal* 47, no. 3 (2008): 48–65.
Alvarez, Gus. "[Interview with] Andrés Wood." 6degreesfilm. http://www.6degreesfilm.com/features/AndresWood.htm (accessed April 4, 2006).
Anderson, Benedict. "Imagined Communities: Nationalism's Cultural Roots." In *The Cultural Studies Reader*. 3rd ed., edited by Simon During, 253–63. New York: Routledge, 2007.
———. *Imagined Communities: Reflections on the Origin and Spread of Nationalism*. New York: Verso, 1991.
Andrés Lagos, Juan. "Las 'complicaciones' del Alto Mando." *El Siglo*, May 10, 2002, 6.
Ang, Ien. *Desperately Seeking the Audience*. New York: Routledge, 1991.
Antze, Paul, and Michael Lambek, eds. *Tense Past: Cultural Essays in Trauma and Memory*. New York: Routledge, 1996.
Appadurai, Arjun. "Disjuncture and Difference in the Global Cultural Economy." In *The Cultural Studies Reader*. 2nd ed., edited by Simon During, 220–30. New York: Routledge, 1999.
———, ed. *Globalization*. Durham, NC: Duke University Press, 2001.
———. *Modernity at Large: Cultural Dimensions of Globalization*. Minneapolis: University of Minnesota Press, 1996.
Arancibia, Nancy. "Gladis Marín: Entre la hoz y Pinochet." *La Nación*, May 2, 2002, 35.
Armando Sánchez, Patricio. "Los héroes de la película, ¿quiénes somos?" *El Siglo*, May 24, 2002, 2.

Ascencio D., Rubén. "El príncipe de la Tinieblas." *El Siglo*, June 23, 2006.
Ashuri, Tamar. "The Nation Remembers: National Identity and Shared Memory in Television Documentaries." *Nations and Nationalism* 11, no. 3 (2005): 423–42.
Associated Press. "Pinochet to keep immunity." March 25, 2005. http://www.guardian.co.uk/chile/story/0,13755,1445453,00.html (accessed December 24, 2008).
Atkinson, Michael. "Couped Up: Self-Regard Trivializes Chilean Historical Memoir: *Machuca*." *The Village Voice*, January 18, 2005. http://www.villagevoice.com/generic/show_print.php?id=60094&page=atkinson&issue (accessed March 1, 2006).
Aufderheide, Patricia. "The Importance of Historical Memory: An Interview with Patricio Guzmán." *Cineaste* 27, no. 3 (Summer 2002): 22–25.
Autor Colaboradores. "Detienen a periodistas por cubrir Funa a asesino." *El Clarín de Chile*, August 22, 2007. http://www.elclarin.cl/index2.php?option=com_content&task=view&id=8156&Itemid=4. (accessed December 24, 2008).
Avila, Roberto. "El voto contra Cuba." *La Nación*, May 2, 2002.
Ayala, Ernesto. "Machuca: En la herida de Chile." *El Mercurio*, August 6, 2004.
Ayala Castro, Leslie. "Concluye masiva notificación por Operación Colombo." *La Nación*, May 29, 2008. http://www.lanacion.cl/prontus_noticias_v2/site/artic/20080528/pags/20080528211531.html (accessed December 24, 2008).
———. "Operación Colombo: Recurren de amparo cinco procesados." *La Nación*. May 30, 2008. http://www.lanacion.cl/prontus_noticias_v2/site/artic/20080529/pags/20080529231157.html (accessed May 30, 2008).
BBC News. "Bank payout to Pinochet victims," February 26, 2005. http://news.bbc.co.uk/go/pr/fr/-/2/hi/business/4300841.stm (accessed December 24, 2008).
———. "Judge questions Chile cult head." March 15, 2005. http://news/bbc.co.uk/go/pr/fr/-/1/hi/world/americas/4349593.stm (accessed December 24, 2008).
———. "New charges for Chile cult head." March 22, 2005. http://news.bbc.co.uk/go/pr/fr/-/2/hi/americas/4370607.stm (accessed December 24, 2008).
———. "Pinochet murder case blocked." March 24, 2005. http://news.bbc.co.uk/go/pr/fr/-/1/hi/world/americas/4380123.stm (accessed December 24, 2008).
———. "Pinochet report welcomed in Chile." March 17, 2005. http://news.bbc.co.uk/go/pr/fr/-/1/hi/world/americas/4356777.stm (accessed December 24, 2008).
———. "Pinochet 'stowed $13m in banks.'" March 16, 2005. http://news.bbc.co.uk/go/pr/fr/-/2/hi/americas/4353801.stm (accessed December 24, 2008).
BBC Mundo.com. "Chile: habla Contreras," May 14, 2005. http://news.bbc.co.uk/hi/spanish/latin_america/newsid_4545000/4545829.stm (accessed December 24, 2008).
Bannister, Ramón Carlos. "The AFDD Conjunto: Commemoration, Pain, and Memory." Master's thesis, Indiana University, 2004.
Barnhart, Anne. "Mensaje, A Voice for the Oppressed: A Translation of Five Articles with a Critical Introduction." Master's thesis, Indiana University, 1996.

Becerra Arce, Ana Graciela. "Una sobreviviente." *El Siglo*, Feburary 8, 2002.
Benaroyo, Mónica. "La mujer que nadie buscó en 30 años." *The Clinic*. http://www.theclinic.cl/c_reportajes/rep_02.php (accessed August 14, 2008).
Benavides, Sergio. "Alejandro Guillier se baja del avión y vuelve a TVN." *La Nación*, October 17, 2008. http://www.lanacion.cl/prontus_noticias_v2/site/artic/20081016/pags/20081016214337.html (accessed December 26, 2008).
Bennett, Tony. "Texts, Readers, Reading Formations." *Bulletin of the Midewest Modern Language Association* 16, no. 1 (Spring 1983): 3–17.
Blanchet, Raúl. "Cerro Chena: El terror continúa." *El Siglo*, Feburary 8, 2002.
———. "Cerro Chena: Presiones contra una magistrada." *El Siglo*. March 29, 2002.
———. "Jueces especiales: La operación fracaso." *El Siglo*, May 3, 2002.
Borzutzky, Silvia, and Lois Hecht Oppenheim, eds. *After Pinochet: The Chilean Road to Democracy and the Market*. Gainesville: University Press of Florida, 2006.
Bresnahan, Rosalind. "Radio and the Democratic Movement in Chile 1973–1990: Independent and Grass Roots Voices During the Pinochet Dictatorship." *Journal of Radio Studies* 9, no. 1, (2002): 161–81.
Buckman, Robert. "Chilean Media Face Ethical Growing Pains." *Quill Magazine*, March 2004, 28–30.
Burr, Ty. "Coming of Age in Allende's Chile." *Boston Globe*, March 4, 2007.
Burton, Julianne. *Cinema and Social Change in Latin America*. Austin: University of Texas Press, 1986.
———. "Politics and the Documentary in People's Chile: An Interview with Patricio Guzmán on *The Battle of Chile*." Somerville: New England Free Press. Reprinted by permission of *Socialist Review*. Originally published as "Politics and Documentary in People's Chile," September–October 1977.
———, ed. *The Social Documentary in Latin America*. Pittsburgh: University of Pittsburgh Press, 1990.
Bustos B., Ernesto. "'Machuca' batió record de taquilla." *La Nación*, August 10, 2004.
C., Y. (Valparaíso). "Juez Guzmán supervisó la exhumación de un niño." *La Nación*, May 3, 2002.
Cahiers du Cinéma, ed. "John Ford's *Young Mr. Lincoln*." In *Film Theory and Criticism*. 2nd ed., edited by Gerald Mast and Marshall Cohen, 778–831. New York: Oxford University Press, 1979.
Caiozzi, Silvio. *Fernando ha vuelto*. VHS. Santiago: Andrea Films, 1998.
———. Personal interview. Santiago, March 27, 2002.
Caldwell, John Thornton. *Televisuality: Style, Crisis, and Authority in American Television*. New Brunswick, NJ: Rutgers University Press, 1995.
Canal.cl. "Videotestimonio por Rucia Sucia." http://blog.canal.cl/2006/12/videotestimonio-por-rucia-sucia.html (accessed May 11, 2007).
Carlson, A. Cheree. "Limitations on the Comic Frame: Some Witty American Women of the Nineteenth Century." *Quarterly Journal of Speech* 74 (1988): 310–22.
Carmona, Ernesto. "Amenazan de muerte a dos periodistas." *El Siglo*, September 24, 2004.
———, ed. *Morir es la noticia*. Santiago: 1997.

———. "Y los periodistas chilenos pidieron perdón." *El Siglo*. http://www.elsiglo.cl/noticia.php?id=3717&sec=0&subsec=0&area=agencia (accessed July 3, 2008).
Carrasco M., Lito. "Exonerados políticos: Justicia y reparación." *El Siglo*, March 29, 2002.
Castillo, María Isabel, and Isabel Piper, eds. *Voces y ecos de violencia: Chile, El Salvador, México y Nicaragua*. Santiago: Ediciones ChileAmérica CESOC, 1998.
Cautivo, Dolores. "La rebeldía de Víctor." *El Siglo*. http://www.elsiglo.cl/noticia.php?id=3573&sec=0&subsec=0&area=agencia&num=31 (accessed December 24, 2008).
Cavallo, Ascanio, Pablo Douzet, and Cecilia Rodríguez. *Huérfanos y perdidos: El cine chileno de la transición 1990–1999*. Santiago: Editorial Grijalbo S.A., 1999.
Cavallo, Ascanio, and Virginia Herrera. "Ojo con el cine chileno: 20 estrenos el 2000." *El Sábado de El Mercurio*, June 24, 2000.
Chanan, Michael, ed. *Chilean Cinema*. London: British Film Institute, 1976.
Chaparro Solís, Andrea. "Nombran director interino del SML para enfrentar aguda crisis del organismo." *La Nación*, June 21, 2006.
Chilean Commission of Human Rights. *Nunca más en Chile: Sintesis corregida y actualizada del Informe Rettig*. Santiago: LOM Ediciones, 1999.
The Clinic. "Las mujeres que desafían a carabineros." http://www.theclinic.cl/c_reportajes/rep_02.php (accessed June 23, 2008).
———. "El salvaje 'Wena N' en un colegio de La Pintana." http://www.theclinic.cl/c_reportajes/rep_01.php (accessed June 23, 2008).
Colectivo Londres 38. "Intervención conmemorativa en Londres 38." http://www.londres38.cl/1937/article-82027.html (accessed August 7, 2008).
Colectivo 119. "Londres 38: Casa de la Memoria."
Collier, Barnard, and Jonathan Kandell. "A Devastating End for a Unique, Troubled Venture."
New York Times, September 16, 1973.
Collins, Joseph, and John Lear. *Chile's Free-Market Miracle: A Second Look*. Oakland, CA: Institute for Food and Development Policy, 1995.
"Comunicado de Funa Chile – 11/01/2007." http://www.redh.org/index2.php?option=com_content&task=view&id=721&pop=721&pop=1&pag (accessed July 30, 2008).
Conquergood, Dwight. "Poetics, Play, Process and Power: The Performative Turn in Anthropology." *Text and Performance Quarterly* 9, no. 1 (January 1989): 82–95.
Contreras, Eduardo. "Asesinos y cobardes." *El Siglo*, April 12, 2002.
———. "Pinocheyre." *El Siglo*, March 29, 2002.
———. "¿Qué pasa con Pinochet?" *El Siglo*, February 8, 2002.
Cordero, Rodrigo, Stefan Tomicic, and Pablo Vildósola. "Radiografía a las fuentes públicas de información." In *Las lecciones de los medios*, edited by Abraham Santibáñez and Pablo Vildósola, 115–24. Santiago: University of Diego Portales School of Journalism, 2005.
Corvalan Carbone, Patricio. "El padre de los Machuca." *La Tercera*, August 8, 2004.
Cruz-Coke M., Eduardo. "Chile y el Tribunal Penal Internacional." *La Nación*, May 9, 2002.

Curiel, Jonathan. "Machuca." *San Francisco Chronicle*, July 15, 2005. http://www.sfgate.com/cgi-bin/article.cgi?file=/c/a/2005/07/15/DDGKGD-NJ6P1.DTL&type=p (accessed March 1, 2006).
D., R. "Elena Varela: Recurren a ente interamericano por caso de documentalista." *Elmercurio.com*, July 3, 2008. http://diario.elmercurio.com/2008/07/03/nacional/nacional/noticias/impresion17D43F69- (accessed July 3, 2008).
del Río, Matías. Personal interview. Santiago, July 11, 2006.
del Sarto, Ana, Alicia Ríos, and Abril Trigo, eds. *The Latin American Cultural Studies Reader*. Durham, NC: Duke University Press, 2004.
DemocraticUnderground.com. "Bank to compensate victims." March 11, 2005. http://www.democraticunderground.com/discuss/duboard.php?az=view_all&address=102x1302284 (accessed December 24, 2008).
DeNegri, Claudio. Personal interview. Santiago, March 1, 2002. *El día en que murió Pinochet*. http://www.ics.cl/icsweb/movs/El_dia_en_que_murio_Pinochet.mov (accessed February 6, 2008).
Derechos Chile. "Londres 38." http://www.chipsites.com/derechos/campo_santiago_londres_38_eng.html (accessed July 30, 2008).
El día en que murió Pinochet. http://www.youtube.com/watch?v=WgonGqUpdxs (accessed February 6, 2008. Díaz, Victoria. Personal conversations. Santiago, 2002–2008.
———. Personal interview. Santiago, July 1, 2006.
Díaz, Victoria, Mónica Pilquil, and Mireya Rivera. Personal interview. Santiago, July 14, 2006.
Dinges, John. "The Curious Case of Victor Pey." *Columbia Journalism Review* (May–June 2007): 43–47.
Dinges, John, and Saul Landau. *Assassination on Embassy Row*. New York: Pantheon Books, 1980.
Dittborn, Pablo. "¿Qué le pasa a Marco Enríquez-Ominami con *The Clinic*?" *The Clinic*, January 4, 2007.
Dooner, Patricio. *Periodismo y politica: La prensa de derecha e izquierda 1970–1973*. Santiago: Hoy Ediciones, Editorial Andante, 1989.
Dorfman, Ariel. "Behind the Sunglasses." *Index on Censorship* 1 (2005): 67–71.
Drake, Paul W., and Ivan Jaksic, eds. *The Struggle for Democracy in Chile*. Lincoln: University of Nebraska Press, 1995.
Dreifus, Claudia. "The New Battle of Chile: Keeping Memory Alive." *New York Times*, September 6, 1998.
E., J. "Sentencias para los últimos días de mayo." *La Nación*, April 29, 2002.
Echevarria, Ignacio. "Niños." *La Nación Domingo*, August 15–21, 2004.
Elena, Alberto, and Marina Díaz López, eds. *The Cinema of Latin America*. London: Wallflower, 2003.
Errázuriz, M. José, and Pilar Molina A. "El fallo expansivo del Tribunal Constitucional." *El Mercurio*, April 12, 2002.
Escalante, Jorge. "Abren nueva brecha en EE.UU. contra Pinochet." *La Nación*, February 22, 2002.
———. "Colegio pide perdón por periodistas que mintieron." *La Nación*, June 19, 2008. http://www.lanacion.cl/prontus_noticias_v2/site/artic/20080618/pags/20080618222544.html (accessed June 19, 2008).
———. "El conflicto no resuelto entre el Estado y la Colonia Dignidad." *La Nación*, May 3, 2002.

———. "Documento 'secreto' de la CNI revela razón de matar a Tucapel." *La Nación*, April 29, 2002.
———. "El gobierno defiende el rol del general Juan Carlos Salgado." *La Nación*, May 9, 2002.
———. "El golpe más grande a la represión." *La Nación*, May 27, 2008. http://www.lanacion.cl/prontus_noticias_v2/site/artic/20080526/pags/20080526213404.html (accessed May 28, 2008).
———. "Informe de derechos humanos critica al Gobierno y al Estado." *La Nación*. http://www.lanacion.cl/prontus_noticias_v2/site/artic/20080819/pags/20080819221712.html (accessed August 20, 2008).
———. "Izurieta comprometió 'gestos' del Ejército por crimen de Prats." *La Nación*. http://www.nacion.cl/prontus_noticias_v2/site/artic/20080707/pags/20080707222255.html (accessed July 8, 2008).
———. "Juez reabrió caso Víctor Jara." *La Nación*, June 4, 2008. http://www.nacion.cl/prontus_noticias_v2/site/artic/20080603/pags/20080603213224.html (accessed June 4, 2008).
———. "Juez sobreseyó a Paul Schäfer." *La Nación*, May 2, 2002, 2.
———. *La misión era matar: El juicio a la caravana Pinochet-Arellano*. Santiago: LOM Ediciones, 2000.
———. "Notifican a oficiales (R) procesados por crimen de Huber." *La Nación*, August 15, 2008. http://www.lanacion.cl/prontus_noticias_v2/site/artic/20080814/pags/20080814213424.html (accessed August 15, 2008).
———. "Querellados periodistas por mentir en caso Rinconada." *La Nación*, July 3, 2008. http://www.lanacion.cl/prontus_noticias_v2/site/artic/20080702/pags/20080702213825.html (accessed July 3, 2008).
———. "Sentencia establece responsabilidad institucional de mandos del ejército." *Lanacion.cl*. July 18, 2008. http://www.lanacion.cl/prontus_noticias_v2/site/artic/20080717/pags/20080717233226.html (accessed July 18, 2008).
Estrada, Daniela. "General in Hiding a 'Coward,' Say Activists." *Inter Press Service News Agency*, June 14, 2007. http://www.ipsnews.net/print.asp?idnews=38178 (accessed July 6, 2007).
Farias, Cristian. "Farándula y politicos se unieron para ver Machuca." *La Tercera*, August 3, 2004.
Faundez, Julio. *Democratization, Development, and Legality: Chile, 1831–1973*. New York: Palgrave Macmillan, 2007.
———. "In Defense of Presidentialism: The Case of Chile, 1932–1970." In *Presidentialism and Democracy in Latin America*, edited by Scott Mainwaring and Matthew Soberg Shugart, 300–20. Cambridge: Cambridge University Press, 1997.
Fernandez, Francia. "'Lloro cuando veo Machuca': Andrés Wood y su nueva película ambientada en los tiempos de la UP." *La Nación Domingo*, August 8–14, 2004.
Fernández, Patricio. Personal interview. Santiago, February 20, 2002.
Fernando Ha Vuelto. http://www.bazuca.com/bazucaE-GetComent-prrfnbr=34531&prod=pelicula-mas-comentarios-de-Fernando-Ha-Vuelto (accessed Jan. 22, 2008).
———. http://www.bazuca.com/pelicula-34531-Fernando-Ha-Vuelto (accessed November 20, 2007).

———. http://www.youtube.com/watch?v=J0UPK6NjmTc. (accessed February 6, 2008).

———. http://www.youtube.com/comment_servlet?all_comments&v=J0UPK6NjmTc&fromurl=/watch%3Fv%3DJ0UPK6NjmTc (accessed February 6, 2008).

Fox, Ken. "Machuca." *TV Guide*. http://online.tvguide.com/movies/database/Movie-Review.asp?MI=45877 (accessed March 1, 2006).

Franklin, Jonathan. "Pinochet Interview Revives Trial Hope." *Guardian*, December 5, 2003. http://globalpolicy.igc.org/intljustice/wanted/2003/1205hope.htm (accessed May 14, 2007).

Fraser, Nancy. "Rethinking the Public Sphere: A Contribution to the Critique of Actually Existing Democracy." *The Cultural Studies Reader*, 2nd ed., edited by Simon During, 518–36. New York: Routledge, 1999.

Funa Chile. "Declaración de La Funa: No tenemos nada que esconder." http://www.geocities.com/jrme_chile/delcaracion_de_la_funa.htm?200830 (accessed July 30, 2008).

———. "Funa a el príncipe," May 25, 2006. http://www.flickr.com/photos/22202937@N00/2498696343/ (accessed July 30, 2008).

———. "Funa a Pablo Rodriguez Grez, Fundador de Patria y Libertad y actual abogado de Augusto Pinochet," September 13, 2006.

Gálvez, Mario. "Informe sobre DD.HH. y drogas: Lagos rechaza críticas de Estados Unidos." *El Mercurio*, March 7, 2002.

García Márquez, Gabriel. *Clandestine in Chile*. New York: Henry Holt and Company, 1986.

Getino, Octavio. *Cine y televisión en América Latina: Producción y mercados*. Santiago: LOM Ediciones, 1998.

Golding, Peter, and Phil Harris, eds. *Beyond Cultural Imperialism: Globalization, Communication and the New International Order*. Thousand Oaks, CA: Sage, 1997.

Gómez-Barris, Macarena. *Where Memory Dwells: Culture and State Violence in Chile*. Berkeley: University of California Press, 2009.

González, Lola (wife). "Detenido Desaparecido: El doctor Godoy." *The Clinic*, March 21, 2002.

Gonzalez M., Rodrigo. "Machuca consagra a la actriz Manuela Martelli." *La Tercera*, August 5, 2004.

———. "Los niños de septiembre." *La Tercera*, August 6, 2004. *El Siglo*. "'Gordon fue . . .'" April 12, 2002.

Gripsrud, Jostein. *The Dynasty Years: Hollywood Television and Critical Media Studies*. New York: Routledge, 1994.

———. *Understanding Media Culture*. New York: Oxford University Press, 2002.

Guardian Unlimited. "Pinochet's web of bank accounts exposed." March 16, 2005. http://www.guardian.co.uk/business/story/0,3604,1439031,00.html (accessed December 24, 2008).

Guillier, Alejandro. Personal interview. Santiago, April 8, 2002.

Hall, Stuart. "Encoding, Decoding." In *The Cultural Studies Reader*. 2nd ed., edited by Simon During, 507–17. New York: Routledge, 1999.

Hartman, Geoffrey, ed. *Holocaust Remembrance: The Shapes of Memory*. Cambridge: Blackwell, 1994.

Herman, Edward S. *Manufacturing Consent: The Political Economy of the Mass Media*. New York: Pantheon Books, 2002.
Herman, Edward S., and Robert W. McChesney. *The Global Media: The New Missionaries of Global Capitalism*. Washington: Cassell, 1997.
Hermosilla, Inelia. Personal conversations. Santiago, 2002–2006.
Hermosilla Silva, Inelia. Personal interview. Santiago, June 6, 2006.
Hitchens, Christopher. *The Trial of Henry Kissinger*. New York: Verso, 2001.
Holden, Stephen. "Morally Accountable for the 'Disappearances' and the Atrocities: *The Pinochet Case*." *New York Times*, September 11, 2002.
Holzmeyer, Cheryl. "Exploring the Im/Possibilities of Boyhood Friendship During the Last Days of the Allende Government: Film Screening: 'Machuca' with Director Andrés Wood. March 13, 2006." http://socrates.berkeley.edu:7001/Events/spring2006/03-13-06-machuca/index.html (accessed April 4, 2006).
Hormazábal, Guillermo. Personal interview. Santiago, February 12, 2002.
Human Rights Watch. *Los límites de la tolerancia: Libertad de expresión y debate público en Chile*. Santiago: LOM Ediciones, 1998.
Huyssen, Andreas. "Present Pasts: Media, Politics, Amnesia." In *Globalization*, edited by Arjun Appadurai, 57–77. Durham: Duke University Press, 2001.
———. *Twilight Memories: Marking Time in a Culture of Amnesia*. New York: Routledge, 1995.
Independent. "The Personal is Political & Political is Personal Awards: Paulina & Chile: Obstinate Memory." April 1998.
"Informe de la comisión nacional sobre prisión política y tortura." http://www.gobiernodechile.cl/comision_valech/index.asp (accessed May 11, 2007).
"Informe de la comisión nacional sobre prisión política y tortura." http://www.comisiontortura.cl/listado_informes.html (accessed August 1, 2008).
Internet Movie Database. "Machuca (2004)." http://imdb.com/title/tt0378284/ (accessed July 20, 2007).
Iturrieta, Claudia. "Las Fosas." *El Siglo*, March 7, 2002.
Jalil F., Gazi. "Ex alumnus que inspiraron la película *Machuca* cuentan su experiencia." *La Tercera*, August 5, 2004.
Jelin, Elizabeth. *State Repression and the Labors of Memory*. Minneapolis: University of Minnesota Press, 2003.
Johnson, Glen M. "Performing Access: Tim Miller, Larry Sanders, and Jay Leno." *Text and Performance Quarterly* 18 (1998): 137–46.
Jonas, Stacie. "Pinochet: Fit to Be Tried." *Foreign Policy In Focus*, February 2005. http://www.fpif.org/papers/0502pinochet.html (accessed February 4, 2005).
José López, María. "Medina, Montes y *The Clinic*." *Qué Pasa*. http://www.quepasa.cl/medio/articulo/0,0,38039290_101111578_357835192,00.html (accessed June 17, 2008).
Kael, Pauline. Review of *The Battle of Chile*, directed by Patricio Guzmán. *New Yorker*, January 23, 1978.
Kaiser, Susana. *Postmemories of Terror: A New Generation Copes with the Legacy of the "Dirty War."* New York: Palgrave Macmillan, 2005.
Kennicott, Philip. "The Pinochet Case." *Washington Post*, December 13, 2002.
Kinsbruner, Jay. *Chile: A Historical Interpretation*. Evanston, IL: Harper & Row, 1973.

Kirmayer, Lawrence J. "Landscapes of Memory: Trauma, Narrative, and Dissociation." In *Tense Past: Cultural Essays in Trauma and Memory*, edited by Paul Antze and Michael Lambek, 173–98. New York: Routledge, 1996.
Klady, Leonard. Review of *Chile: Obstinate Memory*, directed by Patricio Guzmán. *Variety*, November 10–16, 1997.
Klawans, Stuart. "A Whole World Disappeared." *The Nation*, September 28, 1998.
Klinger, Barbara. *Melodrama and Meaning: History, Culture, and the Films of Douglas Sirk*. Bloomington: Indiana University Press, 1994.
KNIGHTLine International. "Ken Dermota—Overcoming Obstacles: Investigative Reporting Where There are Few Press Freedoms." Summer 2001.
Kornbluh, Peter. "The *El Mercurio* File: Secret Documents Shine New Light on How the CIA Used a Newspaper to Foment a Coup." *Columbia Journalism Review* (September–October 2003): 14–19.
Krauss, Clifford. "Pinochet Case Reviving Voices of the Tortured." *New York Times*, January 3, 2000.
Kuhn, Annette. *Family Secrets: Acts of Memory and Imagination*. New York: Verso, 1995.
———. "'That Day Did Last Me All My Life': Cinema Memory and Enduring Fandom." In *Identifying Hollywood Audiences: Cultural Identity and the Movies*, edited by Melvyn Stokes and Richard Maltby, 135–46. London: British Film Institute, 1999.
Lagos, Claudia, and Patrick J. McDonnell. "Fugitive Ex-General Stirs 'Dirty War' Animosities in Chile." *Los Angeles Times*, June 16, 2007. http://www.americas.org/item_32868 (accessed July 6, 2007).
Lagos G., Andrea. "Machuca pasa hambre." *The Clinic*, September 30, 2004.
Lagos Lira, Claudia. *Aborto en Chile*. Santiago: LOM Ediciones, 2001.
Landau, Saul, and Sarah Anderson. "Payout for Pinochet Victims Shines in Dark Times for Human Rights." *ZNet*, March 16, 2005. http://www.fpif.org/pdf/gac/0503pinochet.pdf (accessed December 24, 2008).
Larroulet, Cristián, ed. *The Chilean Experience: Private Solutions to Public Problems*. Washington, DC: Center for International Private Enterprise, 1993.
Larsen, Neil. "The Cultural Studies Movement and Latin America: An Overview." In *The Latin American Cultural Studies Reader*, edited by Ana del Sarto, Alicia Ríos, and Abril Trigo, 728–35. Durham, NC: Duke University Press, 2004.
Lazzara, Michael J. "The Poetics of Impossibility: Diamela Eltit's *El Padre Mío*." Prepared for SUNY Albany's "Democracy in Latin America: Thirty Years after Chile's 9/11," conference, Albany, NY, October 10, 2003.
Leal V., Angelina. "Nuevo Canal 24 Horas parte en enero." *La Nación*, December 9, 2008. http://www.lanacion.cl/prontus_noticias_v2/site/artic/20081208/pags/20081208200216.html (accessed December 26, 2008).
León-Dermota, Ken. *. . . And Well Tied Down: Chile's Press Under Democracy*. Westport, CT: Praeger, 2003.
Lescornez, Macarena R. "La Crítica española aplaude el estreno mundial de 'Machuca.'" *El Mercurio*, June 12, 2004.
Leyton, Rodrigo. Personal interview. Santiago, March 26, 2002.
Lopez, Ana M. "*The Battle of Chile*: Documentary, Political Process, and Representation." In *The Social Documentary in Latin America*, edited by Julianne Burton, 267–87. Pittsburgh: University of Pittsburgh Press, 1990.

Loveman, Brian. *Chile: The Legacy of Hispanic Capitalism.* New York: Oxford University Press, 2001.
Lull, James. *China Turned On: Television, Reform, and Resistance.* New York: Routledge, 1991.
Macari, Mirko. "Chilean Media Work in the Long Shadow of Pinochet." *Nieman Reports* 53, no. 2 (Summer 1999): 33–35.
Mankekar, Purnima. *Screening Culture, Viewing Politics: An Ethnography of Television, Womanhood, and Nation in Postcolonial India.* Durham, NC: Duke University Press, 1999.
Marré, Ximena, Rodrigo Lara, and Hernán Ávalos. "Schaefer en Buenos Aires: El fin de una larga clandestinidad." *ElMercurio.com*, March 11, 2005. http://diario.elmercurio.cl/detalle/index.asp?id=%7B79267bd8-953c-4c54-bc18-6ede32434484%7D (accessed March 11, 2005).
Mast, Gerald, and Marshall Cohen, eds. "A Collective Text by the Editors of *Cahiers du cinema*: John Ford's *Young Mr. Lincoln.*" In *Film Theory and Criticism: Introductory Readings*, 2nd ed., 778–831. New York: Oxford University Press, 1979.
Mathews, Jack. "From Chile, a Coup of a Different Variety." *New York Daily News*, January 19, 2005. http://www.nydailynews.com/archives/entertainment/2005/01/19/2005-01-19_from_chile__a_coup_of_a_diff.html (accessed March 1, 2006).
Matus, Alejandra. *El libro negro de la justicia chilena.* Buenos Aires: Editorial Planeta Argentina S.A.I.C., 1999.
Matus, Alejandra, and Marcela Ramos. "Spiniak B." In *Las lecciones de los medios*, edited by Abraham Santibáñez and Pablo Vildósola, 27–30. Santiago: University of Diego Portales School of Journalism, 2005.
May, Catalina. "'Todos los rostros de la dictadura hoy tienen voz.'" *The Clinic*, January 10, 2007.
McSherry, J. Patrice. *Predatory States: Operation Condor and Covert War in Latin America.* New York: Rowman & Littlefield, 2005.
Mena, Rosario. "Andrés Wood, director de Machuca: 'El clasismo hoy es más exacerbado que en esos días.'" *Nuestro.cl*, August 2004. http://www.nuestro.cl/notas/noticias/machuca.htm (accessed March 1, 2006).
———. "Los herederos de la prensa satírica." *Nuestro.cl*, August 2003. http://www.nuestro.cl/notas/rescate/clinic1.htm (accessed July 4, 2008).
Mendez, Juan M. "Recuerdos de un golpe de estado, 25 años después." *El Diario*, September 11, 1998.
El Mercurio. "72° aniversario de la Fuerza Aérea." March 22, 2002.
———. "Benavides cumple arresto domiciliario." February 23, 2005.http://diario.elmercurio.cl/detalle/index.asp?id={3f0f3d97-81f0-438f-b522-654da9b46fce (accessed December 24, 2008).
———. "Causas de desaparecidos: Rechazan excluir al programa de DD.HH." April 12, 2002.
———. "Envían a Texas restos óseos del Patio 29." June 24, 2008. http://diario.elmercurio.com/2008/06/24/nacional/nacional/noticias/impresion-B56FA556- (accessed June 24, 2008).
———. "Familiares de Prats y Schneider van a traspaso." March 7, 2002.
———. "Festival: Filmes chilenos en Montevideo." March 22, 2002.
———. "'La Nación': Presión de PS y PPD gatilla salida de director." March 22, 2002.

———. "Nueva crisis en el SML." June 22, 2006.
———. "Peritos del SML declararán en juicio contra hijo de nuevo director." June 22, 2006.
———. "Querella contra periodistas." July 3, 2008. http://diario.elmercurio.com/2008/07/03/nacional/nacional/noticias/impresionAD778B12 (accessed July 3, 2008).
———. "Sepultan restos de ejecutado en 1973." February 10, 2002.
Miranda, Rodrigo. "Cine: El género documental explora por primera vez el discurso pinochetista." *El Mercurio*, March 30, 2002.
———. "Machuca rompe marca como la cinta chilena más vista en su primer día." *La Tercera*, August 7, 2004.
Molina Sanhueza, Jorge. "Cómo se gestó la detención de Paul Schäfer en Buenos Aires." *La Nación.cl*, March 11, 2005. http://www.lanacion.cl/prontus_noticias/site/artic/20050310/pags/2005 (accessed March 11, 2005).
Montecinos, C., and V. Mondaca. "Cancillería dice que exhortos los decide el Poder Judicial." *La Nación*, February 22, 2002.
Moraga L., Marcos. "No tengo nada que celebrar." *La Nación*, August 18, 2008. http://www.lanacion.cl/prontus_noticias_v2/site/artic/20080817/pags/20080817202556.html (accessed August 18, 2008).
Morley, Dave. "Texts, readers, subjects." In *Culture, Media, Language: Working Papers in Cultural Studies, 1972–79*, edited by Stuart Hall, Dorothy Hobson, Andrew Lowe, and Paul Willis, 163–73. Birmingham, AL: Center for Contemporary Cultural Studies, 1980.
Morley, David, and Charlotte Brunsdon. *The Nationwide Television Studies*. London: British Film Institute, 1980. New York: Routledge, 1999.
Mouesca, Jacqueline. *Plano secuencia de la memoria de Chile: Veinticinco años de cine chileno (1960–1985)*. Madrid: Ediciones del Litoral, 1988.
Mouesca, Jacqueline, and Carlos Orellana. *Cine y memoria del siglo XX*. Santiago: LOM Ediciones, 1998.
Muga, Ana. "Patricia Silva, Presidenta de la AFEP: 'Aún no tenemos razones para confiar en la justicia.'" *El Siglo*, Feburary 15, 2002.
Mujica, Enrique. "Periodismo web en Chile: En búsqueda de su ADN." In *Las Lecciones de los Medios*, edited by Abraham Santibáñez and Pablo Vildósola, 131–36. Santiago: University of Diego Portales School of Journalism, 2005.
Mujica Olea, Alejandro. "Carta abierta a Michelle Bachelet." *El Siglo*, February 8, 2002.
Muñoz, Ernesto, and Darío Burotto. *Filmografía del cine chileno*. Santiago: Ediciones Museo de Arte Contemporáneo, Facultad de Arte, Universidad de Chile, 1988.
La Nación. "Carmen Hertz ratifica responsabilidad penal de ex ministros de Pinochet." February 23, 2005. http://www.lanacion.cl/prontus_noticias/site/artic/20050223/pags/20050223093430.html (accessed December 26, 2008).
———. "Colombo: Corte otorga libertad a 16 procesados." June 6, 2008. http://www.lnd.cl/prontus_noticias_v2/site/artic/20080605/pags/20080605223309.html (accessed June 6, 2008).
———. "Corte marcial rechaza impugnación de jueza exclusiva." May 3, 2002.
———. "Corte rechaza seis recursos de amparo de procesados en Operación Colombo." June 5, 2008. http://www.lanacion.cl/prontus_noticias_v2/site/artic/20080604/pags/20080604213727.html (accessed June 5, 2008).

———. "DD.HH.: Jefe del Ejército descarta salida de Bustos." July 18, 2008. http://www.lanacion.cl/prontus_noticias_v2/site/artic/20080718/pags/20080718112929.html (accessed July, 19 2008).

———. "Las dos caras en la muerte de Pinochet." December 8, 2007. http://www.lanacion.cl/prontus_noticias_v2/site/artic/20071204/pags/20071204160213.html (accessed June 18, 2008).

———. "Especial: Un año sin Pinochet," December 8, 2007. http://www.lanacion.cl/prontus_noticias_v2/site/artic/20071205/pags/20071205131014.html (accessed June 18, 2008).

———. "El intrincado nexo entre los detenidos desaparecidos de 1987, el secuestro del coronel Carreño y el tráfico de armas." July 19, 2008. http://www.lanacion.cl/prontus_noticias_v2/site/artic/20080718/pags/20080718162103.html (accessed July 20, 2008).

———. "Lavín: Destaca actitud de 'hombre' y la integridad de Sergio Fernández." February 23, 2005. http://www.lanacion.cl/prontus_noticias/site/artic/20050223/pags/20050223133448.html (accessed February 23, 2005).

———. "Machuca desplaza a costosa cinta *Yo, Robot*." August 18, 2004.

———. "Niegan excarcelación de carabinero (R)." February 7, 2002.

———. "Los nudos de la dictadura: Carreño, Famae, Karin Eitel y los cinco." July 18, 2008. http://www.rie.cl/lanacioncl/?a=106404 (accessed July, 19 2008).

———. "Procesan a general (R) de la FACH." February 7, 2002.

———. "El pueblo desbordó las calles para despedir a Gladis Marín." March 8, 2005. http://www.lanacion.cl/prontus_noticias/site/artic/20050308/pags/20050308082720.html (accessed March 8, 2005).

———. "Renunció Administradora de Cine en Osorno." August 10, 2004.

———. "Sinclair seguirá recluido al menos hasta el lunes." July 18, 2008. http://www.rie.cl/lanacioncl/?a=106361 (accessed July 19, 2008).

———. "SML envía a EEUU muestras de ADN de desaparecidos." June 24, 2008. http://www.lanacion.cl/prontus_noticias_v2/site/artic/20080623/pags/20080623211418.html (accessed June 24, 2008).

Navarro, Patricia (daughter). "Detenido desaparecido: El embelequero." *The Clinic*, April 4, 2002.

New York Times. "Gladis Marín, 63, Opponent of Pinochet Dictatorship in Chile, Dies." March 7, 2005. http://www.nytimes.com/2005/03/07/obituaries/07marin.html (accessed March 7, 2005).

Newcomb, Horace, ed. *Television: The Critical View*. 5th ed. New York: Oxford University Press, 1994.

Nichols, Bill. *Representing Reality: Issues and Concepts in Documentary*. Bloomington: Indiana University Press, 1991.

Nordenstreng, Kaarle, and Herbert Schiller, eds. *Beyond National Sovereignty: International Communication in the 1990s*. Norwood, NJ: Ablex, 1993.

Núñez, Iván. Personal interview. Santiago, July 16, 2003.

Oliva García, Julio. "Derechos humanos: Los avances de la ofensiva militar." *El Siglo*, May 10, 2002.

———. "Derechos humanos: La conspiración contra los Jueces Especiales." *El Siglo*, March 29, 2002.

———. "Manuel Ahumada, sobreviviente de Cerro Chena: 'Yo estuve con los ferroviarios fusilados.'" *El Siglo*, April 5, 2002.

———. "Los torturadores de Tejas Verdes." *El Siglo*, February 1, 2002.

———. "Tribunales de justicia: El retorno de los generales." *El Siglo*, April 12, 2002.

———. "Walter Araya, torturado en Copiapó en 1988: 'Cheyre nos negó ante el Obispo Ariztía.'" *El Siglo*, March 15, 2002.

Oliva García, Julio, and María Luz Zacconi Palacín. "Doctor Adam Schesch, sobreviviente del Estadio Nacional: 'Los fusilados fueron al menos 400.'" *El Siglo*, May 24, 2002.

Oppenheim, Lois Hecht. *Politics in Chile: Democracy, Authoritarianism, and the Search for Development*. Boulder, CO: Westview, 1993.

———. *Politics in Chile: Socialism, Authoritarianism, and Market Democracy*. 3rd ed. Boulder, CO: Westview, 2007.

Ormeño, José. Chilean Commission of Human Rights. Personal interview. Santiago, March 21, 2002.

Orrego, Claudio. "Los herederos de Machuca." *La Tercera*, August 15, 2004.

Ortolani, Diego. Funa Commission. Personal interview. Santiago, May 7, 2002.

Ossa Coo, Carlos. *Historia del cine chileno*. Santiago: Empresa Editora Nacional Quimantu Limitada, 1971.

Ossandón, Fernando, and Sandra Rojas. *La epoca y Fortín Mapocho: El primer impacto*. Santiago: ECO-CEDAL, 1989.

Otano, Rafael. "Una opaca transparencia." In *Las Lecciones de los Medios*, edited by Abraham Santibáñez and Pablo Vildósola, 125–29. Santiago: University of Diego Portales School of Journalism, 2005.

Oyarzo L., Quintín. "Fin a denominación 'capitán general.'" *La Nación*, February 22, 2002.

Pavez, Cristián. "Amante Eledín Parraguez: 'Machuca' y el sueño de 'la integración.'" *El Siglo*, September 10, 2004.

Peralto, Álvaro. "Cuando Pérez Yoma quiso machucar a Víctor Jara." *The Clinic*, September 2, 2004, 19.

Pérez G., Ximena. "Carroza otorga libertad a general ® Sinclair." *Elmercurio.cl*, July 19, 2008. http://diario.elmercurio.com/2008/07/19/nacional/nacional/noticias/impresion5752E802- (accessed July 19, 2008).

———. "Condenan a Schaefer a 3 años de cárcel." *Elmercurio.com*, July 3, 2008. http://diario.elmercurio.com/2008/07/03/nacional/_portada/noticias/impresion9DC15D85(accessed July 3, 2008).

Pérez Guerra, Arnoldo. "'Cheyre destruyó nuestras vidas.'" *El Siglo*, March 22, 2002.

———. "La 'doble desaparición' de los ejecutados de La Moneda." *El Siglo*, May 3, 2002.

———. "El testimonio de Luisa Stagno: 'Varias veces me violaron y aplicaron corriente en la parrilla . . . '" *El Siglo*, February 1, 2002.

———. "Violaciones a los derechos humanos: La responsabilidad de Cheyre." *El Siglo*, March 15, 2002.

Petras, James F. *Latin America: Bankers, Generals, and the Struggle for Social Justice*. Totowa, NJ: Rowman & Littlefield, 1986.

Petras, James, and Fernando Ignacio Leíva. *Democracy and Poverty in Chile: The Limits to Electoral Politics*. Boulder, CO: Westview, 1994.

Pick, Zuzana. "Chilean Documentary: Continuity and Disjunction." In *The Social Documentary n Latin America*, edited by Julianne Burton, 109–30. Pittsburgh, PA: University of Pittsburgh Press, 1990.

———. *The New Latin American Cinema: A Continental Project*. Austin: University of Texas Press, 1993.

Pilquil, Elizabeth. Personal conversations. Santiago, 2006–2008.

Pilquil, Mónica. Personal conversations and e-mail correspondence. Santiago, 2006–2008.

Pino, Soledad. "Alejandro Amenábar, Director de Cine Chileno-Español: 'Machuca me ha gustado muchísimo.'" *The Clinic*, September 16, 2004.

Pizarro, Claudio. "La dictadura habló a través de la Bolocco." *The Clinic*, May 31, 2007.

Pizarro Fernández, Rodrigo. "La vigencia de los desaparecidos de El Salvador." July 19, 2008. *Lanacion.cl*. http://www.lanaciondomingo.cl/prontus_noticias_v2/site/artic/20080718/pags/20080718155420.html (accessed July 19, 2008).

Poblete, Juan. "Culture, Neo-Liberalism and Citizen Communication: The Case of Radio Tierra in Chile." *Global Media and Communication* 2 (2006): 315–34.

Porteous, Clinton. "Fugitive Chile Cult Leader Held." *BBC News*, March 11, 2005. http://news/bbc.co.uk/go/pr/fr/-/2/hi/americas/4338825.stm (accessed December 26, 2008).

Publimetro. "Suprema interviene en caso Patio 29." June 17, 2006.

R., M. "¿Quieren terminar con la delincuencia? Legalicen el aborto." *The Clinic*, June 29, 2006.

Radio Tierra. http://www.radiotierra.com/ (accessed May 25, 2007).

"Rating Minuto a Minuto." Martes 15/7/2003. Rating Todos. Canal: 11. Programa: EL TERMOMETRO.

Rechtshaffen, Michael. "Machuca." *Hollywood Reporter*, November 5, 2004. http://hollywoodreporter.printthis.clickability.com/pt/cpt?action=cpt&title=Machuca&ex (accessed March 1, 2006).

Remedi, Gustavo A. "The Production of Local Public Spheres: Community Radio Stations." In *The Latin American Cultural Studies Reader*, edited by Ana del Sarto, Alicia Ríos, and Abril Trigo, 513–34. Durham, NC: Duke University Press, 2004.

Rendall, Steve. "*Missing* the Chile Story at the *New York Times*." *Extra!: The newsletter of FAIR (Fairness and Accuracy in Reporting)* (May–June 2000): 22.

Richard, Nelly. *Cultural Residues: Chile in Transition*. Minneapolis: University of Minnesota Press, 2004.

———. "Intersecting Latin America with Latin Americanism: Academic Knowledge, Theoretical Practice, and Cultural Criticism." In *The Latin American Cultural Studies Reader*, edited by Ana del Sarto, Alicia Ríos, and Abril Trigo, 686–705. Durham, NC: Duke University Press, 2004.

Riding, Alan. "Telling Chile's Story, Even if Chile Has Little Interest." *New York Times*, October 3, 2002.

Ripley, Regina. "The United States Involvement in Chile's Coup of 1973 as Interpreted Through *The Execution of Charles Horman: An American Sacrifice*." Graduate presentation. Indiana University, Bloomington, IN, 1996.

Rojas, Ana. Association of Relatives of the Detained-Disappeared. Personal interview. Santiago, May 23, 2002.

———. Personal conversations. Santiago, 2002–2006.

Roniger, Luis, and Mario Sznajder: *The Legacy of Human-Rights Violations in the Southern Cone: Argentina, Chile, and Uruguay.* New York: Oxford University Press, 1999.
Rooney, David. "Machuca." *Variety*, May 25, 2004. http://www.variety.com/ac2005_review/VE1117923951?nav=reviews&categoryid=1798 (accessed March 1, 2006).
Ruiz Cerda, Enrique, and María Olga Cabello López. "Siempre presentes: Edith en la Cuesta." *El Siglo*, February 15, 2002.
Russell, Adrienne. "Local Struggle in a Global Environment: Computer Mediated Communication and the Zapatista Movement." PhD diss. (Defense Draft). Indiana University, March 6, 2001.
Salazar, Carlos J. "Errores en el Patio 29: Nadie sabe más que los muertos." *El Sur*, May 2, 2006 http://www.elsur.cl/edicion_hoy/secciones/ver_rep.php?id=2662&dia=1146542400 (accessed November 20, 2007).
Santa Cruz A., Eduardo. *Analisis historico del periodismo chileno.* Santiago: Nuestra América Ediciones, 1988.
Santibáñez, Abraham, ed. *Doce diarios regionales: Una semana construida.* Santiago: National Association of the Press and University of Diego Portales School of Journalism, 2005.
———. *Entre el horror y la esperanza.* Santiago: Edebé, 2003.
———. Personal interview. Santiago, May 8, 2002.
Santibáñez, Abraham, and Pablo Vildósola, eds. *Las lecciones de los medios.* Santiago: University of Diego Portales School of Journalism, 2005.
Schiattino, Roberto. "Lenin Guardia: 'López Candia logró engañarme.'" *El Mercurio*, April 12, 2002.
Schiller, Herbert I. *Culture, Inc.: The Corporate Takeover of Public Expression.* New York: Oxford University Press, 1991.
———. *The Ideology of International Communications.* New York: Institute for Media Analysis, 1992.
———. *Mass Communications and American Empire.* 2nd ed. Boulder, CO: Westview Press, 1992.
Scott, A. O. "'Machuca': History Through the Eyes of a Frightened Child." *New York Times*, January 19, 2005. http://movies2.nytimes.com/2005/01/19/movies/19mach.html?ei=5070&en=943abaa4c2e (accessed March 1, 2006).
Senerman, Nicole. "El día en que murió Pinochet." 2006. http://www.ics.cl/icsweb/movs/El_dia_en_que_murio_Pinochet.mov (accessed May 11, 2007).
———. Personal e-mail interview. May 17, 2007.
Sepúlveda, Carmen. "Breaking news." *La Nación*, November 9, 2008. http://www.lanacion.cl/prontus_noticias_v2/site/artic/20081108/pags/20081108192922.html (accessed December 26, 2008).
Sepúlveda C., Alfredo. "Los 'Machucazos' de Wood." *Wikén; Revistas El Mercurio* 6 (August 2004): 6–9.
Serra, Sonia. "The Killing of Brazilian Street Children and the Rise of the International Public Sphere." In *Media Organisations in Society*, edited by James Curran, 151–72. London: Arnold, 2000.
Siavelis, Peter M. "Executive-Legislative Relations in Post-Pinochet Chile: A Preliminary Assessment." In *Presidentialism and Democracy in Latin America*, edited by Scott Mainwaring and Matthew Soberg Shugart, 321–62. Cambridge: Cambridge University Press, 1997.

El Siglo. "A 11 años del Informe Rettig, exigimos verdad y justicia." March 1, 2002.

———. "AFEP por la Verdad y la Justicia." Announcement for a demonstration for 'truth and justice' by the Association of Relatives of the Executed Political Prisoners. March 15, 2002.

———. "Aportando al rescate de la memoria: Nuevo sitio web de derechos humanos." April 12, 2002.

———. "Campaña por el procesamiento de Pinochet en EE.UU." May 10, 2002.

———. "Carta de General Bachelet a su hijo: '. . . Traiciones de personas que uno creía que eran sus amigos.'" February 8, 2002.

———. "Cheyre sabe como se dice tortura en inglés, castellano y francés: Ahora estudia mapudungún, el que no aprendió en los diecisiete años del general." *Margarita* cartoon, March 28, 2002.

———. "Cheyre y la censura." April 12, 2002.

———. "Combatientes por la vida, constructores de la libertad." June 23, 2006.

———. "Continúa paro en el servicio médico legal." June 23, 2006.

———. "Escuela de Caballeria." February 15, 2002.

———. "Funa a Cheyre." March 22, 2002.

———. "Funa el 22." March 15, 2002.

———. "Funa en Cerrillos." May 3, 2002.

———. "Funa por Daniel Menco Prieto: 'Tu nombre está en las calles gritando libertad.'" May 24, 2002.

———. "Hallazgos de osamentas en Melipilla," February 15, 2002.

———. "Hasta ahora nadie se ha acordado de indemnizar a todo el país por el bombardeo de La Moneda: Malversación como esa no hay otra!" *Margarita* cartoon, February 21, 2002.

———. "Homenaje a los héroes de Calle Conferencia," May 10, 2002.

———. "Homenaje a Víctor Díaz." May 10, 2002.

———. "La Identidad de El Príncipe." http://www.elsiglo.cl/noticia.php?id=3578&sec=0&subsec=0&area=agencia&num=31 (accessed May 30, 2008).

———. "Luciano Fouilloux: Un operador descalificado." March 29, 2002.

———. "Marcha de los ex P.P." March 22, 2002.

———. "Marcha de exonerados políticos." April 5, 2002.

———. "Mucho más caros que los F-16 le resultaron al país los P-17 (los 17 de Pinochet, papito de la UDI)." *Margarita* cartoon, February 21, 2002.

———. "Nuevos procesados por desaparecidos." February 8, 2002.

———. "Nueva querella criminal contra Pinochet." February 15, 2002.

———. "Otro funado muerde el polvo." January 25, 2002.

———. "Otro triunfo de la FUNA." May 10, 2002.

———. "Viven Guerrero, Nattino y Parada en la conciencia de Chile," April 4, 2002.

———. "¿Y qué pasó con la objetividad?" April 26, 2002.

Smith, Russell Scott. "Chile Tale a Real Coup." *New York Post*, January 19, 2005. http://www.nypost.com/movies/38377.htm (accessed March 1, 2006).

Spigel, Lynn, and Michael Curtin, eds. *The Revolution Wasn't Televised: Sixties Television and Social Conflict*. New York: Routledge, 1997.

Sragow, Michael. Review of *Chile: Obstinate Memory*, directed by Patricio Guzmán. *New Yorker*, September 14, 1998.

Sreberny-Mohammadi, Annabelle. "The Many Cultural Faces of Imperialism." In *Beyond Cultural Imperialism: Globalization, Communication and the New International Order*, edited by Peter Golding and Phil Harris, 49–68. Thousand Oaks, CA: Sage, 1997.

Sreberny-Mohammadi, Annabelle, and Ali Mohammadi. *Small Media, Big Revolution: Communication, Culture, and the Iranian Revolution*. Minneapolis: University of Minnesota Press, 1994.

———. "Small Media and Revolutionary Change: A New Model." In *Media in Global Context: A Reader*, edited by Sreberny-Mohammadi et al., 220–35. New York: Arnold, 1997.

Staiger, Janet. *Interpreting Films: Studies in the Historical Reception of American Cinema*. Princeton, NJ: Princeton University Press, 1992.

Stern, Steve J. *Battling for Hearts and Minds: Memory Struggles in Pinochet's Chile, 1973–1988*. Durham, NC: Duke University Press, 2006.

———. "De la memoria suelta a la memoria emblemática: Hacia el recorder y el olvidar como proceso histórico (Chile, 1973–1998)." In *Memoria para un nuevo siglo: Chile, miradas a la segunda mitad del siglo XX*, edited by Mario Garcés, Pedro Milos, Myriam Olguín, Julio Pinto, María Teresa Rojas, and Miguel Urrutia, 11–33. Santiago: LOM Ediciones, 2000.

———. *Remembering Pinochet's Chile: On the Eve of London, 1998*. Durham, NC: Duke University Press, 2004.

Stone, Judy. "Passionate Documentary on the Chilean Coup." *San Francisco Chronicle*, April 20, 1977.

Storey, John. *An Introduction to Cultural Theory and Popular Culture*. 2nd ed. Athens: University of Georgia Press, 1998.

Straubhaar, Joseph D. "Distinguishing the Global, Regional and National Levels of World Television." In *Media in Global Context: A Reader*, edited by Sreberny-Mohammadi, Annabelle et al., 284–98. New York: Arnold, 1997.

Streeter, Thomas. *Selling the Air: A Critique of the Policy of Commercial Broadcasting in the United States*. Chicago: University of Chicago Press, 1996.

Sturken, Marita. *Tangled Memories: The Vietnam War, the AIDS Epidemic, and the Politics of Remembering*. Berkeley: University of California Press, 1997.

———. *Tourists of History: Memory, Kitsch, and Consumerism from Oklahoma City to Ground Zero*. Durham: Duke University Press, 2007.

Sunkel, Guillermo. "La prensa en la transición chilena." In *Prensa y transición democrática: Experiencias recientes en Europa y América Latina*, edited by Carlos H. Filgueira and Dieter Nohlen, 160–77. Madrid: Egartorre Libros, 1994.

Tanner, Eliza. "Chilean Conversations: Internet Forum Participants Debate Augusto Pinochet's Detention." *Journal of Communication* 51, no. 2 (June 2001): 383–403.

Tanner Hawkins, Eliza. "Creating a National Strategy for Internet Development in Chile." *Telecommunications Policy* 29 (2005): 351–65.

Taylor, Diana. *The Archive and the Repertoire: Performing Cultural Memory in the Americas*. Durham, NC: Duke University Press, 2003.

———. *Disappearing Acts: Spectacles of Gender and Nationalism in Argentina's "Dirty War."* Durham, NC: Duke University Press, 1997.

Teletrece Internet. "Cinco altos oficiales del Ejército procesados por caso Huber." August 12, 2008. http://teletrece.canal13.cl/t13/html/Noticias/Chile/351126Iimprimirq1.html (accessed August 13, 2008).

La Tercera. "Corte de apelaciones rechaza recursos de amparo en Operación Colombo." June 5, 2008. http://www.latercera.cl/contenido/25_18670_9.shtml (accessed June 5, 2008).
———. "Cúpula de la DINA fue sometida a careos." February 14, 2002.
———. "Eliminada la censura cinematográfica en Chile." October 31, 2002. http://www.tercera.cl/diario/2002/10/31/42.CUL.CENSURA_OT.html (accessed October 31, 2002).
———. "Familias de víctimas de caso Rinconada de Maipú presentaron querella contra periodistas." July 3, 2008. http://www.latercera.cl/contenido/25_27049_9.shtml (accessed July 3, 2008).
———. "Fotógrafo Ricardo Portugueis recibió premio Rodrigo Rojas Denegri 2008." August 16, 2008. http://www.latercera.cl/contenido/29_40252_9.shtml (accessed Aug. 16, 2008).
———. "Kissinger cancela visita a Brasil por temor a protestas en su contra." February 27, 2002.
———. "Machuca supera los 59 mil espectadores." August 10, 2004.
———. "Paul Schaefer es condenado a tres años por infracción a la ley de control de armas en Colonia Dignidad." http://www.latercera.cl/contenido/25_27080_9.shtml (accessed July 3, 2008).
Time. "Chile: The Expanding Left." October 19, 1970.
Tironi, Eugenio. "Fin de un silencio." *La Tercera*, August 8, 2004.
Tomlinson, John. *Cultural Imperialism: A Critical Introduction*. Baltimore: Johns Hopkins University Press, 1991.
———. *Globalization and Culture*. Chicago: University of Chicago Press, 1999.
Torres López, Pía. "La película perdida del cura Hasbún." *The Clinic*, April 5, 2007.
Turan, Kenneth. "'Machuca': Although set in Chile in the 1970s, this story of children swept into a vortex of terrible events is universal." *Los Angeles Times*, April 29, 2005. http://www.calendarlive.com/movies/turan/cl-et-machuca29apr29,2,5737381.story (accessed March 1, 2006).
Turow, Joseph. *Breaking Up America: Advertisers and the New Media World*. Chicago: University of Chicago Press, 1997.
TVN Web site. "Reabren causa por Víctor Jara." June 3, 2008. http://noticias.tvn.cl/detalle_imprimir.aspx?IdC=253461&IdS=2 (accessed June 4, 2008).
Valdés, Hernán. *Tejas Verdes: Diario de un campo de concentración en Chile*. Santiago: LOM Ediciones, 1996.
Valenzuela, J. Samuel, and Arturo Valenzuela, eds. *Military Rule in Chile: Dictatorship and Oppositions*. Baltimore: Johns Hopkins University Press, 1986.
Varas A., Lidice. "Machuca Apuesta por el Cine." *La Nación Domingo*, August 8–14, 2004.
Vejar, Patricio. Personal interview. Santiago, May 9, 2002.
Vera, Luís R. "*Fiestapatria*: ¿Censura o calificación?" *The Clinic*, April 5, 2007.
Verdugo, Patricia, ed. *De la tortura no se habla: Agüero versus Meneses*. Santiago: Catalonia, 2004.
Villalobos Vergara, César. "Leonardo 'Barba' Schneider: El agente clave en la desarticulación del MIR." *El Siglo*, May 3, 2002.
Volk, Steven. "Seeking Justice in Chile: A Personal History." http://www.oberlin.edu/news-info/observations/observations_steven_volk1.html (accessed August 13, 2008).

White, Bill. "Machuca." *Seattle Post-Intelligencer*, January 13, 2006. http://seattlepi.nwsource.com/printer2/index.asp?ploc=b&refer=http://seattlepi.nwsource (accessed March 1, 2006).

Wikipedia. "Londres 38, Cuartel Yucatán." http://es.wikipedia.org/wiki/Londres_38 (accessed July 30, 2008 and December 24, 2008; page last modified on December 15, 2008).

Wiley, Stephen B. Crofts. "Assembled Agency: Media and Hegemony in the Chilean Transition to Civilian Rule." *Media, Culture & Society* 28, no. 5 (2006): 671–93.

———. "Transnation: Globalization and the Reorganization of Chilean Televisión in the Early 1990s." *Journal of Broadcasting & Electronic Media* 50, no. 3 (September 2006). http://findarticles.com/p/articles/mi_m6836/is_3_50/ai_n24999198/print (accessed May 30, 2008).

Wilmington, Michael. "Movie review: 'Machuca.'" *Chicago Tribune*. http://www.chicagotribune.com/entertainment/movies/mmx-0501208-movies-review-machuca,0,7776144.story (aaccessed March 1, 2006).

Wright, Thomas C. *State Terrorism in Latin America: Chile, Argentina, and International Human Rights*. New York: Rowman & Littlefield, 2007.

Wright, Thomas C., and Rody Oñate. *Flight from Chile: Voices of Exile*. Albuquerque: University of New Mexico Press, 1998.

Wilkinson, Kenton T. "Cultural Policy in a Free Trade Environment: Mexican Television in Transition." *Journal of Broadcasting and Electronic Media* 50, no. 3 (September 2006): 482–501.

Wilkinson, Kenton T. "A Mexican-American Mediascape?" Presented at the National Communication Association conference, *Rethinking Communication within Changing Global Contexts*, June 28–30, 2007.

Young, James E. *The Texture of Memory: Holocaust Memorials and Meaning*. New Haven, CT: Yale University Press, 1993.

You Tube. http://www.youtube.com/comment_servlet?all_comments&v=WgonGqUpdxs&fromurl=/watch%3Fv%3DWgonGqUpdxs (accessed February 6, 2008).

Zavala, Fernando. "Ariel Mateluna y Matías Quer: Las futures estrellas del cine chileno." *El Mercurio*, August 1, 2004.

———. "Lo de 'Machuca' ya es fenómeno." *El Mercurio*, August 10, 2004.

Zuñiga, Gabriela. Association of Relatives of the Detained-Disappeared. Personal interview. Santiago, May 23, 2002.

Index

abortion, 125
Acosta, Tamara, 86
advertising, 109, 115, 128, 148
Allende Gossens, Salvador, 2, 33, 54, 58, 83; and *Battle of Chile*, 77; and *Machuca*, 85; media coverage of, 10; and *El Mercurio*, 114; sponsorship of filmmakers, 59
Alliance coalition, 40
alternative media, 8–9, 17; and commercial media, 17, 149; documentary as, 58–59; print media, 109–10, 113, 118–32
Althusser, Louis, 34
Alvarado, Pablo, 41–44, 47, 52–53
Alvarado E., Rodrigo, 130
Alvarez, Gus, 92
amnesia, 20
Amnesty International, 17
Anderson, Benedict, 14, 105
Anderson, Sarah, 146
Appadurai, Arjun, 15
Arancibia, Nancy, 120
Argentina, 134
arpilleras, 12
Association of Relatives of the Detained-Disappeared (AFDD), 12, 26, 115; and *Fernando ha vuelto*, 63, 67; and *Machuca*, 99–101; media visibility of, 78; and public protest, 133–34
Atkinson, Michael, 97
Au Revoir Les Enfants, 98

Ávila, Benjamín, 136
Ayala, Ernesto, 94

Bachelet, Michelle, 2, 6, 8, 48, 70, 79, 111, 115, 125
Battle of Chile, The, 19, 53, 58, 75–77, 86, 133
Bayas, Hernan, 4
Bazuka.com, 65
Benaroyo Pencu, Monique Cristin, 127
Berman, M., 108
Bertolucci, Don, 66
bloggers, 128
Bolocco, Cecilia, 126
Brazil, 15–16
Bresnahan, Rosalind, 12
Britain, 117
broadcast networks, 37–39
Burr, Ty, 97
Burton, Julianne, 58–59
Bustamante Gómez, Héctor, 136
Bustos B., Ernesto, 93

cable television, 31–32
Caiozzi, Silvio, 27, 59–60, 62–65, 67, 72–73
Caldwell, John, 42, 54
camera images, 77, 102–3, 115
Canal 13, 37–38, 42, 125–26
Canal 24 Horas, 32, 51
Canepa, Marco, 66
CanWest Global Communications, 39
"Caravan of Death," 121

Carlson, A. Cheree, 123
Carmona, Ernesto, 114, 117–18, 136
Carter, Jimmy, 112
Catholic Church, 38, 111, 125
Catholic Organization of Cinema, 62
Catholic University of Chile, 37–38
Caucato, Nelson, 51
Cavallo, Ascanio, 79, 81
censorship, 17–18; film, 79; and globalization, 107–9, 131; print media, 106–7, 114, 117. *See also* self-censorship
Center for National Information (CNI), 112, 135
Central Intelligence Agency (CIA), 11, 22, 46
Chacal de Nahueltoro, El, 80
Chávez, Hugo, 46
Chelloveck, Prestoopnik, 67
Cheyre, Juan Emilio, 121
Chilean Commission of Human Rights, 1–2
Chile: Obstinate Memory, 19, 75, 143
Chilevisión, 20–21, 27, 37, 39–52; and Bachelet government, 49; *Ciento*, 52; control and ownership of, 39–40; and DINA case, 53; self-promotional images, 40–41; *El Termómetro*, 41–50; viewer share, 42–43
China, 25–26
Ciento, 52
cinema, 76–81; censorship of, 79–80; funding for, 80–81; and national meaning, 102–3, 115; themes of, 81
Cisneros, Gustave, 39–40
Claro, Ricardo, 38–39
Claxson Interactive Group Inc., 40
Clinic, The, 1, 8, 27–28, 106, 109–10, 122–28, 149

CNN Chile, 31–32
Cohen, Marshall, 54
Colegio de Periodistas, 117
collective memory, 76. *See also* historical memory
Colonia Dignidad, 45, 119–20
commercial media, 17, 149. *See also* mainstream media
Concertación, 3
Conquergood, Dwight, 123
Conquistadores del fin del mundo, 41
Consorcio Periodístico de Chile S. A. (COPESA), 108
consumers; and alternative media, 8–9; social disarticulation of, 44
Contreras, Manuel, 121
COPESA media group, 39
Correa, Tiago, 85
Costa-Gavras, Constantin, 10–11
counterprogramming, 41–42
counterpublics, 16–17
Cuba, 57, 59
cueca sola, 134
cultural imperialism, 13–15
cultural memory, 77. *See also* historical memory
Curtin, Michael, 35–36, 54
Cuthbert, Sofia, 4

Day Pinochet Died, The, 2, 27, 68–72, 82–83
delinquency, 125
del Río, Matías, 43, 47–51
DeNegri, Claudio, 106, 109, 122, 131
detained-disappeared, 124–25, 128. *See also* Association of Relatives of the Detained-Disappeared (AFDD)
"Devastating End for a Unique, Troubled Venture," 10
día en que murió Pinochet, El, 2, 27, 68–72, 82–83
Díaz, Víctor, 53
Díaz, Victoria and Viviana, 53, 100

Díaz Palma, Fernando, 117
Dimter Bianchi, Edwin, 121
Directorate of National Information (DINA), 53, 112, 116
documentary, 57–73; as alternative media, 58–59; *Battle of Chile, The*, 19, 53, 58, 75–77, 86, 133; *Chile: Obstinate Memory*, 19, 75, 143; *día enque murió Pinochet, El*, 2, 27, 68–73, 82–83; and family memory, 57–58; *Fernando ha vuelto*, 27, 59–68; and human rights, 61–62, 73; and national consciousness, 57; and Pinochet regime, 59, 77–78; responses to, 67; witnessing technique, 62
Doordarshan, 26
Douzet, Pablo, 79, 81
Dubó, Luís, 87

Edwards family, 108, 114
Eledín Parraguez, Amante, 83–84, 90
emblematic memories, 20–22, 54, 65
"Encoding, Decoding," 24
"En la mira," 120
Escalante, Jorge, 119–20
Estadio Chile, 51

Fahrenheit 9/11, 57
Farias, Alvaro, 66
Fernández, Patricio, 106, 108, 122–23, 128–29, 131
Fernando ha vuelto, 27, 59–68; responses to, 62, 64–67, 73; structure of, 60–64
film festival, Vina del Mar, 58
films, 78–81. *See also* documentary; *Machuca*
Fondo Nacional de Desarrollo Cultural y las Artes (FONDART), 80

Fraser, Nancy, 16, 44, 148–49
Frei Montalva, Eduardo, 4, 40
Frei Ruiz-Tagle, Eduardo, 40, 51
Freud, Sigmund, 77
Funa organization, 28, 113–14, 135–37

Garcés, Juan, 146
García-Huidobro, Andrea, 85
García-Huidobro, Ricardo, 66
Garzón, Baltasar, 1, 146
geocultural market, 15
globalization, 11–16; and alternative/local cultures, 11, 14–15; benefits of, 13–14; and global cultural flow, 15; and international response to Chile, 146; and languages, 13; and media censorship, 107–9, 131
Global Media, The, 9
Gómez-Barris, Macarena, 22
González, Ángel, 39
Gripsrud, Jostein, 18
Guerra, Mónica, 114
Guillier, Alejandro, 30–32, 49, 51–52, 55, 112
Gutierrez, Pamela, 66
Guzmán, Jaime, 17
Guzmán, Patricio, 19, 58, 75, 82, 133, 143
Guzmán Tapia, Juan, 3, 22, 32, 145

Habermas, Jürgen, 15–16
Hall, Stuart, 24
Hasbún, Raúl, 125–26
Hauser, Thomas, 10
Henrichsen, Leonardo, 136
Henríquez, Jorge Tomás, 125
Herman, Edward, 9–11, 108
HIJOS-Chile, 135
Hiriart, Lucía, 2
historical memory, 18–27; emblematic memories, 20–22, 54, 65; and human rights, 23; and media omissions, 26–27,

historical memory (*continued*) 145; and media professionals, 144; and personal identity, 19; as power struggle, 24; and television, 25–26, 82; and visual media, 19–20, 76–77, 102–3
Hitchens, Christopher, 146
Hitler, Adolf, 57
homeless children, 16
Horman, Charles, 10, 22
Hormazábal, Guillermo, 106–7, 120
Hoy, 111
Huber, Gerardo, 21
human-interest stories, 124–25
human rights, 5–11, 150; and Catholic Church, 38; and documentary, 61–62, 73; and feature films, 78–79; and historical memory, 23; and print media, 109–11, 113–22, 129–31; and television, 30, 32–33, 37–39, 45, 49–50, 147
Huyssen, Andreas, 6, 75–76

Ibermedia, 80–81
images, 77, 102–3, 115, 127
"imagined community," 14
Independent Democrat Union (UDI) party, 40
India, 26
Insulza, José Miguel, 40
Interferences, 126
international film festivals, 58
Internet, 8–9, 12, 140, 151; and globalization, 15; and mainstream media, 72–73; newspaper outlets, 118, 129; online chat, 116; online films, 68; as programming grid, 72
Iran, 25
Iturriaga Neumann, Raúl, 4
Izurieta, Óscar, 4

Jara, Victor, 17, 51, 121, 135
Jelin, Elizabeth, 23–24, 72, 107
Jiménez, Tucapel, 119
John Paul II (pope), 113
Johnson, Glen M., 123
judicial cases; and international concern, 146; and mainstream media, 21–22; post-Pinochet, 4–5; TV coverage of, 38
juvenile delinquency, 125

Kaiser, Susana, 134, 141
Kandell, Jonathan, 10
Kennedy, Ted, 112
Khomeini, Ayatollah, 25
Kirmayer, Lawrence, 33
Kissinger, Henry, 116, 146
Krögh, Pablo, 89
Kuhn, Annette, 19
Küppenheim, Aline, 84

Lagos, Ricardo, 1, 33, 46, 116
Landau, Saul, 146
language; of Chilean television, 36–37; and imperialism, 13
Larraín, Pablo, 130
Latin America; documentaries in, 58; Spanish language media in, 15; and United States, 9–11, 46, 146
Lemmon, Jack, 10
León-Dermota, Ken, 38–39
Letelier, Orlando, 112, 119
Levitt, Steven, 125
LGBTQ issues, 50, 120
Littín, Miguel, 80
Londres 38, 28, 137–40
"los 199," 69
Lübbert, Orlando, 26, 82
Lull, James, 25
Luppi, Federico, 84

Macherey, Pierre, 147
Machuca, 27, 66, 75–103, 133; and AFDD, 99–101; Chilean

reception of, 83, 93–95, 102; Internet responses to, 98–99; synopsis, 84–92; U.S. reception of, 95–98, 102
mainstream media, 8–10; and Chilean coup, 10–11; and hegemonic domination, 149; and Internet, 72–73; and judicial coverage, 21–22; newspapers, 114–18; ownership of, 9, 34–35, 108–9. *See also* print media; television
Malbrán, Ernesto, 84
Malle, Louis, 98
Mankekar, Purnima, 26
"Many Faces of Cultural Imperialism, The," 13
Mapuche Indians, 113, 138
Marín, Gladys, 120
Martelli, Manuela, 85
Mast, Gerald, 54
Mateluna, Ariel, 84, 95
Matte, María Olga, 89
McChesney, Robert, 9–11, 108
media; agenda-setting function of, 6; and collective memory, 76; deregulation of, 12; geocultural market for, 15; globalization of, 11–16; and historical context, 18–19; and historical memory, 19–20, 76–77, 102–3; and human rights, 5–11, 145, 147; imperialism, 14–15; and nationalism, 14; ownership of, 34–35, 108–9, 148–49; and public sphere, 16–17; research, 150–51; self-censorship in, 18, 47, 50, 80, 107, 114; Western control of, 11–12. *See also* documentary; print media; television
media professionals, 144, 147–48, 150
Medina, Gabriela, 89
Megavisión, 37–39, 42

memory, 19, 101–2. *See also* historical memory
memory knots, 20–21, 82–83, 102, 144
memory remains, 143–45
memory symbolic, 22–23
Mena, Rosario, 93, 122–23
Mercurio, El, 21, 28, 103, 114–18; CIA funding of, 11; ownership of, 108–9; structured absences in, 26
Metrópolis-Intercom, 38
Missing, 10–11, 22
Moffitt, Ronni, 112, 119
Mohammadi, Ali, 25
Mondaca, V., 119
Moneda, La, 75, 88–89, 124, 144
Montecinos, C., 119
Moore, Michael, 57
Moraga L., Marcos, 130
Morande, Felipé, 51
Mothers of the Plaza de Mayo, 134
Movimiento Izquierda Revolucionario (MIR), 63, 90
Mujica, Enrique, 130
Müller Silva, Jorge, 53
museums, 75–76

Nación, La, 106, 109, 118–20
nation, concept of, 15
National Commission for Truth and Reconciliation, 4–5, 32
National Commission on Political Prison and Torture, 5
nationalism, 14
National Renovation Party, 40
newspapers; *The Clinic*, 1, 8, 27–28, 106, 109–10, 122–28, 149; *El Mercurio*, 11, 21, 26, 28, 103, 108–9, 114–18; on Internet, 118, 129; *La Nación*, 106, 109, 118–20; *La Tercera*, 21, 27–28, 39, 108–9, 114–18; *Las Últimas Noticias*, 114, 117

New World Information and
    Communication Order
    (NWICO), 11
New York Times, 10–11
Nichols, Bill, 57, 62
Non-Aligned Movement (NAM),
    11
Nueva Canción, 51
Núñez, Iván, 43, 46–47, 52

online chat, 116
*Orphaned and Lost: Chilean Cinema
    of the Transition 1990–1999*, 79
Orrego, Claudio, 101
Oyarzo L., Quintin, 119

Pascal Allende, Andrés, 90
Patio 29, 49, 67
Patria y Libertad, 88
Paulsen, Fernando, 51
Pavez, Cristián, 84, 90
Paz Santibáñez, María, 126
Pepsi, 11
Pilquil, Mónica, 99–100
Piñera, Sebastián, 27, 40, 47–49, 51
Pinochet Case, The, 82
Pinochet Ugarte, Augusto, 1–4,
    6, 8, 54; *Clinic* image of,
    127; death of, 2, 79–80, 111,
    145; detention in the United
    Kingdom, 1, 20, 22, 31–33,
    36, 122, 145; dictatorship of,
    29–30, 111–14; international
    connections, 146; and media
    ownership, 34–35; military
    coup of 1973, 2–3, 75, 83;
    La Nación coverage of, 119;
    television coverage of, 37–38,
    45–46, 77; *La Tercera* coverage
    of, 116–17
Pizarro, Claudio, 126
Pizarro, Macarena, 43, 47
Poblete, Juan, 12
police violence, 46, 135
polling, TV, 43

Popular Unity government, 59, 77,
    85–86
Portugueis, Ricardo, 27
Postmemories of Terror, 134
Prats, Carlos, 4
printing press, 105
print media, 105–32; alternative,
    109–10, 113, 118–32;
    censorship of, 106–9, 114, 117,
    131; and electronic media, 110;
    and globalization, 107–9, 131;
    and human rights, 109–11,
    113–22, 129–31; ownership of,
    108–9, 113; and photographs,
    115; and Pinochet dictatorship,
    111–14; practical constraints
    on, 105–6; and reader attitudes,
    130. *See also* newspapers
Protagonistas de la música en Bruto, 41
protests, 133–41; Funa
    organization, 135–37; locations
    of, 140; *Londres 38*, 137–40;
    student, 101
public sphere, 16–17, 149
Purdy, Frederick, 22

Quercia, Boris, 93

radio, 12
Reagan, Ronald, 12, 113
"reality" TV, 41
Red, La, 37, 39, 42
repression, psychological, 77
Rettig Report, 4–5, 32
Revolution Wasn't Televised, The,
    35–36
Reyes, Francisco, 84
Richard, Nelly, 78–79, 82
Riefenstahl, Leni, 57
Riggs Bank, 146
Rivera, Mireya, 99, 101
Rodíguez, Cecilia, 79, 81
Rojas DeNegri, Rodrigo, 27
Roniger, Luis, 30–31
Ruiz, Raúl, 125

Salas, Víctor, 130
Salvador Allende, 82
Sandoval Arancibia, Enrique, 135
San Martín Vergara, Luis, 4
Santibáñez, Abraham, 109–13, 130
Schäfer, Paul, 45, 119–20
Schiller, Herbert, 11
Scott, A. O., 97–98
screen memory, 77
self-censorship, 18, 47, 50; by filmmakers, 80; by journalists, 107, 114. *See also* censorship
Senerman, Nicole, 2, 27, 68–73, 82
Serra, Sonia, 15
Servicio Medico Legal, 67
Sexo con amor, 93
sexual abuse, 45, 127
shah of Iran, 25
Siglo, El, 106, 109, 120–22
social inequality, 44
Spacek, Sissy, 10
Spigel, Lynn, 35–36, 54
Sreberny-Mohammadi, Annabelle, 12, 25, 108
State Repression and the Labors of Memory, 107
Stern, Steve J., 20–22, 24, 54, 65, 82, 102, 144
Storey, John, 147
Straubhaar, Joseph, 14–15
structured absences, 26–27, 34–36, 54, 76, 147
student protest of 2006, 101
Sturken, Marita, 19, 76–77, 102, 106, 115, 143
survivors, 32–33
Synajder, Mario, 30–31

Tangled Memories, 106, 144
Tanner, Eliza, 116
Taxi para tres, 26, 82
Taylor, Diana, 138
Tejas Verdes, 121
Televisa, 38–39
television, 15, 29–55; broadcast networks, 37–39; cable, 31–32; *Canal 13*, 37–38, 42, 125–26; Canal 24 Horas, 32, 51; in China, 25–26; commercial sponsors of, 35; and controversial programming, 35–36; counterprogramming, 41–42; domestic and imported programming, 31–32; and freedom of expression, 52–53; and historical memory, 25–26, 82; and human rights, 30, 32–33, 37–39, 45, 49–50, 147; in India, 26; and international stories, 36; and Internet, 72; in Iran, 25; language of, 36–37; and market capitalism, 37; *Megavisión*, 37–39, 42; and military, 31; ownership of, 34–35; and Pinochet regime, 29–30, 34–35, 37–38, 77; polling, 43; "reality," 41; *La Red*, 37, 39, 42; and structured absences, 26–27, 34–36, 54, 76; subversive potential of, 54; in United States, 35–36. *See also Chilevisión*
Televisión Nacional de Chile, 21, 26, 32, 36–38, 42, 51
Televisuality, 42
Tercera, La, 21, 27–28, 39, 108–9, 114–18
Termómetro, El, 41–50, 129, 147; commercials during, 47; guests on, 48; and human rights, 45, 49–50; and Pinochet regime, 45–46; and police violence, 46; polling, 43; ratings, 49; self-censorship, 47; topics covered by, 47–48; and Venezuelan coup, 46; viewers of, 42–44, 49
Thatcher, Margaret, 1
Tiananmen Square, 25
Time magazine, 10

Tironi, Eugenio, 95
Tolerancia Cero, 20, 51
Tomlinson, John, 13
Toribio Merino, José, 127
Torres Aránguiz, Jorge, 115
Torres López, Pía, 126
torture; centers, 53, 137; media coverage of, 5, 32, 45, 78, 129; survivors of, 33, 110
Trejo, Alejandro, 85
Tres años para nacer, 83–84
Trial of Henry Kissinger, The, 146
Truth and Reconciliation Commission Report, 4–5, 32
Turan, Kenneth, 97
Twilight Memories, 75

UC13, 37–38, 42, 125–26
Última Mirada, 50–51
Últimas Noticias, Las, 114, 117
Undurraga Gómez, Beatriz, 117
United Kingdom, 117
United States; and Chilean coup, 22, 96, 124; controversial TV programming in, 35–36; delinquency in, 125; and Latin American dictatorships, 9–11, 46, 146; sexual abuse by clergy in, 45
University of Chile, 39

Valdivia film festival, 64

Valech Report, 5, 111, 129
Varas A., Lidice, 94
Venda, La, 65
Venevisión, 39–40
Venezuela, 46
Ventura, Zuenir, 107
Victor Jara Foundation, 17
video, 12
Vina del Mar film festival, 58
violence; police, 46; TV coverage of, 48

"Wealthy in Chile Still Find Beef and Scotch," 10
Western Hemisphere Institute for Security Cooperation, 124
Whelan, Gerardo, 84, 90
White, Bill, 97
Wiley, Stephen Crofts, 30, 35, 39, 44
Wilmington, Michael, 96
women; and Indian television, 26; and public protest, 133–34
Wood, Andrés, 27, 82, 83, 86–87, 90, 92–96, 102, 133

Xelpupla, 68

YouTube, 73

Zavala, Fernando, 95
Zuñiga, Gabriela, 65